THE BRITISH IMAGE OF INDIA

ALLEN J. GREENBERGER

The British Image of India

A Study in the Literature of Imperialism 1880–1960

London
OXFORD UNIVERSITY PRESS
NEW YORK TORONTO
1969

Oxford University Press, Ely House, London W.1

GLASGOW NEW YORK TORONTO MELBOURNE WELLINGTON
CAPE TOWN SALISBURY IBADAN NAIROBI LUSAKA ADDIS ABABA
BOMBAY CALCUTTA MADRAS KARACHI LAHORE DACCA
KUALA LUMPUR HONG KONG TOKYO

Printed in Great Britain by
The Camelot Press Ltd., London and Southampton

To my parents

PREFACE

The relationship between literature and history is clearly an intimate one. Literature is particularly important in spreading ideas and images about things which are unfamiliar to the general reading public, thus helping to shape opinion and through it policy. At the same time it is an expression of views about many subjects. Thus from several angles literature can serve as an important source for this historian.

This study was originally suggested to me by Gerald S. Brown of the University of Michigan in a seminar in British Imperial History. He encouraged me to continue to work on this topic and to enlarge the seminar paper into a doctoral dissertation which formed the basis of the present study. He was also most helpful in serving as an interested and critical observer in the development of my work. I cannot possibly express adequate thanks for both his initial suggestion and continued encouragement, as he has enabled me to see a new dimension of historical research.

The insights which John H. Broomfield of the University of Michigan shared with me regarding the position of the British in India were most exciting and often set me thinking in a new line of thought. His generosity in reading parts of the manuscript even while he was involved in his own work in India is appreciated. Even though I have not been able to follow all of his advice, his thoughtfulness has in no small measure contributed to my research.

Albert Feuerwerker and Jacob M. Price of the University of Michigan's Department of History and Warner G. Rice of the English Department at Michigan have also read the manuscript and given me criticism which has helped me to clarify some of my vague thoughts. I am grateful to them for their careful reading of a not too clear manuscript.

It was a pleasure to work with Jon Stallworthy of Oxford University Press and with John Lloyd, each of whom helped to clear up a number of queries. Under the pressure of a deadline, Frances Eaton has done a fine job of typing. My deepest thanks, however, are due to my aunt, Jeannette Scoblow, for spending many harried hours over early drafts, in proof reading and correcting my English. I suspect that, if I were to have given it to her to rewrite completely, it would read far better than it does.

Claremont, California   A. J. G.
October, 1967

CONTENTS

Literature and art are not the field of the literary or art critic only; they are also the concern of the sociologist, of the social historian, or anthropologist, and of the social psychologist. For through literature and art men seem to reveal their personality and, when there is one, their national ethos.

Gilberto Freyre, *Brazil: An Interpretation*

*

Important writing, strange to say, rarely gives the exact flavour of its period; if it is successful it presents you with the soul of man, undated. Very minor literature, on the other hand, is the Baedeker of the soul, and will guide you through the curious relics, the tumbledown buildings, the flimsy palaces, the false pagodas, the distorted and fantastical and faery vistas which have cluttered the imagination of mankind at this or that brief period of its history.

George Dangerfield, *The Strange Death of Liberal England*

*

... it is the image which in fact determines what might be called the current behaviour of any organism or organization. The image acts as a field.

Kenneth Boulding, *The Image*

I

INTRODUCTION

The British connection with India is one of the most fascinating occurrences of history. This relationship between two far distant areas took place not only in the spheres of law and administration, but also in the realm of ideas. A more complete understanding of British policy towards India can be gained through a recognition of the ideas and images which the British rulers held about their Indian subjects and Indian possessions.

There have been studies of the higher intellectual sphere through which ideas flowed between the two countries, but the popular sources of these ideas have largely been overlooked. Probably the major source of ideas concerning India came from fiction set in that country. 'Literature is the one field of Indo-British culture which has provided a comparatively large harvest, though the average quality is not very good.'[1]

Although there were earlier works of fiction which dealt with India, it was only after the great success of Kipling that novels and stories set in the sub-continent were published in large number. From Kipling's time to the present, the British public has been deluged by a vast amount of writing on the subject of India.

Literature can be valuable evidence for the historian in many ways. In the study of British relations with India it is particularly valuable. First, it is one of the major sources of information which the public receives. Writing about one of the most popular of the early authors who employed Indian settings in his stories, Mark Nadis notes: 'Henty impressed a whole generation of English-reading schoolboys (and presumably some adults) with his special image of British India. Since imperial policy in late Victorian times was usually made by an

[1] Geoffrey Theodore Garratt, 'Indo-British Civilization', in G. T. Garratt, ed.. *The Legacy of India*, London, 1937, p. 410.

inner circle which came exclusively from the public schools, Henty's idea of India fell on fertile soil.'[1]

Second, since many of the authors were only vocal members of the public rather than full-fledged intellectuals, they give a broad picture of how people in general were thinking at a given time.

Third, the images created by these authors were bound to have their effect not only in England, but also in India itself. It was these images, that people coming out to India held, which influenced the way in which they saw India. Edmund Candler, who later became a well-known writer of fiction dealing with India, recounts how, before he went out to India as a teacher, he read all about that country from the viewpoint of authors like Kipling. With this background, he believed not only that he understood the country, but also that he would find there exactly what had been described in the stories.[2] A man who was to become an officer in the army in India similarly describes the influence of Kipling's writing. 'I happened to go out to India as a lad when the first Kipling books in their green paper covers were taking the world . . . by storm. . . . They inspired me once and for all with that romance of the East.'[3]

Writing of the 1920s another commentator on the Indian scene noted that for a woman going out to the East there was still an aura of romance about the trip. These women were going out there because that was where the young men of their social class were to be found. Around these men 'hung the spell, authentic in those days, of Maud Diver's uncomfortable and splendid heroes, all sunburn and stern renunciation'.[4]

In addition, the British in India often tended to take the fictional types as their ideals. One author writes in regard to 'the cult of the strong silent man', that when he came out to the Punjab at the turn of the century, this cult was being worshipped in all the clubs and messes.[5] Similarly, Leonard Woolf

[1] Mark Nadis, 'G. A. Henty's Idea of India', *Victorian Studies*, VII, September 1964, p. 50.

[2] Edmund Candler, *Youth and the East: An Unconventional Autobiography*, London, 1924, pp. 27–8.

[3] George MacMunn, 'Some Kipling Origins: The Irish Soldier', *Kipling Journal*, I, March 1927, p. 13.

[4] J. K. Stanford, *Ladies in the Sun: The Memsahibs' India, 1790–1860*, London, 1962, p. 37.

[5] Edwin Haward, 'Kipling Myths and Traditions in India', *The Nineteenth Century*, CXXV, February 1939, p. 199.

found his life as a government official in Ceylon not unlike a Kipling story. 'The white people were also in many ways astonishingly like characters in a Kipling story. I could never make up my mind whether Kipling had moulded his characters accurately in the image of Anglo-Indian society or whether we were moulding our characters accurately in the image of a Kipling story.'[1] Even in the post-Independence period an old Englishwoman living in one of the remaining hill stations told a visiting university student that if he really wanted to understand India he should read the works of Maud Diver.

There can be little doubt that the images that came to England through fiction had their effect. Edward Thompson feels that one of the major reasons for the lack of understanding between the British and Indians which led to political conflicts is the mistreatment of the Indians in fiction. 'The tension existing in India has been bad for our race; and a conception of Indian life based upon the writings of Ethel M. Dell or Maud Diver, or even Kipling, has not helped'.[2]

It is difficult to pinpoint the precise effects of these images, but it is certain that they did have some influence on policy-making. In two of the most important studies of historical images of non-Western people, Philip Curtin and Harold Isaacs agree that 'beyond the world of despatches, there was also a world of unstated assumptions'.[3]

It can, of course, be argued, that the prominence of an idea in British thought as a whole is no guarantee that any particular body of administrators were moved by it in their decisions. This is quite true: it is no *guarantee*. But it is extremely likely that people who share a common educational background and who are subject to common intellectual influences will share a common denominator of ideas and attitudes.[4]

Writing of the American scene Isaacs says much the same thing:

---

[1] Leonard Woolf, *Growing: An Autobiography of the Years 1904–1911*, London, 1961, p. 46. See also p. 151 where he notes the same thing in more detail.

[2] Edward Thompson, *The Other Side of the Medal*, London, 1925, p. 114.

[3] Philip D. Curtin, *The Image of Africa: British Ideas and Action, 1780–1850*, Madison, Wisconsin, 1964, p. vii.

[4] Ibid., p. viii.

I have never discovered any reason to credit the government policy-maker as a type with any superior mental discipline, any unique capacity to separate his concepts of his own and other peoples from the so-called international facts of life. . . . Events are shaped by social forces that are normally much larger and more powerful than any individual policy maker, but insofar as policy makers do play a role, then their images of the people concerned (like their images of themselves and their own nation) have some part in the process.[1]

The number of authors and works dealing with India from the 1880s onward is unbelievably large. In his study of Anglo-Indian fiction Bhupal Singh lists sixteen pages of titles of works on India and this only covers the period to the mid-1930s.[2] Since that time hundreds of additional works set in India have been published. The inclusion of men like Kipling and Forster raises the literary tone of the works studied, but on the whole, the literary value of this genre is slight. There is little distinction between the ideas of men like Forster, who are acknowledged giants in the field of fiction, and the writers of popular potboilers. This is despite Dangerfield's assertion, cited above, that important writing rarely gives the flavour of its age.

In this study a few authors have been included who are basically concerned with either Burma or Ceylon. Although these areas are usually thought of as being beyond the boundaries of India, most Englishmen did not look on them as being any different from India itself. Burma was, of course, administered as a part of the Indian Empire for most of the period during which it was ruled by the British. It was merely another province being governed from Calcutta. Ceylon, while under a separate civil service, was a part of the same English society which filled all of the sub-continent. The images held of these two areas are similar to those held of India proper.

The backgrounds of the authors discussed in this study are given in the Biographical Notes on pp. 205–13. One point in common to most of the authors who wrote about India is that they had a first-hand knowledge of the area. Although a few of them, like Forster, were there for only a short period, many of

[1] Harold R. Isaacs, *Images of Asia: American Views of China and India*, New York, 1962, p. 405.
[2] See the bibliography in Bhupal Singh, *A Survey of Anglo-Indian Fiction*, London, 1934, for a complete listing.

these writers spent a goodly portion of their lives in India. Thus the readers were particularly treated to the images held by the Anglo-Indian community itself. There is, however, little difference between the writings of those who were most familiar with the area and those who knew it only through secondary sources.

In historical terms, the period since Kipling's first works appeared in the 1880s is a short one. However, in terms of the history of the British Empire, these years cover the enormous changes from a secure world-wide empire at its height, through the first serious attacks on it, to its dissolution. The writers of fiction mirrored this development.

These authors fall into three periods—The Era of Confidence, 1880–1910; The Era of Doubt, 1910–1935; and The Era of Melancholy, 1935–1960. (In such a short span of years there is bound to be some element of arbitrariness in any division.) Authors who wrote in one period often continued to write similar stories in a later period. Furthermore, old images, like old generals, rarely die. They only slowly fade away or are slightly transformed. Finally, there were many writers who foreshadowed later developments. Still, these different periods are marked by quite different tones and points of emphasis.

The Era of Confidence is dominated by writers who presented the image of a confident and secure empire. The authors of this period all shared a common faith in the value of British civilization. It was from this belief that almost every other aspect of the British image of India was derived. Starting with this confident approach to their own civilization, these authors believed in their position as rulers and the complementary Indian position as subordinates. As interesting as the things that the authors of this period wrote about, and their style, is what they did not discuss. Such problems and developments as racial relations and the rise of Indian nationalism are almost totally ignored.

In The Era of Doubt these two topics became the major areas of interest. This period is somewhat less internally coherent than the preceding one. Here there are three groups of writers who share a common feeling of doubt, but differ in their reaction to this doubt. The supporters of the Raj reacted in an aggressive way to their loss of confidence. They turned to strong attacks on anything that threatened the continued British

control of India. Although their basic images remained similar
to those of the authors of the first period, their recognition that
forces were opposing the Raj made it impossible for them to
continue to hold on to these older images in an unselfconscious
way. A second group, who attacked the Raj, not only doubted
the value of Western civilization but actually hated it. From
this point of view they carried on an attack on the entire institution of the Empire. The third group of writers in this period
stands in the middle, oscillating between opposition to, and
support for, the existence of the Empire in India. These authors
saw both a good side to the imperial connection which they
admired and a bad side that they hated. Above all else, they
doubted that it was possible for there to be a successful relationship between the British and Indians.

Derived from this third group are the writers of the next
period—The Era of Melancholy. Their foundation was based
on the position that the Empire in India was at an end, although
in fact it was still a living institution. With this belief as their
starting point they felt that they no longer had to attack the
institution or even to defend it. Although most of these writers
were friendly towards the historical Empire they were not particularly concerned with evaluating the successes or failures of
the British in India. To them the position of the Empire in
India was no longer a living question. More than this they were
interested in the personal position of the English in India. They
show a one-sided concern with their own fates. Through this
they express a deep love for their India and also a conflict
between their love and their recognition that India no longer
wants them.

Through each of these periods certain generalizations concerning the relationship between the image and reality stand
out. The present study will not attempt to analyse this matter
in any detail, but a few general concepts have emerged.[1] The
emphasis is always on England rather than on India. It is events
in England, and in the West in general, which determine the
image held of India at any particular time. From this it follows
that the images were not changed by the Indian reality. It is

---

[1] See Bhupal Singh, *A Survey of Anglo-Indian Fiction, passim.* Singh has attempted
to show how inaccurate most of the British authors were in their picture of India
and the Indian people.

far more likely that the images have influenced the way in which the reality was seen. The changing images appear to have had little to do with developments in India.

In his recent study of the British image of Africa, Philip Curtin has come to this same conclusion.

Perhaps the most striking aspect of the British image of Africa . . . was its variance from the African reality. . . .

Reporters went to Africa knowing the reports of their predecessors and the theoretical conclusions already drawn from them. They were therefore sensitive to data that seemed to confirm their European preconceptions, and they were insensitive to contradictory data. . . . Data that did not fit the existing image were most often simply ignored. As a result, British thought about Africa responded very weakly to new data of any kind.

It responded much more strongly to changes in British thought. The travellers (and even more, the analysts at home) took the European *Weltanschauung* as their point of departure. They did not ask, 'What is Africa like, and what manner of men live there' but, 'How does Africa, and how do the Africans, fit into what we already know about the world'. In this sense, the image of Africa was far more European than African. . . .

The image of Africa, in short, was largely created in Europe to suit European needs—sometimes material needs, more often intellectual needs. . . . Their errors, nevertheless, did as much to mould the course of history as their discoveries.[1]

---

[1] Curtin, *Image of Africa*, pp. 479–80. Curtin repeatedly brings out the point that, no matter how much reality might depart from the original image, the British refused to change their ideas about Africa. For example, they believed that all tropical areas had to be good for agriculture. When attempts at farming failed in Sierra Leone, everything was blamed on the developers because according to the image it had to succeed. See pp. 127, 132, and 254.

The Era of Confidence
1880–1910

II

THE BRITISH SELF-IMAGE

The Late Victorian Age saw cracks beginning to grow in the consensus of public opinion about domestic affairs, but in the imperial sphere there was a continued feeling of confidence. Most British felt that they possessed the virtues necessary to dominate the world, and history seemed to bear them out. Until the end of the Boer War their superior position was evident, and it was from this position of confident superiority that they looked at India.

In order to rule, the novelists believed it was necessary for an individual to be British and to possess certain characteristics which were felt to be natural to that 'race'. The ideal British hero of this 'era of confidence' is brave, forceful, daring, honest, active, and masculine. A French student of imperialism has noted:

> The legal sources of imperialism are to be sought in the old mood of the Anglo-Saxon soul, in the ideal of the *gentleman* who was the standard type of culture and good manners. The gentleman is not only the polite and polished man; he is more especially the man who knows how to command; the imperial man in a certain sense, who, having powers, makes it his duty and his right to use them for the common welfare. The ideas of authority-as-power and authority-as-duty are the heritage of an aristocratic tradition.[1]

In short, he is a physical being or, in Victorian terms, 'manly'.

The noun 'manliness' and its objective 'manly' are words rarely encountered today. In the nineteenth century, however, and during the Edwardian age, they were part of the common descriptive vocabulary of the period; so common, indeed, that one might

[1] René Maunier, *The Sociology of Colonies: An Introduction to the Study of Race Contact*, London, 1949, p. 31.

reasonably conclude that manliness was one of the cardinal Victorian virtues.[1]

In the Indian context the ideal English hero of this period always 'works like an ox'[2] and is 'indomitable, unfailing, always fulfilling his duties with machine-like regularity, stern, impenetrable, hard as granite'.[3] To a large degree he is only an overgrown public school boy.

Diana Barrington describing her husband, Hugh, comes closest to depicting this culture hero.

I should hate a man who took an hour over his tie, lolled on a sofa reading poetry, or sat hand in hand with me looking at the moon, and criticized my dress like a milliner. I like to know that my husband is a man, and not an old woman. He shoots tigers, plays polo, and rides races, with my *full* approval.[4]

When a small British community in India is about to be attacked and the women are warned, they react as if it were the most natural thing in the world. 'There was no excitement, no heroics'.[5] Constantly we are given pictures of British under attack being concerned only with the making and drinking of a cup of tea. Life on The Ridge overlooking Delhi during the Mutiny is described in terms that make the whole thing seem as if it must have been something of a game.

Between the rain-showers too, men, after the manner of Englishmen, began to talk of football matches, sky races, and bewail the fact of the racquet court being within the range of walls.[6]

And so the messes talked of games, of races; and men, fresh from seeing their fellows killed by balls on one side of the Ridge, joined those who on the other side were crying 'Well bowled!' as wickets went down before other balls.[7]

Not only are they brave and daring, but they are also gentlemen who have a firm knowledge of the difference between what

[1] David Newsome, *Godliness and Good Learning: Four Studies on a Victorian Ideal*, London, 1961, p. 195.
[2] Ethel M. Dell, *The Way of an Eagle*, London, 1914, p. 86.
[3] Ethel M. Dell, 'The Safety Curtain', in *The Safety Curtain and Other Stories*, London, 1917, p. 49.
[4] Bithia Mae Croker, *Diana Barrington: A Romance of Central India*, London, 1888, vol. 3, p. 63.
[5] Flora Annie Steel, *The Hosts of the Lord*, London, 1900, p. 253.
[6] Flora Annie Steel, *On the Face of the Waters*, London, 1897, p. 293.
[7] Ibid., p. 321.

is fair and what is unfair. During the Mutiny, Harry Wylam
comes upon a fakir defending a mosque where a treasure is hidden. He could easily kill the fakir by using his pistol, but since the
Indian has only a sword this would not be fair. He is willing to
be killed rather than to take advantage of the situation.[1]

An understanding of the ideal character of the Englishman
can be gained by looking at those rare English characters who
do not possess it. Mark Jervis, one of Croker's 'typical' heroes, is
accompanied to India by Clarence Waring who, by contrast, is
shown to be worthless. He is a ladies' man and he loves to
gamble.[2] In keeping with the masculine bias of this period, any
man who chases women is no good. It is expected that a 'hero'
will treat English women respectfully, but he is not supposed to
be particularly interested in or to know a great deal about them.
Rather he should have more 'worthwhile' things to do than to
become involved with women. When Waring cheats Jervis it is
not surprising from a man of his character. Another of this rare
breed of villainous Englishmen is Phillip Lamond in *Flotsam*.
Unlike Waring he does not chase women or gamble; rather
he is dishonest, untrustworthy, and places money above principles.[3]

Possession of the characteristics they felt were so valuable
gave the British both the right and the obligation to rule.
Leadership was looked upon as being the true test of an individual's or, more importantly, a race's worth. The crucial
thing is that the British saw the ability to lead in terms of race.
It was the British blood which gave them their unique position.
Kipling's Kim *must* order his Bengali friend to follow him and
Huree Chunder Mookerjee must accept the order *because* Kim
is British and hence the natural leader. Similarly Harry Wylam
in Merriman's *Flotsam* is described as 'a fair scion of the northern
race which knows no rest or fear'[4] and, even though he is only
an orphaned child, he shows 'the masterfulness of the dominant
race' over his 'passive ayah'.[5] The British believed that the
position of majesty 'is a position which comes naturally to most
Englishmen'.[6]

---

[1] Hugh S. Scott, *Flotsam: The Study of a Life*, London, 1906, p. 213.
[2] See Bithia Mae Croker, *Mr. Jervis*, London, 1894, *passim*.
[3] In Scott, *Flotsam, passim*.   [4] Ibid., p. 6.   [5] Ibid., p. 19.
[6] Steel, *On the Face of the Waters*, p. 2.

In 'Namgay Doola', Kipling depicts a red-haired Tibetan named Namgay Doola who is the son of Timlay Doola 'which is Tim Doolan gone very wrong'. Although he does not even know he is of British descent, this is demonstrated by the fact that he is the most capable man in the little kingdom and emerges as its accepted leader.[1] Harry Lindsay, in a similar story, is raised as a Maratha after the murder of his parents. He does not suspect that he is English, but is stronger and more fond of exercise than the other boys who soon expect him to be and accept him as their leader.[2] When he tells Bajee Rao that he is English, the Maratha leader replies that he had always noted that Harry was different from the Maratha boys with 'his energy and readiness . . . to take responsibilities on his shoulders and to be so full of resource'.[3] Based on the same discovery Nana Furnevees recognizes that although he did not know that Harry was English it must have been because he felt intuitively that he had always been able to confide in the youth.[4]

Even a drop of English blood is, in the absence of a full-blooded Briton, sufficient to bring out the leadership qualities in an individual. Ma Sein, the half-caste daughter of an Englishman, is the leader of all the children's games and the arbiter of what is right and wrong for her Burmese playmates.[5]

Michele d'Cruz in Kipling's 'His Chance in Life', who is 'very black' and has 'seven-eighths native blood in his veins', finds the power of his one-eighth English blood in a time of crisis. As an employee of the Telegraph Department of the Indian Government he is sent to a small village and while there a riot occurs.

The native Police Inspector ran in and told Michele that the town was in an uproar and coming to wreck the Telegraph Office. The Babu put on his cap and quietly dropped out of the window; while the Police Inspector, afraid, but obeying the old race-instinct which recognizes a drop of White blood as far as it can be diluted, said, 'What orders does the *Sahib* give?'

The 'Sahib' decided Michele. Although horribly frightened, he

---

[1] See Rudyard Kipling, 'Namgay Doola', in *Life's Handicap: Being Stories of Mine Own People*, London, 1891, pp. 222–34 *passim*.

[2] G. A. Henty, *At the Point of the Bayonet: A Tale of the Mahratta War*, London, 1902, p. 30.

[3] Ibid., p. 98.   [4] Ibid., p. 121.

[5] A. E. W. Mason, *The Sapphire*, London, 1935, p. 72.

felt that, for the hour, he, the man with the Cochin Jew and the menial uncle in his pedigree, was the only representative of English authority in the place.[1]

So he puts down the riot alone, although he later loses his courage as 'the White drop in Michele's veins' died out.

Since the British *must* rule they have an obligation to use every possible means to make their rule secure. The English hero of Henty's tale of the Maratha War thinks that it is unethical to have anyone spy on the British, but there is absolutely nothing wrong with having someone spy on the Indians because the British cause is the just one.[2] The American, but completely Anglo-Saxon, Tarvin in *The Naulahka* uses the passions of the Indian princess to trap her. There is nothing ungentlemanly about pretending to be in love with her in order to gain information and then to throw her over despite the fact that she loves him. It is merely a proper method of taking advantage of the weaknesses that the Indian character contains.[3]

Usually this is brought out by the willingness of the British to use force. Rarely is it actually necessary to use warfare, but the existence of the threat and willingness to do so must always be kept in the forefront. When the Mutiny occurs Scott's hero, Frederick Marqueray, explains why his regiment will stand firm while everyone else's will revolt. 'They trust to kindness. We don't, we trust to fear.'[4] If it takes firmness and fear or even deceit to make the Indians recognize that they must follow the British, then the British see no reason why they should not be used.

The keystone to maintaining their position of leadership is not to be found in the treatment of the Indians. It is, after all, in the English *blood* and the important thing is to keep the blood 'pure'. For this reason intermarriage is dangerous. Equally dangerous, however, is the adoption of Indian customs and attitudes. There is something of a contradiction in this feeling that, despite the emphasis on pure blood, it is equally important to keep 'culturally pure'. Although, as will be seen below, the

---

[1] Rudyard Kipling, 'His Chance in Life', in *Plain Tales from the Hills*, London, 1913, p. 66.

[2] Henty, *At the Point of the Bayonet*, p. 121.

[3] Rudyard Kipling and Wolcott Balestier, *The Naulahka: A Story of West and East*, London, 1898, pp. 201–2.

[4] Scott, *Flotsam*, p. 139.

possession of a British culture alone was not sufficient to give one the quality of leadership, but when culture and blood were found together the individual's capabilities could not be questioned. Indian culture must therefore be rejected as a destructive element. The strength of the British lay in being British through and through.

The giving up of any part of the British way of life was believed to be the worst thing that one could do. Croker introduces a character into *Mr. Jervis* only to prove this idea. On a trip the heroine of the novel meets a woman who is posing as an Indian and living in complete seclusion. It turns out that she is actually a 'Mutiny Lady'—a woman who had accepted the Indian faith and way of life at Cawnpore in order to avoid being massacred. She is totally ashamed of this fact and is unwilling therefore to try to take her place in English society again.[1] To the present-day reader she is a strange character who is tragic because of her inability to live the kind of an English life that she wants, but a critic of the late nineteenth century saw the scene in terms far closer to what the author must have meant her readers to feel. That writer feels that the 'Mutiny Lady' 'gave way' and that this is the tragedy. 'So far as our recollection goes, fiction has few more pathetic figures than this renegade Englishwoman. . . . There were many lives ruined by the Mutiny, but the saddest by far were those of the men and women who had ruined them by their own fault.'[2] The right kind of a woman would rather accept death than give up her position as an Englishwoman. In *The Devil's Wind* it turns out at the end of the book that Adela was not killed in the Cawnpore Massacre, but rather had accepted marriage to an Indian in order to save her life. Her husband, who has remarried, is horrified at the thought. He talks about it with his new wife, who says: 'If it had been I ——' and he responds with the statement: 'It could never have been you. There was always a choice—always death.'[3] Death before dishonour was the way the British believed they had to act in India.

Tarvin, the hero of Kipling's *The Naulahka*, has gone to the

[1] Croker, *Mr. Jervis*, vol. 2, 190–3.
[2] 'The Indian Mutiny in Fiction', *Blackwood's Edinburgh Magazine*, CLXI, February 1897, p. 226.
[3] Patricia Wentworth, *The Devil's Wind*, London, 1912, p. 319.

Cow's Mouth, an ancient Indian shrine, to search for the neck-
lace whose name provides the title of the novel. There he faces
the crisis of the total negation which Kipling sees as the soul of
India. This crisis is both the structural and narrative climax of
the novel. This action is preceded by a poem summing up the
fear of the Indian unknown.

> This I saw when the rites were done,
> And the lamps were dead and the Gods alone,
> And the gray snake coiled on the altar stone—
> Ere I fled from a fear that I could not see,
> And the Gods of the East made mouths at me.[1]

Tarvin first hears rather than sees the Cow's Mouth as 'he
heard a malignant chuckle, half suppressed, which ended in a
choking cough, ceased, and broke out anew'.[2] This sound comes
from the rushing of water through 'the formless jaws'[3] of the
carving which causes the Cow's Mouth to chuckle 'as it had
chuckled since the making of the tank, and that was at the
making of time'.[4] The pool in which the holy spot is located is so
dark, lying at the bottom of 'a path that led from the sunlight
to the chill and mould of a vault'[5] that 'never in his life had
Tarvin so acutely desired the blessed sunshine'.[6] Although
there is actually 'nothing' there, Tarvin feels a strong sense of
physical horror and flees back to the sun where he fills his
hands with 'the wholesome jungle grass'.[7] His terror was so
great that 'never again, for any consideration, under the wholesome light of the sun, would he, who feared nothing, set foot in
the Cow's Mouth'.[8]

Tarvin, frightened by his discovery, believes that he had to
flee in order to save not only his physical, but also his psycholo-
gical self. His discovery does not, however, cause him to give up
his deep commitment to progress. He had wanted the jewels in
order to finance a railroad which would bring prosperity to his
home-town of Topaz, Colorado—a town to which he is attached

---

[1] Kipling and Balestier, *The Naulahka*, p. 125.   [2] Ibid., p. 135.
[3] Ibid., p. 136.   [4] Ibid., p. 139.   [5] Ibid., p. 136.   [6] Ibid., p. 137.
[7] Ibid., p. 138.
[8] Ibid., p. 141. For a good discussion of this see Stanley Cooperman, 'The
Imperial Posture and The Shrine of Darkness: Kipling's *The Naulahka* and E. M.
Forster's *A Passage to India*', *English Literature in Transition*, 6, 1963, *passim*.

with a patriotic fervour properly becoming to an Anglo-Saxon
hero in this period.

This account demonstrates two things. First, it shows that
Kipling believed that there was a basic difference between the
East and West—a difference that can be summarized in the distinction between a passive negative world and an active positive
one. Second, and more important, is his reaction to his perception. This perception inspires both fear and repulsion in the person
of the hero and author. Tarvin fears the power in the 'nothingness' of India as embodied in the Cow's Mouth, but he is confident enough of the value of his own Western civilization to reject
India. He is not destroyed by his experience, but rather is even
further convinced of the rightness of his own position.

Kim's reaction is similar when he is faced with the vision of
the Himalayas where the individual is dwarfed by the inhuman
non-rational forces of the mountains. Like Tarvin, Kim is
impressed by his discovery of the soul of India but rejects his
vision to work for the protection of the Frontier.[1]

A problem like this is not unique to Kipling. In Perrin's novel
Idolatry there is a contrast and conflict shown between Dion
Dervasse and Oliver Wray. The former is an 'excellent speci-
men of his type—that of the well-bred, unaffected, but not
highly intellectual British soldier'[2] who does not even know
what the letters U.P. and N.W.P. mean when he goes out to
India. He had little desire to understand the country and after
months there he is still unable to distinguish between a Brahman
and a coolie. Instead Dervasse thinks of them all as 'niggers'
although he is too well-bred to use this term. When, in one of
his rare fits of curiosity about things Indian, he goes down to the
river to watch a Hindu rite, he feels he has to flee. 'Of a sudden
he felt anxious to get away quickly, to be outside this atmosphere that stifled him mentally and physically.'[3] Dion is so
unthinking that he believes Anne is in love with him, although
it is clear that she has rejected him.

His rival in both love and cultural attitude is Oliver Wray, a
young and handsome missionary. Wray is devoted to the propa-
gation of Christianity in India despite the continual failure of

---

[1] Mark Kincead-Weekes, 'Vision in Kipling's Novels', in Andrew Rutherford,
ed., *Kipling's Mind and Art*, Edinburgh and London, 1964, p. 228.
[2] Alice Perrin, *Idolatry*, London, 1909, p. 27.   [3] Ibid., p. 36.

his endeavours. He has sworn not to become involved with women because this will limit his evangelical activities. Anne falls in love with him, but finally realizes that it is impossible to marry him or even to take him away from his *duty*. She returns to England after also breaking off with Dion. Oliver, who believes that Christianity will have to be Easternized, ends up by going out among the Indians dressed in the rags of a Hindu fakir. Anne finally realizes that she is really in love with the completely English, if rather dull, Dervasse, rather than with the half-Indianized Wray and is going to marry him. The missionary has lost his rights to the girl because, in his effort to understand India, he has become Indianized while the soldier has triumphed by remaining true to his culture.

When he comes out to India, a missionary in one of Steel's short stories believes that he should dress like an Indian in order to gain more converts. As he learns more about India, however, he says: 'The more I saw of these people, the more necessary it seems to me that we should be ourselves at all points before beginning the attack.'[1]

Thus, the British in this period, at least relatively confident about the value of their culture, imagined that they had to reject everything Indian in order to retain their own individual identity and to succeed in whatever their endeavours might be. In addition there is an element of fear—fear of Indian powers which could conquer the English if they allowed themselves to go even part of the way towards accommodating themselves to the Indians.

If the British had convinced themselves that they had a right to rule provided they kept their racial and cultural characteristics pure, there still remains the question of what they were doing in India.

In looking at their activity in India the British judged their most important obligation to be to do their duty, whatever it might be. Work in and of itself was a good thing. 'The idea that the exercise of power is in itself a good thing; action, struggle, even sport itself are proposed as ideals; the vision of the *gentleman* again! To strive, to play games, to win, that is the destined part for the perfect man to play; all expansion is sound

---

[1] Flora Annie Steel, 'For the Faith', in *The Flower of Forgiveness*, London and New York, 1894, vol. i, p. 87.

and good, for it deploys the energy of the strong.'[1] The value of empire building seems to have less to do with the Empire itself than with the development of certain qualities in the empire builders.[2] Above all else, it was thought that the Englishman in India should not be a shirker. 'It's sheer pluck that counts, nothing else—the pluck to hang on and worry, worry, worry, till you get your heart's desire.'[3]

A group of Kipling's English surveyors get together occasionally from their individual isolated posts in the arid wastes of Rajputana. The rest of the time they live totally isolated lives in the harshest of environments, spitting on sextants to keep them cool, trying to avoid the opthalmia which they are certain to get, and trying to convince their Indian assistants that an error of five degrees in an angle is not as small as it looks. Talking about their difficulties finally leads one of them, Hummil, to say that suicide seems to be the only way out of the thankless life he is living.

'You take a pill,' said Spurstow, who had been watching Hummil's white face narrowly. 'Take a pill, and don't be an ass. That sort of talk is skittles. Anyhow, suicide is shirking your work. If I were Job ten times over, I should be so interested in what was going to happen next that I'd stay on and watch.[4]

Between the collapse of his personal life and the July heat on the Plains, one of Steel's characters finds life so difficult that he does kill himself. The author treats the man as if, despite all his problems, he should have been stronger.

Maybe a fiery furnace and a red-hot bungalow are trying to even the best of clay when it is fresh from the moulder's hand; but that is neither here or there. The fact remains that George had run away from truth and untruth, from himself and his fellow-men, but most of all from Hodinuggar and the crazy, irresponsible creator. . . . And as he lay dead, with a bullet through his heart, the barometer upon the mantel-piece was falling faster and faster . . ., but the only one who could have understood the silent warning had *deserted* his post.[5]

---

[1] Maunier, *The Sociology of Colonies*, p. 34.
[2] See Andrew Rutherford, 'Officers and Gentlemen', in Rutherford, *Mind and Art*, p. 185.
[3] Dell, *The Way of an Eagle*,p. 187.
[4] Rudyard Kipling, 'At the End of the Passage', in *Life's Handicap*, p. 154.
[5] Flora Annie Steel, *The Potter's Thumb*, London, 1894, vol. 2, pp. 206–7. My italics.

It is far more admirable to sacrifice oneself in the doing of one's chosen task, like Hunter's Old Missionary who goes blind working on a dictionary of an obscure hill tribe's language even after his health has been broken. Although it will be impossible for anyone else to take up where he has left off, he struggles on with his task. In the end, he gives not only his eyes, but his life, as testimony to his faith in what he is doing.[1] The Linforth family is more successful in that A. E. W. Mason imagines that the road into the mountains of north-west India is going to be successfully pushed through to the foot of the Hindu Kush. This success, however, is achieved at the cost of three generations of Linforth men. Although no one is certain that the road is not causing more trouble than it is designed to prevent, these men feel that it is their *duty* to stick to the job they and their ancestors have begun. Even the Pathan Shere Ali realizes this when he says: 'The power of the Road is great, because it inspires men to strive for its completion.'[2]

The British acceptance of what they see to be their duty is one of the major marks of their superiority. One of A. E. W. Mason's late novels is set partly in Burma where an Englishman named Crowther has become a Buddhist priest. The narrator of the story is impressed for a while with Crowther's choice of a life until someone criticizes the Englishman for having become a monk, although there was nothing of service in what he was doing. The narrator loses his respect for this man as he thinks: 'Service was no part of their creed. Service meant nothing and I could not remember anything worth devoting a life to into which service did not enter.'[3] Despite the sympathetic treatment given by Kipling, the same thing is true of the lama in *Kim* who seeks to leave the world. Kim must depart from him in order to work for the protection of India despite the love he has for the lama.

The chief reason for the British to be in India was that it was their mission or their duty. 'It was simply a necessity imposed upon England by some organic determinism.'[4]

---

[1] Sir William W. Hunter, *The Old Missionary*, London, 1895, *passim*.
[2] A. E. W. Mason, *The Broken Road*, London, 1907, p. 60.
[3] A. E. W. Mason, *The Sapphire*, p. 229
[4] Michael Edwardes, 'Rudyard Kipling and the Imperial Imagination', *The Twentieth Century*, CLIII, June 1953, p. 450.

Although all other reasons for being in India are of far less importance, the British did offer, in their literary imagination, more concrete reasons for being in India. There is pride in being a 'ruling race which, with all its eccentricities, rules better than even the fabled Vicramiditya himself!'[1] Henty fills his boys' books with the claim that the British had brought peace and prosperity to India. The Burman Meinik says that Burma would be better off under the British than under their native rulers since they could not possibly be taxed any more heavily[2] and the Kashmiri Akram Chunder says that when the British take the valley 'it will be a blessed day for the people'.[3]

The most common explanation, however, is that the British were 'the mere fraction of white faces responsible for the safety of those millions of dark ones'.[4] Safety from what? Largely it is safety from attacks by the 'barbarians beyond the passes' acting either independently or with the help of a foreign power like Russia. Kim is running all over the mountains playing 'The Great Game' of intrigue and counter-intrigue against the enemies of British India and Mason's road is being built to protect against invasions from the north. 'It will go on to the foot of the Hindu Kush, and then only, the British rule in India will be safe.'[5] Occasionally the British see themselves as protecting the Indians from themselves as in the case of communal riots or, even more basically, from the danger of the Indian's own character with its purported tendency towards rioting and pillaging.

Unique to this period is the British feeling that it was not necessary for them to define concretely what they were doing. Unlike the succeeding years it was not uncommon for the British to see themselves merely enjoying what they were doing in India. Kipling's *Kim* is very much the story of a boy, and an author, in love with India.

When thinking of Kipling's India one quite often thinks of

---

[1] Steel, *The Potter's Thumb*, p. 16.

[2] G. A. Henty, *On the Irrawaddy: A Story of the First Burmese War*, London, 1897, p. 186.

[3] G. A. Henty, *Through the Sikh War: A Tale of the Conquest of the Punjab*, London, 1894, p. 129.

[4] Flora Annie Steel, 'The Squaring of the Gods', in *In the Guardianship of God*, London, 1900, p. 26.

[5] A. E. W. Mason, *The Broken Road*, p. 55.

the army and militarism, but, interestingly, there is very little actual fighting. Kipling actually saw no real fighting until after he had published his Indian stories. Only during the Boer War did Kipling have to face the reality of war. 'His India was an assured world in which the only fighting was on the frontier or in Upper Burma.'[1] It has been noted that one of the major attractions of *Kim* is that in that novel Kipling wrote about India as if it were a stable society. 'The British Raj was established and taken for granted. Subversive movements and foreign intrigues on the frontier might be introduced in order to make the plot of a story more exciting. But there was no question of such movement succeeding or changing the nature of society.'[2] This is seen not only in his novel, but also in his stories of army life. Only three of the twenty-four stories in *Soldiers Three* and *Military Tales* deal with troops fighting at any length. He is basically concerned with 'the garrison army at rest'.[3] Even in the accounts that he gives of battles there is a large element of self-enjoyment and fun on the side of the soldiers. 'The Taking of Lungtungpen' describes British troops swimming naked across a Burmese river to take a town.

'Thin we halted an' formed up, the wimmen howlin' in the houses an' Lift' nint Brazenose blushin' pink in the light av the mornin' sun. 'Twas the most ondaisint p'rade I iver tuk a hand in. Foive-and-twenty privits an' a orficer av the Line in review ordher, an' not as much as wud dust a fife betune 'em all in the way of clothin'! Eight av us had their belts an' pouches on; but the rest had gone in wid a handful av cartridges an' the skin God gave thim. They was as naked as Vanus. . . . The Headman av Lungtungpen, who surrinder'd himself, asked the Interprut'r—'Av the English fight like that wid their clo'es off, what in the wurruld do they do wid their clo'es on?'[4]

Even more than in battle he shows the common soldiers in India playing tricks on each other or just relaxing in unmatched idyllic surroundings.

We shot all the forenoon, and killed two pariah-dogs, four green parrots, sitting, one kite by the burning-ghaut, one snake flying, one

---

[1] Stanford, *Ladies in the Sun*, p. 132.
[2] Christopher Hollis, 'Kim and the apolitical Man', *Kipling Journal*, 119, October 1956, p. 6.
[3] Eric Solomon, 'The Regulars: A Note on "Soldiers Three" and "Military Tales"', *Kipling Journal*, 139, June 1959, p. 8.
[4] Rudyard Kipling, 'The Taking of Lungtungpen', in *Plain Tales*, pp. 96–7.

mud-turtle, and eight crows. Game was plentiful. Then we sat down to tiffin—'bull-mate an' bran-bread,' Mulvaney called it—by the side of the river, and took pot shots at the crocodiles in the intervals of cutting up the food with our only pocket-knife. Then we drank up all the beer, and threw the bottles into the water and fired at them. After that, we eased belts and stretched ourselves on the warm sand and smoked. We were too lazy to continue shooting.[1]

As long as India seemed to be a somewhat friendly place in which to live and work, the British could see themselves having a good time.

To live this kind of a life and to do all of the other things that they saw themselves doing the British had to have the right kind of a leader. How is the ideal English leader to be found? Most likely he will be in the army—preferably as an officer. Although others may be able to fit this pattern it is far more difficult in civilian life where the rules of conduct are dictated from elsewhere and men are chosen for their posts by examination. A youth in England receives a letter from his uncle in the Punjab telling him that being good in school and pleasing to the schoolmasters is of no benefit in ruling India.[2] On the boat bringing him out to India he is told that the use of examinations to choose officials for India would be terrible since courage is far more important than book learning.[3]

Likewise Steel has a sympathetic 'military magnate' worry about the future of British rule on the eve of the Mutiny in identical terms.

Poor old Haileybury! I only hope competition will do as well, but I doubt it; these new fellows can never have the old *esprit de corps*; won't come from the same class! One of the Rajah's people was questioning me about it only this morning—they read the English newspapers of course—'So we are not to have Sahibs to rule over us,' he said, looking black as thunder. 'Any krani's son will do, if he has learned enough.'[4]

The ideal type is a person like Merriman's Harry Wylam who in school 'was never the boy to mope in the corner of the playground with a book'.[5] Rather, 'he was vigorous and active—as

---

[1] Rudyard Kipling, 'The Madness of Private Ortheris', in *Plain Tales*, pp. 230–1.
[2] Henty, *Through the Sikh War*, pp. 18–19.   [3] Ibid., p. 30.
[4] Steel, *On the Face of the Waters*, p. 41. '*Krani*' literally means 'low-caste English'.
[5] Scott, *Flotsam*, p. 32.

successful in the play-ground as he was unfortunate in the class-room. The boys admired him for his daring—the masters had a fondness for his honesty.'[1] With this kind of a background, when Harry sets out on a dangerous expedition, he does it with the spirit of a schoolboy.

Clearly there is a close correlation between all of these ideas and the type of an educational system which was prevalent in England in the late Victorian period. The public school system had begun to change radically in the 1870s when 'godliness' was replaced by 'manliness' as the ideal of the public school system. 'Muscular Christianity was firmly establishing itself'[2] as the guiding principle in this, the golden age of the public schools. The whole emphasis had changed from freedom and support of the individual to a more disciplined and collectivist ethos. 'And this change was implicit . . . in the change which was coming in the nature of British Imperialism. If the pre-Arnold generation had provided the world pioneers of Empire, the post-Arnold generation was to provide the obedient governors.'[3] With this went a new emphasis on games, as the idea grew that the development of a group spirit was the most important thing that could be gained from an education.[4] This was of particular value in the colonial services, such as India, where the individual Englishman often found himself isolated from members of his own race and class.[5] Erich Fromm has noted that the lone Englishman who dressed for dinner in his isolated jungle outpost was thus able to maintain a feeling of group solidarity with the English community at home.[6] Through their physical existence—'unheated dormitories, cold baths and monastic isolation' —the public schools also provided early experiences for the physical discomforts of life in the colonial service.[7]

The anti-intellectual bias and glorification of action which is shown by almost all of the authors of this period also had its roots in the public schools. A headmaster at Harrow expressed this well: 'The business of a school is to work and get on with its

---

[1] Ibid., p. 33.   [2] Newsome, *Godliness and Good Learning*, p. 198.
[3] T. C. Worsley, *Barbarians and Philistines: Democracy and the Public Schools*, London, 1940, p. 36.
[4] Rupert Wilkinson, *The Prefects, British Leadership and the Public School Tradition*, London, 1964, p. 19.
[5] Ibid., p. 52.   [6] Erich Fromm quoted in Ibid., p. 62.   [7] Ibid., p. 16.

life without bothering about whys and wherefores and abstract justice and democratic principles.'[1]

The Home Government, the Calcutta Government, and even the provincial governments are constantly being criticized for their lack of knowledge of India. One must be on the spot to understand fully what the problems of India are. Typical is the action of the Calcutta Government in Mason's novel. Shere Ali has found it impossible single handedly to solve the problems presented by his rapid transition from England to India and a position of leadership. He had requested the Indian Government to bring over his friend, young Linforth, from England to help him. They quickly saw the wisdom of doing this. So far so good, but as soon as he arrived in India, Linforth was assigned to another task and kept busy at it for the next six months while Shere Ali's position continued to deteriorate.

Legislation that is passed under the urging of 'philosophers' or touring Members of Parliament is not only of no use, but will absolutely disrupt proper government.

The Philosophical Radical on the rampage is taking the opportunity afforded by baggage parade to record in his valuable diary the pained surprise at the want of touch between the rulers and the ruled, which is, alas! his first impression of India. In all probability it will be his last also, since it is conceivable that both rulers and ruled may be glad to get rid of him on the approach of the hot weather. Mosquitoes are troublesome and cholera is disconcerting, but they are bearable beside the man who invariably knows the answers to his own questions before he asks them.[2]

Kipling's Pagett, M.P., is the same sort.

Pagett, M.P., was a liar and a fluent liar therewith,——
He spoke of the heat of India as the 'Asian Solar Myth';
Came on a four months' visit, to 'study the East', in November,
And I got him to sign an agreement vowing to stay till September.

The Member of Parliament soon enough, to his discomfort, learns that the heat of India is not the 'Asian Solar Myth'. In monthly succession he comes down with prickly-heat, sunstroke, and 'dysent'ry' until

---

[1] Quoted in Edward Mack, *Public Schools and British Opinion Since 1860*, New York, 1941, pp. 124–5.

[2] Flora Annie Steel, 'For the Faith', in *The Flower of Forgiveness*, vol. 1, p. 70.

He babbled of 'Eastern Exile', and mentioned his home with tears;
But I hadn't seen my children for close upon seven years.

Finally, his 'Eastern Exile' up, the M.P. anxiously flees India.

And I laughed as I drove from the station, but the mirth died out
  on my lips
And I thought of the fools like Pagett who write of their 'Eastern
  trips',
And the sneers of the travelled idiots who duly misgovern the land,
And I prayed to the Lord to deliver another one into my hand.[1]

Not only are they unpleasant people but they do, unfortunately, in the views of the makers of the Indian image, have influence. An aide explains to his District Commissioner:

'Mr. Cox, the member of parliament—perhaps you may remember him——'
'A little red-haired fellow was he? who wrote a book about India on the back of his two-monthly return ticket?'
'Mr. Cox is a man of great influence with his party, and he supports Dya Ram's——'
'Pestilential little fool,' interrupted the Commissioner impartially, impersonally. 'It wouldn't be bad, though—stop his scurrilous tongue for a bit. Favour does you know.'[2]

Kipling gives the Indian Government credit for honestly attempting to create a land law which would favour the peasant proprietor over the money-lender. However, because of a lack of first-hand knowledge the Government is, in fact, about to accomplish the exact reverse. They are saved from their error by a little boy, Tods, who leads them to the truth because he has the knowledge and experience which comes from being on the spot.[3]

Such criticism is more than simply an attack on the people who are not on the spot. As with the rest of the image of the British in India there is a 'clubby' tone to this. People who have not sacrificed their lives to India are not members of 'the club' and therefore, besides not having any knowledge, they have no right to legislate for it. 'One of Kipling's most persistent preoccupations, and a highly conspicuous symbol of his writings,

---

[1] Rudyard Kipling 'Pagett, M.P.', in *Departmental Ditties and Barrack Room Ballads*, London, 1904, pp. 41–2.
[2] Steel, *The Hosts of the Lord*, p. 71. Note his red hair, perhaps implying that he is not 'really' English.
[3] Rudyard Kipling, 'Tods' Amendment', in *Plain Tales*, pp. 159–65, *passim*.

is that of a small and sharply defined community of human beings.'[1] This idea of 'the shared intimacy within a closed circle'[2] is one of the keys not only to an understanding of Kipling, but to this whole period. It is in keeping with the feeling that the whole of the British community in India—at least those who were the 'right kind of people'—were like the members of the same public school class or private club. This gave them a feeling of security which could be found only within the group. It also meant that anyone who did not completely follow the dictates of the group had to be driven out of it for the safety of the group.

The British authors of this period were deeply concerned with the position of the Englishwoman in India. Kipling, of course, is well-known for his sharp criticism of female Anglo-Indian society in his stories of the hill stations where the women are concerned only with having a good time. His criticism of this side of the British in India has sometimes been attacked as merely representing the 'sour grapes approach'. Dennis Kincaid recounts how his grandmother could never hear the name of Kipling without experiencing a feeling of deep disgust. She believed that Kipling was a bounder and cad who was only jealous of the hill-station society because his 'betters' excluded him from it. To her he was never anything but 'a subversive pamphleteer'.[3] This is a highly doubtful interpretation of his criticism. Kipling actually had fair first-hand knowledge of what he was writing about.[4] His criticism is put in even better perspective by similar attacks which appeared in the writings of others.

Bithia Mae Croker is, if anything, harsher in her picture. When Diana Barrington comes out of the idyllic isolation in which she was raised for her first glimpse of Anglo-Indian society, she is rightly horrified. The women there, who are mainly concerned with gossiping and attracting a bevy of

[1] Karl W. Deutsch and Norbert Weiner, 'The Lonely Nationalism of Rudyard Kipling', *Yale Review*, LII, June 1963, p. 501.

[2] C. S. Lewis, 'Kipling's World', *Kipling Journal*, 127, December 1958, p. 8. See also W. L. Renwick, 'Re-reading Kipling', in Rutherford, ed., *Kipling's Mind and Art*, p. 8, and especially Noel Annan, 'Kipling's Place in the History of Ideas', in ibid., pp. 106–9.

[3] Dennis Kincaid, *British Social Life in India, 1608–1937*, London, 1939, p. 228.

[4] Stanford, *Ladies in the Sun*, p. 178.

platonic male admirers, treat her with the utmost cruelty because in her attractive simplicity she is a threat to their position.

This approach to the Englishwoman in India is a criticism of only that part of female Anglo-Indian society which is overly sophisticated, overly feminine, and unproductive. These are the very same criticisms which were made in regard to certain types of Englishmen in India. Many individual Englishwomen are treated well, provided they embody the masculine values which are believed to be correct. Scott's Lady Leaguer is portrayed in glowing terms because her relationship with men is a masculine one. She and her male companions are 'chums' rather than lovers.

Even Violet Oliver who is not shown to be a particularly admirable woman can be relied on when the need is pressing. She has been the victim of an attempted abduction engineered by Shere Khan. The local English official, Ralston, tells her that they must go out and ride through the streets of Peshawar in order to show the Indians how unconcerned the English are. 'It is good for these people here to know that nothing they can do will make any difference—no, not enough to alter the mere routine of our lives.'[1] He tells her that there will be no danger involved—'or at all events no danger that Englishwomen are unprepared to face in this country'.[2] When she finds the pressure of the ride too much and asks to turn back Ralston says:

'We ask much of the Englishwomen in India, and because they never fail us, we are apt to ask too much. I asked too much of you.' Violet responded to the flick at her national pride. She drew herself up and straightened her back.

'No,' she said, and she actually counterfeited a smile. 'No. It's all right.'[3]

In another case when an attack on an isolated British garrison is feared, the Englishwomen react as if it were the most normal thing in the world. In this action they are depicted as being typical of all of the 'right kind' of Englishwomen.

Going to the Hills! Whose fault is it that the phrase conjures up to the English ear a vision of grass-widows, flirtations, scandals,

[1] A. E. W. Mason, *The Broken Road*, p. 290–1.   [2] Ibid., p. 289.
[3] Ibid., p. 292.

frivolities? Surely it is the fault of those who, telling the tale of a
hill-station, leave out the tragedy of a separation, which makes
British rule in India such a marvel of self-sacrifice, both to the
women and to the men.[1]

Consideration of the Englishwoman in India leads naturally
to the problem of isolation. Here it will be discussed from the
side of English isolation from normal English society rather than
English isolation from India—a subject which is dealt with later.
Almost any story of Anglo-Indian society is bound to have a
heart-rending account of the way India destroys the institution
of the European family. Besides causing the women to run off to
the hills where they have nothing to do but flit around, it
demands the separation of parents and children. Kipling's
'Baa Baa, Black Sheep' is an autobiographical story written
from the point of view of a child who has been sent away from
his parents in India to a foster home in England.[2] In addition to
the normal difficulties of adapting to a life without one's parents,
this meant getting used to a completely different kind of life as
far as climate and personal luxuries were concerned.

More often the focus of this theme is on the mother in India
who cannot bear to see her children sent to England alone or who
mourns over the fact that they have been sent there. A character like this is Milly Sladen, who 'had two little girls in England,
whom her heart yearned over—little girls being brought up
among strangers at a cheap suburban school'.[3] Another young
Englishwoman in Dell's novel finds her marriage being destroyed partly because her only child has been sent from India
to England where she dies alone.

If the mother has not sent them away and has held on to them
in India, she has probably seen her children spoiled by the
Indian environment. Because they were being raised in a country where anyone white was better than anyone Indian, and
since most of their companions were Indian servants, they
quickly learned how to give orders and see them accepted.
Their development as little despots was seen to be quickened by
the treatment the children received at the hands of these Indian

[1] Steel, *The Potter's Thumb*, vol. 2, p. 113.

[2] Rudyard Kipling, 'Baa Baa, Black Sheep', in *Wee Willie Winkie*, London, 1913,
pp. 220–52 *passim*.

[3] Croker, *Mr. Jervis*, vol. 1, p. 3.

servants. Ayahs and bearers were constantly shown to be among the most loyal elements in India. Whatever the *baba* desired, the servant would do. The British writers do not reflect upon the possibility that it is the practice of teaching English children that they are superior beings that may be at fault. What they are worried about is that the children use their power over their parents and also that if they stay in India too long they will become Indianized. They worry that the children will pick up Indian speech inflections or lose their English 'racial inheritance' of activity for its own sake because of the ease of the Indian life.

Other groups of English in India, like missionaries and businessmen, are rarely treated. Missionaries do appear as minor characters in several of the stories and novels and Hunter's *The Old Missionary*, Perrin's *Idolatry*, and Steel's *The Hosts of the Lord* are novels which deal with this side of Anglo-Indian society. Generally speaking, however, their characters are not highly developed. The most important point regarding them is that even when they are most optimistic regarding conversion they have little success. The Old Missionary, himself, does not believe that he has made any real converts, but does hope that in the next generation the children of the people he has baptized will become good Christians.[1] In no other case does a missionary even feel this confident about the chance of success.

Usually the missionaries are shown to understand fully what they are doing. No longer is conversion to Christianity being depicted as a major part of the British mission. This is due, in part, to the decreasing evangelical fervour and, in part, to the strong emphasis on the differences between the races. Indians might as well retain their native religions because they cannot, in fact should not, become Westernized through a new religion. The Christianity of these authors no longer holds the idea of the universality of the religion. Rather, Christianity has become another of the badges which the English wear in showing how unique they are.

If missionaries play only a minor role, men who have come to India in order to make their fortunes barely exist at all. Outside of Henty's boys' stories which in several respects, like this, are

---

[1] Hunter, *The Old Missionary*, p. 24.

anachronistic, the few men who are so depicted are shown, like Scott's Phillip Lamond, not to be 'good and true Englishmen'. There is a dislike for imputing any economic motive to the British in India because it detracts from the idea that the British were there in order to work hard and that *that* is a value in itself.

One last group of Englishmen to be considered stands in a different relationship to India than these other groups. This is the Englishman who has left India. Sir John Carson who has returned to England after having served as the Lieutenant-Governor of the United Provinces remarks that where yesterday he had been 'a great ruler . . . with a council and an organized Government, subordinated to his leadership'[1] he was 'now a bore at his club'.[2] In the same novel Colonel Dewes remarks that he no longer feels comfortable in either England or India, saying: 'Out here one remembers the comfort of England and looks forward to it. But back there, one forgets the discomfort of India.'[3] In England 'one had lost one's associations. . . . On the whole it was pretty dull', but 'I had my good time in India— twenty-five years of it, the prime of my life. No; I have nothing to complain of.'[4] Similarly, Mark Jervis' missing father turns out to be unable ever to leave India. 'India is my country, it has got into my blood.'[5] On his death-bed he talks about India as 'the siren' who cannot be escaped by those who have known her. Although he is an admirable figure, the father is shown to be, in Waring's harsh but fitting words, like other Englishmen in India who have 'become fossilized' by the 'easy going life'.[6] Phillip Lamond admits that he has become something of a fatalist because of his long contact with India.[7] In this group one sees something of the same fear which motivated Tarvin and Dervasse.

India might provide an enjoyable experience, but the Englishman was expected also to realize that he is an Englishman first and foremost and that he should not let himself get involved with India. Even if it does not 'fossilize' him or his children, it may well make it impossible for him to return to his 'rightful' place in English society. While Colonel Dewes does

---

[1] A. E. W. Mason, *The Broken Road*, p. 69. [2] Ibid., p. 145. [3] Ibid.
[4] Ibid. [5] Croker, *Mr. Jervis*, vol. 3, p. 49. [6] Ibid., vol. 2, pp. 14–15.
[7] Scott, *Flotsam*, p. 92.

not regret his life in India it has made it impossible for him to plunge, as he should, into civic affairs in England.[1] This is also a comment on the theme of British sacrifice. It is clear that these authors believed that the English in India would have to sacrifice themselves in some way. The important thing was to be careful of what kind of a sacrifice was made. It was proper to sacrifice one's life or health, but not one's racial and cultural purity and traditions.

Despite the generally secure feeling from which the British of this period looked at their position in India, a feeling of melancholy is not totally lacking. The emphasis on leadership may well be an expression of some lack of confidence. As a social psychologist has pointed out: 'We do not know enough about active methods of strengthening man's mental defenses. But we are very conscious of the fact that leadership and identification with the leader play an important role.'[2] The same thing is perhaps true of the concentration of these writers on rules and laws to hold all people within certain limits. This has been taken by one critic to mean that Anglo-Indian society felt itself to be threatened and that, therefore, the forces of social control had to be used to keep their society together.[3]

At times, even before the turn of the century, the British occasionally felt, not necessarily that their position in India was insecure, but that all their work and devotion had not made them a part of India or had an effect on the country they ruled. It is in this tone that the death of the Old Missionary is described.

Next evening we buried him. And amid the ceaseless changes of Anglo-Indian life there is one spot—only one—that is always quiet. Let a man revisit even a large Bengal station after a few years, and which of the familiar faces remain? He finds new civilians in the courts, a new uniform on the parade ground, strange voices at the mess-table, new assistants in the indigo factories. The ladies who bowed languidly elsewhere: as for the groups of children who played

[1] A. E. W. Mason, *The Broken Road*, p. 145.

[2] Joost A. M. Meerloo, 'Brainwashing and Menticide: Some implications of Conscious and Unconscious Thought Control', in Maurice R. Stein, Arthur J. Vidich and David Manning White, eds., *Identity and Anxiety: Survival of the Person in Mass Society*, Glencoe, Illinois, 1960, p. 518.

[3] Noel Annan, 'Rudyard Kipling as a Sociologist', *Kipling Journal*, 111, October 1954, pp. 5–6.

round the band-station, one or two tiny graves are all that is left of them in the station. The Englishman in India has no home, and leaves no memory.[1]

Nonetheless, the overwhelming impression of this period remains one of confidence.

[1] Hunter, *The Old Missionary*, pp. 132–3.

III

THE INDIAN SCENE

The India of which the Late Victorian British authors wrote was far smaller geographically than the daub of red on the map of South Asia in 1890. The limited view that the British had of India is shown by the fact that virtually all the novels of this period are set in north-western Indian—the Punjab, North West Frontier Province, and Himalayan foothills. There are a few cases where the locale is Maharashtra or Burma, but Bengal, Central, and South India are almost completely absent.

There are several possible reasons for the limited area used for settings. Rudyard Kipling here, as in many things concerning the British image of India, provides the starting point. Although he does occasionally set his stories in other areas, it is the Punjab and Himalayas that first come to mind when Kipling's name is thought of. He turned to that part of India which he knew best—the area of his birth and most of his experience. The success which followed from his Indian stories was bound to attract a number of imitators who would write about the same areas.

Yet as important as this may be it is not a sufficient reason for this single-minded concern with the north-west. There certainly were enough British in the rest of India to have written about the India with which they were most familiar, but they did not do this. The Punjab fitted in perfectly with the rest of the British image. It is impossible to say whether the setting caused the image or the image the setting. It is clear, however, that without the large-scale agreement between the two there would not have been this continual emphasis.

These thoughts find corroboration in the treatment that Kipling gives to Burma in some of the stories in *Soldiers Three* and especially in 'Georgie Porgie'. He wrote about Burma not because he knew it, but because, like the Punjab, it was a recent acquisition and one which had not yet been completely brought under the control of the Calcutta Government.

The men who run ahead of the cars of Decency and Propriety, and make the jungle ways straight, cannot be judged in the same manner as the stay-at-home folk of the ranks of the regular *Tchin*. . . . These were the men who could never pass examinations, and would have been too pronounced in their ideas for the administration of bureau-worked Provinces. The Supreme Government stepped in as soon as might be, with codes and regulations, and all but reduced New Burma to the dead Indian level; but there was a short time during which strong men were necessary and ploughed a field for themselves.[1]

Burma was an area where, at least in the recent past, military affairs were of significance and where there was still a place for the strong man operating on his own. It is not that Kipling knew Burma, but rather that it pre-eminently offered room for the practice of the ideals he valued. For Kipling, and virtually his whole generation of writers about the Indian scene, the existence of British rule there was important chiefly as an outlet for action.[2]

The emphasis on the Punjab meant that the image of India in fiction was limited. This is certainly not the most typical area of India, but in the literature of the period it is made to appear as the whole of the country. In this area the solutions to problems were largely those in which the army could play the major role. This was the period of crisis with Russia over the control of the passes and the dangers from Afghanistan were still recent enough to create some interest. It was in the north-west that the British were doing that which seemed best to express the ideals of late nineteenth-century imperialism as they defended the borders of civilization from the primitive Pathans and the always dangerous Russians while bringing material improvements to the local peasants. Because this area was the part of India which had most recently come under British control it also provided the best sphere of activity for the strong individual unhampered by control from without. Not only were the Punjab and surrounding areas unique in terms of the British, but they were equally unique on the Indian side. Here,

[1] Rudyard Kipling, 'Georgie Porgie', in *Life's Handicap*, pp. 307–8.
[2] Edwardes, 'Rudyard Kipling and the Imperial Imagination', p. 444.

in one of the few Muslim majority areas, the war-like Sikhs play an abnormally large role. Hindu society, which in most areas is dominant, here is of less significance, and the division between the Hindu *bunniah* (merchant) and the Muslim or Sikh peasant is clearer than it would be in most places. There also would be far fewer Westernized Indians found in the Punjab than in those areas of India with which the British had had longer contact.

Just as important as the question of why there was this concentration on one area and the effect of such concentration is the question of why the rest of India was completely neglected and what the effect of this was. To answer this is like looking at the reverse side of a coin. Just as the Punjab supplied the area in which British values could be acted out, so in the rest of India they could not be so easily performed. The most surprising omission is Bengal since this was the area of India with which the British had had the longest and deepest relationship. One reason may have been the climate there which discouraged any serious writing. Of equal importance is that there the problems which had to be dealt with demanded the use of values totally alien to those they most admired. Instead of being the home of adventure where the independent soldier or administrator could act vigorously toward the primitive India, Bengal was the centre of a bureaucracy which had little contact with the simple Indian peasant. There was almost no chance for the Briton to exercise forceful independent action there. In Bengal he was limited by rules which were not of his own making. There was no frontier action to take the masculine Englishman out of what had become a rather routine existence in Calcutta or any other place with a large Anglo-Indian settlement. Since it was the escape from this routine which was one of the main attractions of India for the British, any area which did not provide this was not a fit scene of endeavour—and certainly not for the setting of novels of romantic adventure. Simply speaking, there was nothing of the Frontier in most of India and it was the Frontier that the British idealized.

On the Indian side, the problem of dealing with Westernized Indians, who perhaps desired more than irrigation projects, was disconcerting. The Westernized Indians did not fit into the image of how a 'good Indian', or for that matter, a 'real Indian', behaved. The kind of problems which existed in areas like Bengal were bound to be more domestic and administrative than international and military. Furthermore, the problem of relations between the races, a problem which most authors chose to ignore even when they saw it, was of greater significance in the more Westernized areas with their greater number of Englishmen and Anglicized Indians.

Just as the imagined India of the late nineteenth-century British is limited to north-western India, so it is largely limited to non-urban India. Village India is represented, especially in the purely Indian tales, but it is noticeable that there are few stories set in any of the great cities of India—Calcutta, Bombay, Madras, or Delhi. When the cities are not avoided they are described with distaste. Kipling refers to 'the great Calcutta stink'[1] and in ' "The City of Dreadful Night" '[2] his description of Lahore fitfully sleeping in oppressive heat certainly is not a pleasant picture.

The authors far preferred to set their stories in the jungles, mountains, hill stations, small villages, or army cantonments rather than in the cities. In writing about the cities it would be necessary to write about Westernized Indians or the Indian businessmen, neither of which fitted the pattern by which Britain looked at India. These groups could be ignored in village India. Furthermore, there is something non-Indian or not 'really Indian' in the cities. If, as these writers believed, the 'real India' was the India of the Frontier and small villages then urban India could be rejected as being 'false'. Certainly this omission cannot be accounted for by the lack of knowledge by the British of the cities. Again, as in the case of the geographical setting, this preference is both a product of, and an element in, the creation of the over-all image.

Outside the cities and larger towns of India it was possible to write about the country without including more than a few stock characters—the loyal servant, the trusty guide, or the passing salaaming villager. Like Croker's characters, an English girl could presumably be raised in the jungle and have hardly any contact with either Indians or Britons. This author's heroes and heroines might as well be flitting about the jungles of the

---

[1] Cited in Stanford, *Ladies in the Sun*, p. 65.
[2] Rudyard Kipling, ' "*The City of Dreadful Night*" ', in *Life's Handicap*, pp. 299–306, *passim*.

Amazon or Congo in spite of the use of Indian terms. Diana
Barrington is the perfect English heroine living in the jungle.
She loves her life there with good reason because she is truly
'Princess of the Jungle'. The chapter with this title is introduced
by some lines from a poem by Cowper which express one of the
major reasons why life in the jungle was idealized by these
believers in paternalism.

I am monarch of all I survey,
My right there is none to dispute.[1]

In two very popular works set in India, Ethel M. Dell
presents similar situations and characters. The only Indians in
The Way of an Eagle are an ayah and a butler, neither of whom
appear more than a couple of times. This was highly unlikely in
an urban setting. The rural India that the British writers
describe is, indeed, an almost Indianless India. In fact, the only
occasions when these authors express any rapturous sentiments
about the physical India—the only times they show a deep love
for India—is when the India they are writing about has nothing
in it to remind them of India. It is an India in which the problem of racial relations can be avoided because the races meet
only in situations in which both already know how to act. Like
the north-west, rural India was a frontier—an area where the
rules were few and where the strong man had the freedom of
action he deemed necessary to the successful development of
his character. It was an area where physical action rather than
mental work was necessary.

'India is to England what the frontier has been to America.'[2]
Like that other frontier, rural India was a place where the
British could do things which everyone accepted as being valuable. In one way they were again protecting the borders of
civilization from the invasion by barbaric forces, like the tigers,
which only the British are able to stop. Most often it is evident
that the attraction of the countryside was that because of these
reasons of adventure and isolation and need, the British could
feel at home there or at least be comfortable and intellectually
relatively secure.

[1] Croker, *Diana Barrington*, Vol. 1, p. 187.
[2] Herbert Marshall McLuhan, 'Kipling and Forster', *Sewanee Review*, LII,
Summer 1944, p. 334.

D

Though several early writers felt obliged to explain that not all of India is hot and steamy—that there are areas where it gets cold and even snows—the basic image of the climate of the country was one of fantastic heat. A climate in which it would be difficult for any Briton to work up to his capacity—this was India. Kipling's 'At the End of the Passage' or ' "The City of Dreadful Night" ' are meant, with success, to fill the reader with horror at the heat. The cemeteries filled with the graves of young men and women, the continual laments of the mother who has to send her children back to England for the sake of their health, the wife who has to run off to Simla to escape the heat of the Plains, or the husband whose job is made all the more difficult by the necessity to separate himself from his loved ones give constant reminders of the heat. Besides reporting what actually was going on, the stories of the difficulties of adjustment to a harsh climate is part of the British image of themselves as a hard-working, self-sacrificing people who are doing their duty under adverse conditions. Where the climate does not provide a harsh enough background for the labours of the British, diseases like typhoid fever and cholera are called in to make things more difficult.

In spite of the numerous stories in which the environment is depicted as being harsh, the general attitude of these writers to the physical India is one of affection. Kipling's *Kim* and Croker's romances are examples of this kind of writing. Depending upon the type of story being written, the physical environment of India is seen in either positive or negative terms. If they want to show the British at work, the latter prevails; but many of the stories stress more favourable aspects. There is not in this period the stress laid on the filth, disease, and malevolence of the land that is to arise later. This is because of the fact that the British in this period had at least some sense of belonging. They did not stress this point, but it is apparent in the generally kind treatments of physical India. Granted that the India in which they felt they belonged was not necessarily the India of fact; nevertheless, they were still in a position where the India they wanted to see and the India they saw were fairly close.

The geographic area itself is looked upon as possessing certain characteristics. India is the land of adventure and mystery. Kipling's ghost stories and frontier adventure stories are so well known as to make a detailed discussion of them unnecessary. When an author who is almost never associated with India, A. Conan Doyle, created the character of Dr. Watson, he obviously wanted to give him some kind of an adventurous romantic background. The original draft of Doyle's notes show Watson as having served in the Sudan, but this was soon scratched out and replaced by Afghanistan, where he is supposed to have served in the Second Afghan War.[1] There he was wounded and saw his 'own comrades hacked to death' without losing his nerve.[2] With this kind of an experience he apparently was held to be ready to help Sherlock Holmes in his battles against the London underworld.

When the author of Sherlock Holmes wants to introduce something particularly mysterious, he often turns to India as the source of the mystery. The second of the Holmes' stories contains what Harold Isaacs has called 'the standard Indian villain' of this genre of English literature.[3] In this case he is an Andaman Islander who has accompanied his beloved English master to England in order to find the men who had stolen a treasure from his temple.[4] Here, too, we see the old image of India as a land where great wealth could be gained. Like Henty, because of his lack of first-hand knowledge, Doyle here presents an image that had largely passed out of view.

Even more mysterious than this story is 'The Adventure of the Speckled Band' in which a stepfather has murdered one of his stepdaughters and is trying to murder the other. That this man, Dr. Roylott, had practised medicine in Calcutta gives Holmes the lead he needed because anyone who had dealings with the East was thought to hold mysterious knowledge. The doctor was making use of a poisonous snake in just the way 'as would occur to a clever and ruthless man who had an Eastern training'.[5]

The theme of mystery 'appears to be tied up with the fact that the countries of the Far East are known to have a history and culture which go back much further than our own, and of

[1] Cited in Vincent Starrett, *The Private Life of Sherlock Holmes*, London, 1934, p. 10.
[2] A. Conan Doyle, *A Study in Scarlet*, London, 1888, p. 2.
[3] Harold Isaacs, *Images of Asia*, p. 280.
[4] A. Conan Doyle, *The Sign of Four*, London, 1890, *passim*.
[5] A. Conan Doyle, 'The Adventure of the Speckled Band', in *The Adventures of Sherlock Holmes*, London, 1892, p. 208.

which we know little'.[1] Thus, when the British writers emphasized that India was the home of mystery, they were expressing
not only a belief that the East and West were very different, but
also that the British were at something of a disadvantage in that
India possessed knowledge beyond that of the West.

The Indian people play a relatively minor role in the British
image. There are innumerable stories in which they simply do
not appear. In addition, when they do come on the scene they
are drawn as two-dimensional characters who do very little.
They are all types rather than individuals. This is particularly
noticeable when they are compared with the native characters
who occur in French novels dealing with their empire in the
same period.[2]

Just as the British novelists saw their countrymen primarily
in terms of 'racial characteristics' so they saw the Indians.
'Englishmen turn . . . with the mental remark that the race-
characteristics of India were very instructive.'[3] With great
emphasis they made the point that there is no such thing as an
'Indian race', but rather that there are numerous 'Indian
races'—Hindu, Muslim, and Sikh; Bengali, Rajput, or Pathan.
They distinguished carefully between the 'racial characteristics'
of these groups, but at the same time did make certain generalizations under which all Indians were grouped.

The foremost character trait of the Indian people is that they
are like little children. This is a statement which holds true for
all of the British writers in this period who apply it to virtually
all the Indians with whom they deal. Because they are children,
they must be handled in certain ways. In an age when 'sparing
the rod' was the equivalent of 'spoiling the child' it is obvious
that relations with a people considered to be children would
involve a large degree of force. The image of the Indian as a
child fitted in very nicely with the British image of himself as a
strong all-knowing leader. Among people who were looked on as
his equal he might only be the leader because of superior

[1] Dorothy B. Jones, *The Portrayal of China and India on the American Screen, 1896–1955*, Cambridge, Mass., 1955, p. 81.

[2] On French novels of empire see Maunier, *The Sociology of Colonies*, p. 339; Garratt, 'Indo-British Civilization', in Garratt, ed., *The Legacy of India*, p. 417; and the section on French fiction in Susanne Howe, *Novels of Empire*, New York, 1949, *passim*.

[3] Steel, 'In the Guardianship of God', in *In the Guardianship of God*, p. 3.

development. Among people of a childlike 'race' he was the leader by race and he had an obligation to play the father to their child. The British obviously, according to these authors, knew what was right for the Indians just as a father would for his children. Above all he knew that it was dangerous for the Indian child to be given authority over himself or, even worse, others. The child might try to 'usurp' his English father's authority, but if punished immediately, he would recognize the error of his ways. By the 'right of race' the Briton was the leader and father and the Indian the follower and child. Any attempt to upset this was to go against the 'rules of nature'.

Not only did the image of the Indian as a child play a major role in the British image of relations between the two, but it also made for a specific way of looking at the Indians themselves. Looked at in this way they were thought to share the characteristics commonly attributed to children. They lacked self-discipline. It is this trait which made them such poor soldiers when they were officered by fellow Indians, but good soldiers when led by the British.[1] Like children, they were seen to be governed by their emotions rather than by their reasons. The Indian 'is as incapable as a child of understanding what authority means, or where is the danger of disobeying it'.[2] This also meant that they were often felt to be untrustworthy—'These Asiatics are at any time ready to turn traitors, and to join the stronger.'[3] This difference between British and Indians was seen as further proof of British 'superiority'. Related to it are other aspects of the Indian personality such as senseless cruelty, a lack of concern with others, and a tendency towards hysteria.

As George Shepperson has pointed out, there is a mixed valuation in this image of the Indians as children. There are certain good elements in the picture as well as bad ones. In their simplicity and energy, along with their intuitive awareness of people, they possess certain gifts which children have and which adults often lose.[4] Despite this interpretation the image of the Indians as children meant, and gave an excuse for the fact,

---

[1] For example see G. A. Henty, *With Clive in India: or The Beginnings of an Empire*, London, 1884, pp. 119–20.

[2] Kipling, 'His Chance in Life', in *Plain Tales*, p. 65.

[3] Henty, *With Clive in India*, p. 292.

[4] George Shepperson, 'The World of Rudyard Kipling', in Rutherford, ed., *Kipling's Mind and Art*, pp. 130–1.

that the British could govern them as fathers. Furthermore, this image also fitted in with the British emphasis on manliness as a prime value. As Newsome notes, one of the leading sources for this idea was S. T. Coleridge's *Aids to Reflection* where manliness was explained as being in opposition to childishness. In this way there is a definitely positive value put on being manly as opposed to being childlike.[1]

Indians are also believed to be basically conservative. 'Megasthenes' account of his travels through India in the year 300 B.C. . . . might have been written today; for these people do not change, except under pressure from without, and then they disintegrate suddenly.'[2] Although this image was stressed to a larger degree later, it, and the concomitant idea of Indian fatalism, did have some mention here: 'An Oriental crowd was draped in the garb of two thousand years ago, whose thoughts and characteristics had changed almost as little as the fashion of their outward covering.'[3]

Closely related to the childlike image of the Indians held by most of these British writers is the idea that, in a way not unlike children, they were very happy in their life no matter if it might appear harsh to a Westerner. Diana Barrington describes the jungle and its inhabitants:

> I know the malgoozar (or headman) of every village, and many of the inhabitants of the knots of hovels scattered over the land. Perhaps 'hovel' is too harsh a name for those snug and sunny mud abodes, with their thatched roofs covered with melons. . . . What though the mistress of the house labours daily as a coolie for the Biblical price of a sparrow, and carries grain, earth, wood, or water on her head, with high-kilted saree and inimitable grace, and the master spends his time in sitting aloft in a . . . basket, raised on stick in a . . . field, clapping with his wooden clapper, and making the welkin ring with hideous shouts—in short, acting as a scarecrow. . . . Still, when the stone-carrying and parrot-scaring are over for the day, many merry, talkative parties may be met, returning joyously to bake the immortal chupattie and to feast.[4]

Steel looks at the Indian peasant the same way: 'And good pottage is warming, comforting, consoling; for all that the two

[1] Newsome, *Godliness and Good Learning*, p. 196.
[2] Steel, *The Potter's Thumb*, vol. 3, p. 212.   [3] Perrin, *Idolatry*, p. 117.
[4] Croker, *Diana Barrington*, vol. 1, pp. 24–5.

hundred and seventy millions of Indians seldom see it; and yet they are happy.'[1]

Of all the various Indian groups it was the Muslims who were most favoured. 'I am an Occidental, not an Oriental. . . . I think I like Indian Mohammedans, but I cannot go much further in an easterly direction.'[2] The similarities between Christianity and Islam no doubt went some way in making the British feel more at home with the Muslim than with the Hindu. Henty describes how a British soldier came to respect the Muslim servant of his officer. With this personal respect went a toleration for the servant's religion.

> He had come to the conclusion that a man who at stated times in the day would leave his employment, whatever it might be, spread his carpet, and be for some moments lost in prayer, could not be altogether a heathen, especially when he learned . . . that the Mohammedans, like ourselves, worship one God. For the sake of his friend, then, he now generally excluded the Mohammedans from the general designation of heathen, which he still applied to the Hindoos.[3]

This is also interesting as a sign of the loss of evangelical fervour. No longer were the Christian British opposed to the Muslim Indians because of their religion.

At least as important as this, is the image of the Muslims as conquerors. They were an imperial people who, like the British, had captured India from the majority Hindus. In her historical novels dealing with the Great Moguls, Steel often expresses this admiration for the conqueror. She particularly likes Babar because, although he felt himself to be a foreigner in India and didn't particularly like the country, he went ahead and did his work anyway. She describes his attitude on entering India as a conqueror and compares it with those of the more recent English who found themselves in a similar position.

> He felt inclined to cry. A state of mind in which this man of the West and North has the sympathy of thousands upon thousands of others; since there is scarce an Anglo-Indian who has not felt the same on hot, breathless May mornings when the dull eyes, seeking for some object on which to rest, find none, save a wide waste of sand,

[1] Steel, *The Potter's Thumb*, vol. 3, p. 210.
[2] Viscount Morley, quoted in Kincaid, *British Social Life in India*, p. 240.
[3] Henty, *With Clive in India*, pp. 249–50.

an indeterminate *kikar* tree, and an aggressive crow bent on showing you that he is as black inside as he is outside.

'The Most-Clement will forget the unloveliness when he stands once more in the Garden-of-Fidelity,' remarked Kwajah-Kilan with intent; and Babar actually scowled at him. Yet he had not the heart to say in so many words that he had no intention of returning to that Garden-of-Fidelity. The very thought of its beauty made him feel sick; but there was duty as well as beauty to be considered.

And here again he has the sympathy of how many thousand western workers in Hindustan. In truth, Babar should be the patron saint of the Indian Services![1]

Thus the Muslims are seen to have been doing the same thing in India that the British are now doing through their devotion to duty whether they love India or hate it.

Not only are the Muslims seen in a favourable historical light because of their conquests, but they are depicted as possessing the values of activity, masculinity, and forcefulness which, to these writers, were the most important values. The Muslim is represented as being 'smart, capable, and full of resource'.[2] This is particularly true when they are placed against the Hindus for contrast. In Patricia Wentworth's novel of the Mutiny, although the leader of the trouble is the Hindu Sereek Dhundoo Panth, he is incapable of any forceful action. It is the Muslim grey eminence Azimullah who is able to see what he wants and to go ahead and get it. He is most definitely shown in an unfavourable light. Yet he is far more admirable than his Hindu colleagues because, in spite of his being on the 'wrong side', he at least has the strength of character and devotion to action necessary to accomplish something.

Even when the Muslims, particularly the Pathans of the border, fight the British they are respected. According to the British code of honour it was a good thing to fight and be willing to die in the field of battle for what you believed in, even if you might be wrong. After the battle was over it would be possible for 'the two strong men' even perhaps to become friends. Above all else, it would be certain that they understood each other. In Kipling's famous 'Ballad of East and West' a hint of this is

---

[1] Flora Annie Steel, *King-Errant*, London, 1928, p. 273. Note the use of the word 'indeterminate' to describe the tree as another example of seeing India in negative terms.

[2] Croker, *Diana Barrington*, vol. 1, p. 244.

given in the possibility he offers for East and West to be united if 'two strong men' meet.[1] The strength that he and the other British writers of this period are referring to is not only firmness of character, but physical strength. If a man takes part in physical activity he is, by definition, a good man.

This was an era when physical activity of any kind was highly regarded and participation in amateur athletics was held in particular esteem—'amateur sport . . . is the best and soundest thing in England'.[2] It was felt in many circles that a game like cricket was far more than merely a game. In fact it was thought to be as important an institution in the British system as trial by jury or *habeas corpus* because it taught teamwork and the subservience of the individual to the team.[3] Edward Mack in his study of the public schools has noted that 'the question of athletics overshadowed all other aspects of public school life'[4] and it was this public school ethos which lay behind much of the British image of the Indians. Speaking of cricket and tennis, even a missionary like Wray notes: 'It does wonders for them morally and physically, and the next generation will feel the benefit even more of such an innovation.'[5] The reader is told by Merriman that Saránj 'was somewhat remarkable . . . because he . . . had learnt to combine East and West in one clear brain in a manner then little known'.[6] Even if he did not tell us this openly we would know that the Muslim Saránj was a special person because immediately following he is described as having just 'returned from playing polo, of which game he was one of the finest exponents of his day'. Readers of these novels never came across Hindus being singled out for their athletic skill. In all of this the British assurance as to the value of their ideals shines forth. The Muslim was acceptable on the playing fields or the battle fields and therefore he could be admired.

Because they admired the Muslim and believed that they understood him better, the British writers dealt with this group to an abnormally large degree. A list of the Indian characters

---

[1] Rudyard Kipling, 'The Ballad of East and West', in *Departmental Ditties and Barrack Room Ballads*, pp. 185–90.

[2] A. Conan Doyle, 'The Adventure of the Missing Three-Quarter', in *The Return of Sherlock Holmes*, London, 1905, p. 311.

[3] Worsley, *Barbarians and Philistines*, pp. 55–6.

[4] Mack, *Public Schools and British Opinion*, p. 210.

[5] Perrin, *Idolatry*, p. 203.   [6] Scott, *Flotsam*, p. 164.

used by these writers shows the predominance of the Muslim—Mason's Shere Ali; Steel's Fâtma, Shureef, Futteh Deen, Feroza, Mir Ahmed Ali, Azmutoolah Khan, or Roshan Khan; Perrin's Osman or Jan Mahomed; Croker's Hassan; and Wentworth's Imam Bux. This is only a partial listing, but it is impossible to find anything like a roll even this long of Hindu characters—major or minor. Even when it seems to make little dramatic or pedantic difference whether the characters are Hindu or Muslim they are almost invariably the latter. When Hindus do appear it is for some definite purpose as far as the author is concerned.

Hindus, in general, and Bengalis, in particular, are portrayed in a very harsh light. They may be 'mild', but to a Late Victorian this was not a virtue because it carried with it the implication that they lacked the characteristics of force and action which were most highly esteemed. If a person showed a willingness and desire to use force—even if it were for the 'wrong' thing he was respected by the British of the novels. This image is brought out in an interesting comparison between two of Mason's characters—the Prince of Chiltistan, Shere Ali; and the minor personage of Bahadur Gobind, Barrister-at-Law with a B.A. from Cambridge. The Hindu is described as 'the most seditious man in the city'. It is not bad enough in the English eyes that he is seditious, but, in addition, he is 'meanly seditious' because all he does is to write 'letters over a pseudonym in the native papers'.[1] In contrast, after Shere Ali has revolted against the British, the local political agent says that he still admires the Indian. He points out that Shere Ali is unlike one of the weak princes of the south who would have taken to drink when they found that they could not get what they wanted. The border prince, however, has shown himself to be a man by fighting for what he wanted. 'Which of the two is the better man? For me, the man who strikes—even if I have to go up into his country and exact the penalty afterwards.'[2]

Even in passing, the words used to describe the occasional Hindus are negative. Croker's money-lender, Coopoodoo, is money-grubbing, 'supercilious', and has an 'unctuous smile'.[3]

---

[1] A. E. W. Mason, *The Broken Road*, p. 292.
[2] Ibid., p. 302.
[3] Croker, *Diana Barrington*, vol. 3, pp. 76–9.

Perrin's Brahman minister, Krishna, is 'a repulsive-looking old native with a small, evil face'[1] and is 'a crab-like old person with greed and cunning stamped on every wrinkle of his malignant countenance, and in every gesture of his shrivelled little hands'.[2] Gregg describes the *Gentu* (Hindu) *banyans* (*bunniahs*) as cheats in contrast to the rest of the Indians.[3] Guthrie's classic Bengali *babus*, Hurry Bungsho Jabberjee and Chunder Bindabun Ghosh are simply ridiculous.[4] Finally, Kipling gives us the picture of the failure of a Bengali as a ruler on the Frontier.[5]

Why is there so much hatred of the Hindus? 'Intellectually, the European mind was outraged by the Hindus precisely in those three principles which were fundamental to its approach to life, and which it has been applying with ever greater strictness since the Renaissance: that of reason, that of order, and that of measure.'[6] For another thing the British saw the Hindu in a very narrow light as the educated, mercantile, intellectual Indian in contrast to the Muslim soldier and peasant. There are peasant characters who, by their names, are Hindus, but who are not definitely identified as such. When a character is identified as a Hindu he is never a simple peasant. Throughout this period it is this very 'simple peasant' who is most preferred among all Indians and the middle-class Indian who is most disliked. With the identification of the middle class with the Hindu the circle is complete.

Just as the Muslim could be liked because he was thought to possess respected traits, so the Hindu was disliked for the reverse reason. Above all else, he was a coward in the eyes of a people who valued physical bravery. It is not only the Bengali's failure as a governor on the frontier that Kipling is mocking, but the way he turned tail and ran at the first sign of trouble. Guthrie's *babu* takes perverse pride in his lack of courage. As a Bengali, Hurry says in his broken English, that he is 'profusely endowed

---

[1] Perrin, *Idolatry*, p. 108. [2] Ibid., p. 110.

[3] Hilda C. Gregg, *In Furthest Ind*, Edinburgh and London, 1894, p. 44.

[4] Thomas Anstey Guthrie, *A Bayard From Bengal*, London, 1902, *passim*; and *Baboo Hurry Bungsho Jabberjee, B.A.*, London, 1897, *passim*.

[5] Rudyard Kipling, 'The Head of the District', in *Life's Handicap*, pp. 102–29 *passim*.

[6] Nirad C. Chaudhuri, 'On Understanding the Hindus', *Encounter*, XXIV, July 1965, p. 24.

with the fugacious instinct' and is 'not racially a temarious'.[1]
When he goes hunting on the moors of Scotland he hears 'that
the grouse on this moor were of an excessive wildness', and 'was
at first apprehensive that one might fly at my nose or eyes
while I was busied in defending myself against its fellows'.[2]
When Hurry meets an ex-Calcutta judge, the Indian extols the
virtues of Bengalis, saying that they should serve in all important posts.

Wherein his Honour did warmly agree, assuring me with fatherly
benignancy of the pleasure with which he would hear of my appoint-
ment to be Head of a District somewhere on the Punjab frontier, and
mentioning how a certain native Bengali gentleman of his acquain-
tance, Deputy-Commissioner Grish Chunder De, Esq., M.A., had
distinguished himself splendidly (according to the printed testimony
of Hon'ble Kipling) in such a post of danger.

I replied that I was not passionately in love with personal danger,
and that in my case *cedant arma togae*, and my tongue was mightier
than my sword, but that there was no doubt that we Bengalis were
intellectually competent to govern the whole country, provided only
that we were backed up from behind by a large English military
force to uphold out authority, as otherwise we should soon be the
pretty pickles, owing to brutal violence from Sikhs, Rajputs, Marathas, and similar uncivilised coarse races.[3]

Out of his own mouth this Bengali *babu* had condemned his
'race' and himself. Obviously, everyone reading this account
was expected to be familiar with the Kipling story, 'The Head
of the District', which is discussed below and to know that when
Hurry can find in Grish Chunder De the best example of Bengali courage he is absolutely proving the Bengalis to be complete cowards. This is in direct contrast to the respect shown for
the Muslim even when he fights the British. The Hindu is
shown as not even being capable of fighting in this way.
Rather he stands behind the scene stirring the others up and
then runs away if the going gets too tough.

It is not enough that the Hindu, as seen by the authors and
shown to their readers, is not brave, but he is also a poor athlete.
Whereas, the Muslim rode his horse magnificently and became
a fine polo player or cricketer, the Hindu showed no interest or
ability in these sports which were deemed necessary in the

[1] Guthrie, *Baboo Hurry Bungsho Jabberjee*, p. 66.   [2] Ibid., p. 201.
[3] Ibid., pp. 121–2.

development of the Late Victorian gentleman. Just as a non-athlete could not be trusted in Britain, so he could not be trusted in India and if this meant casting out an entire group of people, so be it.

In keeping with the rest of this image, the Hindu was shown to be incapable of exercising authority even when he was given the opportunity. With leadership ability as the premium value, this failure was further proof of the Hindu's innate inferiority. The story 'The Head of the District' by Kipling points up that not only does 'the blood-instinct of the race' run true in bringing those of British blood to positions where they can successfully exercise authority, but that the opposite is just as true. The Viceroy appointed a Bengali as chief administrator of a frontier district and immediately trouble began there because of his inability. The British assistant puts it down while the Bengali flees for his life. Before making post-haste for safety he did as had been predicted early in the story and sought to put all the blame on the British. This story brings out not only the cowardice of the Hindu, and particularly the Bengali, but also his inability to rule and his unwillingness to do his *duty* and stick to his job.

In all of these things there is something non-masculine, in fact, almost feminine, being shown in the Hindu character. In keeping with the significance of the concept of manliness for the British, anything effeminate was bad. Manliness had two sides to it. First, it was the opposite of childishness and, second, it was the opposite of femininity.[1] This concept emphasized physical strength as the most important attribute of man. If he did not make use of it, he was not a full-fledged man.[2] Thus, of all the Indians, the Hindus in particular were believed to be unmanly in both senses of the word—childish and effeminate.

Although all Indians are shown to possess a high degree of fatalism, it is in regard to the Hindu characters that this is most fully developed. India was seen to be the 'home of fatalism' and the Hindus were the most particularly affected by this. When Wentworth's Sereek Dhundoo Panth hesitates over whether or not to take part in the Mutiny, he is persuaded by Azimullah's clever use of the idea that it is his fate to do so. The Hindu yields while thinking: 'Who was he to fight against Fate, that real,

[1] Newsome, *Godliness and Good Learning*, p. 197.
[2] Ibid., p. 209.

unchanging deity of the East.'[1] This attitude towards Fate was believed especially to immobilize the Hindu—this when action in and of itself was thought to be good.

Not only the character of the Hindus, but also the religion that they followed was a reason for this dislike. Whereas Islam could be understood as something Western in basis, Hinduism seemed to the British to be completely in conflict with Western ideas. The religion is seen to be negative and passive—two things which went against British values. This vision often frightened the British.

Hinduism was also seen to be a cruel religion. Ramoo in Henty's *Colonel Thorndyke's Secret* has spent years serving Colonel Thorndyke in England only to regain a jewel taken from his temple. Despite love for his master, the Hindu kills him to regain the jewel. Personal feelings cannot interfere with the demands of his religion. It is further interesting to note that Henty does not condemn him for this act personally—it at least shows a willingness to act rather than to sit around and do nothing. Steel sums up this whole attitude in the words of the Brahman Shevdeo after killing a little Indian albino boy who he feels is a curse on his English master: 'What is a Sudra or two more or less to the Brahman?'[2]

This acceptance and even enjoyment of cruelty is not limited to the Hindus, but is shown to be something that is true of all Indians although it is more marked in the Hindus. It is in direct contrast to the way in which the British tended to see themselves. Whereas Wentworth describes the Indians thinking nothing of, and being little affected by, the murders at Cawnpore, when the English heroine has to kill a bird in order to get food for herself and her companion, she finds herself horrified.

Now she rubbed her hands in the mud, and then washed them clean. She was glad that it was getting dark, so that she could not see. She had a dreadful feeling that her hands were still red, still stained with blood—so much agony. Strange, that after all the horrors of Cawnpore, she should feel like a murderess because she had killed a bird.[3]

---

[1] Wentworth, *The Devil's Wind*, p. 188.

[2] Steel, 'The Bhut-Baby', in *The Flower of Forgiveness*, vol. 1, p. 146. This is one of the few places where a Brahman is shown in terms of loyalty.

[3] Wentworth, *The Devil's Wind*, p. 267.

Actually nothing could be less surprising. This is one part of the British feeling that not only were there differences between themselves and the Indians, but, furthermore, that British sensibilities were loftier in all cases.

The Eurasian community plays only a minor role in the overall image of the Indian people in this early period.[1] Even in the rare references to the character of the Eurasian community it was uniformly presented as unfavourable with no attempt at understanding its complexities. On the occasion of a train wreck, Honor Gordon helps the injured while a Eurasian 'stood by, talking incessantly—but doing nothing else'.[2] 'Typically' Eurasian is the minor nameless character in Perrin's *Idolatry* who is 'obsequious' and looks on the British with 'ingratiating smiles'.[3] Wentworth gives us a real Eurasian villain in Rao Sahib who is known to the English as Francis Manners. In her introduction, the author makes a point of discussing the historical accuracy of the novel. She points out that the Nana Sahib actually did have a nephew known as the Rao Sahib, but adds that she has 'given him a half share of English blood, which is fiction'. As explanation for this addition to fact, she goes on to write: 'Those of my readers who have been in India will understand my motive.'[4] Other than this, she does not make herself very clear as to the reason for this distortion. Clearly this point is made in order to make it clear to the readers that they are supposed to be wary of anything Rao Sahib does because once they have been warned that he is a Eurasian, they should 'know' that he cannot be trusted and is liable to do the most horrible things without caring. Finally, Kipling depicts one of the few Eurasian 'heroes' to appear in any of the novels of India in any period. Michele d'Cruz saves the day when a riot occurs, but it is *because* of his English blood and *in spite* of his Indian blood.[5]

This constantly harsh image of the Eurasian is a reflection of several forces in British thought. There is an element of sexual

---

[1] Throughout this study the words 'Eurasian' and 'Anglo-Indian' are used in their original meanings. The former means a person of mixed blood and the latter is an Englishman domiciled in India. In recent years the former term has come to be used rarely and the latter used to describe that group formerly known as 'Eurasians'.

[2] Croker, *Mr. Jervis*, vol. I, p. 179.   [3] Perrin, *Idolatry*, p. 159.

[4] Wentworth, *The Devil's Wind*, p. 5.

[5] Kipling, 'His Chance in Life', in *Plain Tales*, pp. 62–8, *passim*.

guilt which was bound to find expression in a disavowal of this group. The British were responsible for the creation of the Eurasian community and every attempt by the Eurasians to appear to be more like the English only accentuated this fact. Also, in an age such as this one when the British were basing their superiority purely on racial lines, the Eurasians were a threat to their unique position.[1]

'Fusion in the social sense was allied to fusion in the sexual sense.'[2] The Eurasians broke down the clean lines which divided the races in India offering the possibility that some group might be able to rise up and become like the British without the 'necessary' racial purity. Deutsch and Wiener make an interesting point about Kipling's famous poem 'The Ballad of East and West'. They note that it is based upon an actual occurrence. In reality, however, the 'English' hero was a Eurasian. It is strange that Kipling, who must have known this fact, changed it in his poem when it could have been used to add to the drama of the incident. Their conclusion, which seems to be the proper one, is that Kipling rejected using a Eurasian hero because he would have broken down the clean lines that he saw as dividing the groups in India.[3] This attitude is a sign that a feeling of insecurity was not far below the surface.

Both because of the large number of women writers who dealt with India and also because of the general impression of femininity that India gave to the British, the Indian woman assumes a large role in the image of the Indian people. The dominating factor of their character is believed to be their devotion to their husbands or to the man they love. They are depicted as being deeply sensual and passionate individuals who give everything they have to the one they love. If that love is not returned in full, the Indian woman can turn into an animal-like creature wreaking havoc on her 'betrayer'. Regardless of whether her loved one is Indian or English it is dangerous to cross an Indian woman. Mrs. Steel devotes several stories to the theme of the passionate Indian woman who has been wronged. Lazizan burns down the house of her rival in love[4] and Durga

---

[1] R. Pearson, *Eastern Interlude: A Social History of the European Community in Calcutta*, Calcutta, 1954, pp. 228–9.

[2] Maunier, *The Sociology of Colonies*, p. 340.

[3] Deutsch and Wiener, 'The Lonely Nationalism of Rudyard Kipling', p. 509.

[4] Steel, 'Fire and Ice', in *In the Guardianship of God*, pp. 41–57, *passim*.

poisons her lover when he decides to marry someone else.[1]
In a series of very popular stories known collectively as *Indian Tales*, F. W. Bain gave to his English public a highly romantic image of India. Much of this view is related to the idea that India is a feminine country and, in fact, is the home of true femininity. He is very impressed with the devotion of the Indian wife to her position as a wife, mother, and woman. Despite the fact that all of these tales take place in pre-historic times and deal with the great figures of Indian mythology, Bain makes use of them to attack what he sees as the diminishing femininity of the British woman.[2] This whole idea is closely related to the older romantic tradition which looked to a better life in a distant and exotic area. Although works such as these are highly favourable to Indian ideas like reincarnation and the devotion of a wife to her husband, their result was bound to emphasize the idea that there was a basic difference between the East and the West.

When the Indian woman loves another Indian, the 'wronged woman' will react by destroying the object of her love, but when her loved one is an Englishman she will probably give her life for him. Kipling's 'Georgie Porgie' is a classic statement of this theme. The Briton in Burma takes up with a young Burmese girl although, of course, he does not really love her. After a while he returns to England, marries an Englishwoman, and returns to India without realizing the heartbreak he has caused. His Burmese mistress finds him and ends up standing outside his house watching the happiness within while coughing away her life.[3]

The warning is clear to the English—don't get involved with an Indian woman because it is impossible for a Westerner to comprehend the depth of the passions he has tapped. When an Englishman in one of Steel's novels refuses to kiss an Indian girl, the author points out that it was regrettably due to his sense of racial prejudice, but, at the same time, 'the difference between a brown and a white skin was the outward sign of the most inward gulf between sentiment and sheer passion'.[4]

[1] Steel, 'In the House of a Coppersmith', in *The Flower of Forgiveness*, vol. 1, pp. 1–40, *passim*.
[2] See particularly F. W. Bain, *The Descent of the Sun*, London, 1903, p. 52; and *The Livery of Eve*, London, 1917, p. 31.
[3] Kipling, 'Georgie Porgie', in *Life's Handicap*, pp. 307–16, *passim*. This image is not limited to British literature as can be seen in Puccini's opera *Madam Butterfly*.
[4] Steel, *The Potter's Thumb*, vol. 1, pp. 90–1.

IV

ANGLO-INDIAN RELATIONS

The most striking thing in regard to the image of Anglo-Indian relations in this period is that they are not seen to be a major problem. There is a distinct line drawn between the two communities so that by and large there simply are no relations. One of the leading early critics of Anglo-Indian literature who wrote almost contemporaneously with this period, noted that this class of writing concerned itself with five points.

The first is the ever-present sense of exile; the second an unflagging interest in Asiatic religions, as well as in general religious speculation; the third consists of the humorous side of Anglo-Indian official life; the fourth in Indian native life and scenery; the last and perhaps most important, in the ever-varying phases, comic, tragic, or colourless, of Anglo-Indian life.[1]

To the modern reader of this description the lack of any category about cultural or political relations between the races is surprising.

Although Mrs. Steel can write that 'the mutual assimilation of East and West without injury to either' is 'the greatest social problem the world has ever seen, or is likely to see',[2] in the vast majority of her stories the separation between the two races is so great that this problem does not exist. When she, or almost any other author of this period, writes about Indians there are no Englishmen in the story and when she writes about Englishmen there are virtually no Indians present.

None of those authors who see this division think that it is bad. Not only is there nothing good to be gained from getting to know each other, but, in fact, there is likely to be a bad consequence. Involved in this, from the English side, is the feeling that anything which might cause a change in the British value

---

[1] E. F. Oaten, *A Sketch of Anglo-Indian Literature*, London, 1908, pp. 194–5.
[2] Steel, *The Hosts of the Lord*, p. 84.

structure is wrong. Since they saw the British 'mission' in India as being that of ruling, making friends with the Indians was thought to be a step which might limit the British power. Although not so much is made of the problem for the Indians, nevertheless, the same result is seen. If the Indian loses his basic racial character through contact with the Englishman, he, too, is all the worse for it.

Derived from the British view of themselves as 'natural leaders' and the Indians as children, the paternal ideal of ruling was seen to be correct. Thus we are given innumerable pictures of 'good' Indians who go around salaaming to their English masters whom they love. Many completely loyal Indian servants have no other function in life than to serve and honour their English masters, nor do they desire one. Loll Duss becomes a Christian because of his affection for his master;[1] Meinik, 'the faithful Burman', won't allow 'his Englishman' to take any risks and wants always to remain in British territory;[2] the ayah who cares for the little English children is loyal to her charge at no matter what great cost to her—'there is no nurse so faithful as an ayah';[3] the old servants who 'you see . . . often, these old, anxious-looking retainers, waiting on the Apollo Bunder, or coming aboard in the steam launches with wistful, expectant faces;'[4] or the Andaman Islander of whom his English master says: 'He was staunch and true. . . . No man ever had a more faithful mate',[5] are all cut from the same mould. While Indians are often described in these terms, this is not always pointed out as a virtue. Rather it is a necessity because of their race. 'Dhurm Singh, as a rule, did things *dhurm nâl*—partly because a slow, invincible tenacity of purpose made all chopping and changing distasteful, partly because fidelity to the master is sucked in with the mother's milk: very little, it is to be feared, from conscious virtue.'[6] Thus, an Indian's loyalty to the British did not necessarily make him a morally superior individual—it was simply expected of him.

If the Indians were expected to act like good children and

---

[1] Gregg, *In Furthest Ind*, p. 271.   [2] Henty, *On the Irrawaddy*, p. 215 and p. 297.
[3] Scott, *Flotsam*, p. 26.
[4] Steel, 'For the Faith', in *The Flower of Forgiveness*, p. 54.
[5] Doyle, *The Sign of Four*, p. 272.
[6] Steel, 'For the Faith', in *The Flower of Forgiveness*, p. 54. '*Dhurm nâl*' means 'with faith'.

love their English parents, likewise the English were expected to
be good parents. Rarely are we given English figures who do not
accept their responsibilities. When such characters are encountered, they are harshly shown to lack those basic characteristics of fairness, honesty, and a love of action which mark the
British here. If a man is not a 'pukka sahib' he is not worthy of
being served and the Indians, in a way not unlike that of children, can intuitively tell whether or not an Englishman properly
fits the mould: 'That is the first thing they find out about an
Englishman.'[1]

For the British to do their duty as parents it is naturally most
important that they recognize both their superior position and
the fact that the Indians, because of their 'racial character',
must be treated as dependants. Half of the British mistakes in
India are blamed on the 'false' British notion of kindness in
treating the Indians as the British themselves would like to be
treated. 'And when we come to mere justice! we might as well
give a child the right to appeal against his mother when he has
disobeyed her. What chance would the child have, to begin
with, and then what good would it do?'[2]

When the British are thought to be worthy of being served,
which in the context of this period means that they are 'good
Englishmen', the Indians are shown as looking up to them and
accepting whatever they do with good grace. The British
rarely resort to the use of force although this possibility is always
present in the background. Any 'lowering of the lion's tail' is
thought apt to bring about trouble for the British in India and
the 'Peace with Dishonour' party is felt to be totally mistaken as
to policy.[3] These authors continually stress the necessity for the
British to recognize that because the Indians are like children
and they are the 'natural' leaders, they must be willing and
able to use their position of strength. 'It may be very well to be
lenient when one is dealing with a European enemy, but
magnanimity does not pay when you have to do with Orientals,
who don't care a rap for treaty engagements, and who always
regard concessions as being simply a proof of weakness.'[4]

Particularly in the stories of the Mutiny there is a constant

---

[1] Steel, 'For the Faith', in *The Flower of Forgiveness*, p. 60.
[2] Steel, *The Potter's Thumb*, vol. 3, p. 143.   [3] Ibid., vol. 2, p. 5.
[4] Henty, *On the Irrawaddy*, p. 186.

theme that much of the trouble was due to the British failure to realize their own power and to use it. Marqueray's statement that the reason why his troops remained loyal, unlike those of the other English commanders, was because he relied on fear rather than kindness to control his men is one expression of this idea.

Frederick Marqueray knew something of Asiatic warfare, and that in such a fight as he perhaps foresaw even then, the only course for Englishmen was to dare—and dare—and dare again.

Looking back now to the great Mutiny in the cool repose of historical reflection, we arrive at the same conclusion. It was those who dared who saved India.[1]

In the best known of the Mutiny novels, *On the Face of the Waters*, Steel expresses the same sentiments. Her hero, James Douglas, has 'recognized' this fact from the start as he assures everyone that the only way to stop the spread of false rumours about things like bone dust being put in the flour to defile all the Indians was to thrash those people who were spreading them.[2] When the Mutiny does begin, many of the Indians are described as taking part in the looting and murdering, but at the same time many of them are said to stand aside and wait 'with a certain callousness, to see if the master would come or if folk said true when they declared his time was past, his day done'.[3] Later, Douglas is shown talking to Nicholson and Hodson. He explains to them that the basic problem is that the Indians believe that the British are in 'a blind funk' and are afraid to act. 'I now assert that they had a right to say so. We never stirred hand or foot for a whole month.'[4] Douglas is afraid that the British are too worried about the threat to their rule although he can see nothing for them to really worry about. 'Where has an order to charge, to advance boldly, met with a reverse?'[5] Finally, the heroes of the Mutiny are shown to have realized the truth of what Douglas said.

Some men, however—amongst them Baird Smith and John Nicholson—took no heed of sickness or death. And these two, especially, looked into each other's eyes and said, 'When you are ready I'm ready.' Their seniors might say that an assault would be thrown on the hazard of a die. What of that—if men are prepared to

---

[1] Scott, *Flotsam*, pp. 148–9.   [2] Steel, *On the Face of the Waters*, p. 46.
[3] Ibid., p. 178.   [4] Ibid., p. 355.
[5] Steel, *On the Face of the Waters*, p. 356.

throw sixes, as these two were? They had to be thrown, if India was to be kept; if this bubble of sovereignty was to be pricked, the gas let out.[1]

Although not directed towards an historical occurrence, Mason, too, brings in this idea. In one scene a woman comes to the area posing as a goddess and is being used by the priests to cause trouble. The Political Agent, Ralston, realizes the danger and sees the difficulties in finding a solution without causing additional turmoil. 'To assume that no one questioned his authority was in Ralston's view the best way and the quickest to establish it.'[2] So he merely lets the woman know that he has both the force and the willingness to use it and she leaves.

None of this means that the British believed that force was the only answer to the question of how best to rule India, but there does appear to have been widespread agreement that if ever the British reached the point of being afraid to use this force, they would have doomed themselves. Since, in this period, and for many later authors, British rule was beneficial to both sides, an unwillingness to use force was a bad thing for both the British and the Indians.

More often than force the British are shown using their intelligence to overcome opposition. Just as Kipling's Tarvin showed his intelligence in using the Indian queen's passion to overcome her, so Mason's Ralston shows his 'superiority' in a similar way. He has to settle a feud between Futteh Ali Shah and another Afridi. The problem is a difficult one and he finally decides that he must get Futteh Ali Shah to retreat. In order to accomplish this, he asks the Indian to accompany him on a walk—a request which the Indian must accept because it is an honour. Ralston knows this and also knows that Futteh Ali Shah will have to walk as long as the Englishman wants to or else lose face. This is precisely what does happen until the weary Indian is forced to agree to Ralston's terms in order to stop the walk.[3]

---

[1] Steel, *On the Face of the Waters*, p. 388. See also Edward Shanks, *Rudyard Kipling: A Study in Literature and Political Ideals*, London, 1940, p. 83, on the acceptability of the use of war as a method of control for the authors of this period.

[2] A. E. W. Mason, *The Broken Road*, p. 179.

[3] Ibid., pp. 190–2. In his autobiography Leonard Woolf describes an identical situation in which he took part. The salt contractors had refused to do their work for the going rate and wanted the government to pay more. After Woolf had un-

The interesting thing is that the Indians are shown to *smile* at the British victories over other Indians with the implication being that they know that the British are right and approve of whatever they do to win. Indians are shown to believe that true justice can come only through a personal appeal to the sahib. This is a basic part of the image of paternalistic relations. It brings out the idea that the Indians not only believe the British are efficient and fair, but also that they enjoy the way in which they are ruled. In one case a holy man pretends to a crowd that his spirit has gone inside a cannon while, in fact, he has smuggled a small boy in there. An English officer gets a small Sikh to crawl into the cannon and pull 'the voice' out of it. Not only is the Englishman pleased with the result, but 'after much laughter and congratulations, the crowd parted with *smiles*.'[1]

There is a commonly held feeling that the Indians *expect* the British to utilize force or the threat of it and that only when the rulers do this are they recognized as such by the Indians. When, in Steel's novel of the Mutiny, Jim Douglas orders his female Rajput servant, Tara, to take care of the Englishwoman, Kate, he feels that the Rajput has not agreed quickly enough. He becomes very angry and says that he will kill anyone who threatens the Englishwoman. Tara is shown to *smile* as she compliments Jim on the force of his anger.[2] In all of these approaches to Anglo-Indian relations there is a strong feeling of superiority on the British side and also the idea that the Indians recognized this 'fact'.

Anything which disrupts this relationship is thought to be a bad thing and, likewise, any person who does so is a bad person. Most of the Indians who are shown as having any dealings with the British are characterized as being very loyal, but even in this age of relative security a few disloyal and therefore, in the British eyes, 'bad' Indians are shown.

successfully tried to get one of the leading contractors to agree to working under the old rate, he asked the Ceylonese to go for a walk with him so that they could continue talking. It was impossible for the Ceylonese to turn back although Woolf threatened to keep on walking all night long. He was afraid of losing face. Finally, in Woolf's words: 'He turned to me with a smile: "Well, Your Honour, I'll take . . ." ' the old rate. With this accomplished, they turned back. Note the fact that the Ceylonese is shown to *smile*. Leonard Woolf, *Growing*, London, 1961, pp. 184–5.

[1] Steel, *The Hosts of the Lord*, p. 165. My italics.
[2] Steel, *On the Face of the Waters*, p. 269.

Notably lacking from the image of the disloyal Indian is the
Indian nationalist. There is virtually no discussion of this force
despite the fact that the Congress Party had already been
founded. It is almost as if the British writing about India either
did not recognize its existence or else chose to ignore it. One of
the rare cases where Indian nationalism is discussed is in a short
story by Kipling which is rarely mentioned by his critics. In this
story he again uses Pagett, M.P., as the butt of his attack. In this
attack Kipling presages the following period in which discussions of this phenomenon appear frequently. The story, 'The
Enlightenments of Pagett, M.P.,' opens with a quote from
Burke's *Reflections on the Revolution in France.*

Because half a dozen grasshoppers under a fern make the field
ring with their importunate chink while thousands of great cattle,
reposed beneath the shadow of the British oak, chew the cud and are
silent, pray do not imagine that those who make the noise are the
only inhabitants of the field that, of course, they are many in number
—or that, after all, they are other than the little, shrivelled, meagre,
hopping, though loud and troublesome insects of the hour.[1]

Just as in the poem dealing with this same man, Pagett is
taught 'the truth' about India, the difference being that instead
of learning about the sacrifice of the British, he is enlightened
about Indian nationalism. He is told by his host, Orde, that
despite Pagett's belief to the contrary, 'nothing could be more
tranquil than the state of popular feeling'.[2] When the Member
of Parliament insists that the mass of Indian people are being
affected by the nationalist agitation, Orde explains that 'the
native side of the movement is the work of a limited class, a
microscopic minority' who 'have no practical knowledge of
affairs'.[3] A procession of people including an English radical
who now works in India, a Sikh, an old Muslim, and a simple
Jat farmer, all of whom are either anti-nationalist or totally
unconcerned with the movement, are paraded before the
Parliamentarian. Finally he meets a nationalist in the person of
a young Hindu college student and the boy's glib answers plus
Orde's explanations show him not only that he has a great deal
to learn, but also that Indian nationalism is far from being the

[1] Quoted in Rudyard Kipling, 'The Enlightenment of Pagett, M.P.', in *Under
the Deodars*, New York, N.D., p. 183.
[2] Ibid., p. 188.   [3] Ibid., p. 191.

kind of a progressive popular movement that he had believed it was when he was in England.

There are a relatively large number of stories and novels based on the Mutiny. It is a significant fact that the Mutiny exercised such a fascination for the writers of this period. 'Of all the great events of this century, as they are reflected in fiction, the Indian Mutiny has taken the firmest hold on the popular imagination.'[1] To these writers with their emphasis on adventure and the use of force, the Mutiny offered a good source of plot. Differing aspects of these works like Wentworth's *The Devil's Wind*, Scott's *Flotsam*, and Steel's *On the Face of the Waters* have been discussed above. At this point, it is appropriate to discuss the third of these novels from another point of view. Steel's was the most effective and popular novel of the Mutiny. In her autobiography the author recounts the great impact which the Mutiny had even on children who were completely untouched by the events. This, and her later contact with India, led her to write a novel based upon the uprising. Although the book 'sold like hot cakes' when it first appeared and was still selling in large numbers at the time of Mrs. Steel's death in 1929,[2] this was not what gave her the most satisfaction from it. Rather it was a letter that she received from a stranger saying that after reading her book he now felt himself able to forgive India for the death of his wife in the Mutiny. To Mrs. Steel this was the important thing because she had meant, through her novel, to show that not all Indians were responsible for the brutalities of the Mutiny.[3]

It is true that the novel contains loyal and good Indians like the Rajputs Soma and Tara and criticism of the British for mistakenly believing that every 'black face' was an enemy. Still, the over-all impression of the book goes only a short way towards correcting this kind of an impression. As she describes the English troops marching on Delhi, she imagines them telling themselves that 'there were but two things to be reckoned with in the wide world. Themselves—Men. Those others—Murderers.'[4] She continues to use these two words throughout the rest of the novel without even taking the trouble to put them in

---

[1] 'The Indian Mutiny in Fiction', p. 218.
[2] Steel, *The Garden of Fidelity*, London, 1930, p. 226.   [3] Ibid., p. 191.
[4] Steel, *On the Face of the Waters*, p. 279.

quotation marks. Thus, even while attempting to show that not all Indians were associated with the Mutiny, Steel helps to continue the image of a link between disloyalty and evil.

Outside of the historical novels where characters like Nana Sahib occur, there is a fascinating assessment of the type of Indian who is disloyal. Bengali *babus* are among this group, but they are not believed actually to be dangerous to the British because of their general ineptitude. The real threats are the leaders of the Indian religions—Brahman, *mullahs*, *sadhus*, and even Jain ascetics. The trouble-makers for Mason are the *mullahs* who are able to utilize the deep Indian religious beliefs to get them to attack the British. We have already met the Brahman Krishna in Perrin's *Idolatry* who is keeping the young prince from being Westernized because it would mark a threat to his continued power. During the Mutiny a Jain ascetic tells the English that the rebels are coming down a path which will bring them to the rear of the defenders. The English doctor asks him why he brought this news and receives the answer: 'They come to kill—and I kill nothing.'[1] Fortunately for the British the doctor does not believe him and he is prepared for the attack which comes the other way. Among the bodies left behind by the defeated mutineers Steel sarcastically notes that there was 'the naked body of a Jain ascetic, with a bit of muslin swathed about his mouth lest, inadvertently, he should bring death to the smallest of God's creatures'.[2]

These religious leaders are simply not to be trusted. The Muscular Christianity of the Late Victorian Era was in direct contrast to what the British saw as Indian religiosity. At least to the public school educated English, their brand of Christianity was the kind of religion that any average healthy extrovert could follow. Such things as asceticism, celibacy, excessive piety, or even too much concern with ritual were felt to be harmful to the development of the manly individual—they were all thought to be the worst kind of effeminate practices.[3] In addition, the evangelical fervour of the early nineteenth century had largely disappeared to be replaced by what was only a formal commitment to religion. The man who was deeply tied to things spiritual was looked upon as being rather strange. For another,

---

[1] Steel, 'In a Fog', in *In the Guardianship of God*, p. 218.   [2] Ibid.
[3] Newsome, *Godliness and Good Learning*, p. 199.

the religious men of India, through their ability to tap a part of the Indian soul which was completely closed to the British, emerged as a real threat. Even if they were not actively stirring up the people against the British, by virtue of their existence alone they were a threat. Finally, the *mullah* or Brahman represented a force that was alien to the whole British ideal of rationalism. The mystery of the East as embodied in these people might make it more interesting, but it also made it more difficult for the British to find a place. Thus, these men emphasized the British sense of not belonging—a feeling which they preferred not to see stressed.

Just as harsh as the treatment of the religious leaders of India is the treatment meted out to the Westernized Indian. 'The only effect our civilization has upon some men I know, is to make them want to keep their hats and their boots on at the same time.'[1] This point has been touched on above, but it is necessary here to make some further comments on this theme. Westernization is seen to 'spoil' the Indian. Roshan Khan and especially Shere Ali are basically good—good in the sense that they possess the virtues which the British generally attribute to the Muslims. However, because they have been exposed to Western thought they have lost their 'natural virtues' and *nothing* else can take the place of these characteristics.

There are two elements which lie behind the continual British emphasis on this point. So long as the Indians retain their 'natural virtues' they will work with and for the British because loyalty is one of their virtues. Once they have lost them they are a danger to the British and, by extension, to themselves. 'And it is difficult to say whether the judgements were a product of the belief that India should not rule herself, or whether the judgements produced that belief. In any case, the themes became a conventional part of the unsystematic theory which rationalized the maintenance of the Empire.'[2]

In one of Steel's novels the distinction between the 'good' aborigine Am-ma and the 'bad' aborigine Gu-gu is based completely on this point. Gu-gu conspires with the enemies of the Raj while Am-ma comes to their aid thus lending his support

---

[1] Steel, *The Hosts of the Lord*, p. 72.
[2] Susanne Hoeber Rudolph, 'The New Courage: An Essay on Gandhi's Psychology', *World Politics*, XVI, October 1963, 99–100.

to the British victory. After the trouble is over Am-ma gives an affadavit. 'I, Am-ma, of the river folk, solemnly affirm that, knowing the *Dee-puk-râg* to be in the power of the *Huzoors,* I several times warned Gu-gu not to follow other masters. But he had learned books, and become ignorant.'[1] Basically speaking, what Gu-gu has become ignorant of are the virtues of his people, such as hunting, swimming, and loyalty. It is significant that when he and Am-ma confront each other in the river—their second home—it is Am-ma who triumphs. He is more skilled in the ways of his people and therefore is not only loyal, but also can handle himself better in his native medium, the water.

Even more fundamental, from the British point of view, is that any Westernized Indian, like any Eurasian, is a threat to the heart of their image of India. This image, based as it is on the separation of the races, cannot allow for any group which might stand in an intermediate position either racially or culturally.

Thus, the British influence on India was seen to have been a mixed blessing. It was good in so far as it was limited to the material or physical improvements of the people. It could also be a good thing for the rare Indian like Saránj who was so exceptional as to be able to handle the effects of living with two cultures. Otherwise, it caused trouble or, at least, was ineffective.

For the same reasons as for the dislike of Westernized Indians, inter-marriage or even concubinage between the races is looked on with great disfavour. From the earlier discussion about the Eurasian community it is clear that because the offspring of such a union would be a 'degenerate' race possessing the vices of both, such unions were, in themselves, bad things. They were also thought to be bad because they would be destructive to either one or both of the partners. The Indian women, such as the girl in 'Georgie Porgie', would be destroyed because they would give too much of themselves to their English partners who could not appreciate their sacrifice. The British male would be destroyed by being 'dragged down' into the Indian environment and hence lose his English values. In an exception, ' "Yoked with an Unbeliever" ' by Kipling, the Indian, Dunmaya, helps the Englishman, Phil, to overcome his weak character and

---

[1] Steel, *The Hosts of the Lord*, p. 330.

become a man. However, even here the problem has a solution only because Dunmaya is a Hill-woman and thus has more things in common with the Englishman, including skin colour, than would a woman of the plains. The solution which is generally offered to such romantic liaisons in the novels and stories is that the Indian woman, never the English man, must die—if she is not deserted first. In none of these stories do the authors permit children born of the union to survive. Even true love between the races as in Kipling's 'Without Benefit of Clergy' normally is not enough to overcome the 'impossibility' of such a relationship.

Speaking of the Hindus, who are always equated with the most traditional side of India, a character sums up two of the British rationalizations for saying that Westernization was of no value.

> You cannot really change them. . . . Why, what have the Mohammedans ever actually done in a thousand years towards producing a radical change in Hindu thought, except by violence? And don't we all know that those of the Hindus who are most closely connected with Europeans are the very ones to display the greatest animosity and revolt against our rule and customs? It is the villagers, the peasants who don't come into continual contact with us who regard us with the most tolerance and respect—not the people who know all our habits, and religion, and ways of thought.[1]

In addition to the ideas that they cannot be changed and that Westernization makes them disloyal, the third of these rationalizations, which is not mentioned in this quote, is, of course, that it makes that Indians 'less-Indian' and therefore violates the commandment of being true to one's own race.

Indians educated in the Western traditions could only become partly educated according to these authors. It was thought to be impossible for them truly to understand Western thought because it was so completely foreign to their way of life. When a group of schoolboys who are learning, in English, about Burke and other English thinkers are told by anti-British trouble makers that the canals being opened in the Punjab are operated by 'the hydraulic power of men's brains'—dead men's brains are removed from their bodies and used to work the canal—they believe it. 'There was nothing about the dynamic

[1] Perrin, *Idolatry*, p. 247.

and hydraulic power of a man's brain in their treatises; but, after all, the statement was scarcely so strange to ignorance as many another held in the books under their arms.'[1]

Roshan Khan, who is described as having the potential of being 'a fine fellow—if—if he wasn't so—so civilized'[2] and who thinks of himself as a proper Englishman while he plays cricket, polo, and tennis, carries a silver cigarette case, and feels un-uncomfortable in native clothes, but is still unable to overcome his basic native racial prejudices. When Captain Dering asks him if the local Hindus still worship an old cannon, 'The Mahomedan's face took on the expression of his race and creed; all unconsciously, too, he reverted to his own language' as he refers to the Hindus as 'idolators'.[3] In an argument with Dya Ram, the Hindu says that he will take the case to the High Court. " 'Carry it to the Court of thy god Indra, if need be, Dya Ram," retorted Roshan, and as he strode off he spat deliberately in the dust. That also surprised him faintly, for he had thought he had learned tolerance of the *Huzoors*.'[4] Not only has he not learned tolerance towards Hindus, but, despite himself, his racial drives make it impossible for him to be tolerant of the English. Once he feels that Dering is going to take the Eurasian Laila away from him he becomes violently anti-English. This is made even worse when he sees Dering courting Laila while she is clothed in native dress, since in that costume the feeling that she belongs to him by right of race becomes even stronger. He thinks of the Englishman 'guzzling swine's flesh and bibbing wine' while 'that faint amaze at the presence in his own mind of such antiquated half-forgotten ideas assailed him again at this point'.[5] Finally he identifies all English with his rival and thinks: 'They needed a teacher, needed a lesson; these aliens, these usurpers, these depravers of women.'[6] Roshan Khan's Western veneer thus only partially hid his basic racial characteristics which took command when a crisis occurred. That tragedy resulted was not so much his fault as the fault of those who tried to make something out of him that he was not. In a very perceptive passage, Steel does note that the fact that Roshan Khan, like many other Indians, had been given a cer-

---

[1] Steel, *The Hosts of the Lord*, pp. 149–50.　　[2] Ibid., p. 216.
[3] Ibid., p. 10.　　　　[4] Ibid., p. 48.　　　[5] Ibid., p. 217.
[6] Ibid., p. 224.

tain position and then denied the right to advance as far as his exceptionally fine abilities might take was a hardship. However, she shows the strength of her times, especially in regard to the image of the Indian's character, when she denies that this would cause any real trouble for Roshan Khan.

Roshan himself, being sensible—above all, being of a nation which accepts limitation as a law of God—was, as a rule, satisfied with his future *risaldar* major-ship, and if he was lucky, *Aide-de-Camp to the Queen*, and a few other titles tacked on to it. Like all natives of India he lived largely on the approbation of his immediate superiors.[1]

A more blatant attack along these same lines is given by Hunter through the mouth of the Old Missionary. This man is shown to understand completely the Indian situation so that his thoughts on this subject are given even more emphasis. He explains:

Your State education is producing a revolt against three principles which, although they were pushed too far in ancient India, represent the deepest wants of human nature—the principle of discipline, the principle of religion, the principle of contentment. ... The indigenous schools educated the working and trading classes for the natural business of their lives. Your Government schools spur on every clever small boy with scholarships and money allowances, to try to get into a bigger school, and so through many bigger schools, with the stimulus of bigger scholarships, to a University degree. In due time you will have on your hands an overgrown clerkly generation, whom you have trained in their youth to depend on Government allowances and to look to Government service, but whose adult ambitions not all the offices of the Government would satisfy. What are you to do with this great clever class, forced up under a foreign system, without discipline, without contentment, and without a God?[2]

The strongest and most fully developed discussion of this problem occurs in A. E. W. Mason's *The Broken Road*. This book was written with a very definite purpose. Mason had recently been elected to Parliament and had undertaken a trip to India in order to become recognized as a specialist on Indian affairs.[3] His success in attaining this goal can be seen by the fact that Curzon wrote him a nine-page letter congratulating him on the

---

[1] Steel, *The Hosts of the Lord*, p. 40.
[2] Hunter, *The Old Missionary*, pp. 84–6.
[3] Roger Lancelyn Green, *A. E. W. Mason*, London, 1952, p. 107.

accuracy of the account.[1] The novel's major point is an attack on the Westernization of Indian princes.

At the beginning of the book the old Khan has decided to send his heir, Shere Khan, to Eton and Oxford despite the opposition of the Political Agent, Luffe. Luffe points out the error of this policy.

> You take these boys to England. You train them in the ways of the West, the ideas of the West, and then you send them back again to the East, to rule over Eastern people, according to Eastern ideas, and you think all is well. I tell you, Dewes, it's sheer lunacy. . . . You have to look at the man as he will be, the hybrid mixture of East and West. . . . You take these boys, you give them Oxford, a season in London. . . . You show them Paris. You give them opportunities of enjoyments, such as no other age, no other place affords—has ever afforded. You give them, for a short while, a life of colour, of swift crowding hours of pleasure, and then you send them back—to settle down in their native States, and obey the orders of the Resident. Do you think they will be content? Do you think they will have their hearts in their work, in their humdrum life, in their elaborate ceremonies? . . . . In England he is treated as an *equal*; here, in spite of his ceremonies, he is an inferior, and will and must be so. . . . Will he be content with a wife of his own people? He is already a stranger among his own folk. He will eat out his heart with bitterness and jealousy.[2]

The wisdom of this man who Mason portrays as 'the wisest of the wise' is borne out in Shere Khan's development. When it is time for him to be recalled from the England he has grown to love, he is no longer sure that he thinks of Chiltistan as his home.

> 'Do I belong here?' he asked. 'Or do I belong to Chiltistan?'
> On the one side was all that during ten years he had gradually learned to love and enjoy; on the other side was his race and land of his birth He could not answer the question; for there was a third possibility which had not yet entered into his speculations, and in that third possibility alone was the answer to be found.[3]

The young man's confusion is only heightened by what he finds on his return to India. He discovers that while the Indians

[1] Stanley J. Kunitz, ed., *Twentieth Century Authors*, New York, 1946, p. 523.
[2] A. E. W. Mason, *The Broken Road*, pp. 30–1.   [3] Ibid., p. 95.

do look on him as an Englishman—something he believes is the truth—the English quite definitely treat him as an 'inferior' Indian. On his arrival the official who meets him is quick to give Shere Khan orders 'for his own good'. He finds the answer to the question he had asked on leaving India. 'When I left England I was in doubt. I could not be sure whether my home, my true home was there or in Chiltistan. . . . I am no longer in doubt. It is neither in England nor in Chiltistan. I am a citizen of no country. I have no place anywhere at all.'[1] Shere Khan is finally driven to utter a tragic phrase: 'I wish to heaven that I had never seen England.'[2] This comes from a man who had felt far more at home in his English schools and with his English friends than he did in India. He finally comes to the personal realization of the cause of the tragedy that has destroyed his life and which results in his being sent off to Burma to rot. 'Those who have done me harm are those who sent me, ten years ago, to England.'[3] The harm was done not only to him, but also to the English because the ill-advised plan of sending him to England for his education eventually meant that England was involved in another frontier war.

The little bit of Western education that most of the educated Indians are able to absorb is only enough to leave them between the two worlds. They are either ridiculous petty trouble makers or are tragic characters who don't know where their place is or how they are supposed to act.

Guthrie's *babus* with their inaccurate, if colourful English; misuse of trite phrases—preferably in schoolboy Latin; and lack of understanding of even the most fundamental aspects of English society are the classic illustrations of the ridiculous Westernized Indian. Western literature is virtually destroyed by these *babus* with their vain attempts to demonstrate how educated they are. From 'Daemon and Pythoness' to 'Simpson and Delilah' to 'Mr. Monty Christo'—every possible allusion is used and misused. When Chunder Bindabun Ghosh finds himself confronted with making a decision between accepting a challenge to a duel or else receiving a kicking, he misuses so many trite phrases that it becomes difficult to separate them. 'So, weeping to find himself between a deep sea and the devil of

---

[1] A. E. W. Mason, *The Broken Road*, p. 137. [2] Ibid., p. 148.
[3] Ibid., p. 133.

a kicking, he accepted the challenge, feeling like Imperial Caesar, when he found himself compelled to climb up a rubicon after having burnt his boots.'[1]

In his autobiography Guthrie recounts that from the time he had been at Cambridge he had been attracted to *babu*-English and wanted to write a story using that dialect. Although he did not personally know any Indians, he felt that through his large personal collection of Indo-Anglian literature and information supplied by friends of his who had lived in India he was able to be accurate. Guthrie admits that while the Hurry Bungsho Jabberjee series was appearing serially in *Punch* in 1897, a number of protests were made on the belief that such a series was bound to cause a great deal of ill-feeling among the higher class of Indians. 'I doubt whether these were, or are, accustomed to regard the Bengali Babu with such veneration as all that.'[2]

Although no other author has been able to match him for comic effects, the type of English spoken by most of the Indian characters throughout this period is similar. That Guthrie, who, unlike most of these authors, had no first-hand knowledge of India is unique in his use of comedy is no accident.

'There are few crisp, incisive, humorous books about India. No one feels blithe, gay, or carefree about it.'[3] It has been noted by many commentators on this class of literature that comedies are almost totally lacking. For the English there, much as they might love India, humour played little role. 'Novels about India provide more vicarious discomfort than anyone is entitled to. They are among the unhappiest books in the language. They are long on atmosphere, but short on humour and on hope.'[4] There may be occasionally humorous accounts of Anglo-Indian life, but on the whole there is so little of this approach that it is surprising when it occurs.

The image of the Bengali *babu* which finds its prototype in Guthrie's work is not totally unfavourable. At times the Indian character is used to show the foibles of British society. The over-

---

[1] Guthrie, *A Bayard from Bengal*, pp. 34–5.

[2] Thomas Anstey Guthrie, *A Long Retrospect*, London and New York, 1936, pp. 232–3.

[3] Howe, *Novels of Empire*, p. 33.

[4] Ibid., p. 32. See also Oaten, *A Sketch of Anglo-Indian Literature*, p. 9; and Santha Rama Rau, 'New Voices from Asia', *American Association of University Women Journal*, October 1964, p. 3.

all picture that comes from reading these works, however, shows the Bengali *babu* as a not very bright, pretentious, foolish, if not totally unlikeable, clown.

This constantly harsh image of the Westernized Indian sums up the difficulty which faced him when he met the alien civilization. If he did not become Westernized, it was looked upon as proof of the fact that he was lacking in ability since it was believed that Western civilization was superior to anything the Indians had to offer. On the other hand, if he did try to model himself after his rulers, he was condemned for trying to ape his 'betters' and in so doing was thought to have lost his integrity in this attempt to become something that he was not.[1]

For the authors more familiar with India, these *babus* were less creatures of comedy, although they remained this because of what was seen as their general ineptitude, than people who caused trouble. Hunamân Singh returns from school to the small Muslim village where his godfather is the Hindu money-lender. Although Hunamân has absolutely no interest in religion he is willing to stir up trouble between the hitherto friendly Hindu and Muslim communities. The issue comes to revolve around the erection of an image of the blue monkey god on the top of the small Hindu temple which the Muslims had allowed to be built behind the façade of the mosque. 'But, though Hunamân cared not at all for the blue monkey god, he worshipped liberty—especially his own; and he preferred it, if possible, with a flavour of law about it. What! deprive a citizen, a subject of the Queen Empress, from due exercise of his religious right?'[2] Although the older men of the village are able finally to find a solution to the problem through the use of traditional methods, for a while Hunamân and his friends get what they want. The affair to them is 'a real, solid, Heaven-sent grievance to a small knot of advanced young pleaders'.[3]

Men like this cause trouble, but at the same time are equally as ridiculous as Guthrie's *babus*. When actual physical violence does erupt, Dya Ram, who had been preaching armed

[1] Rudolph, 'The New Courage', p. 103.
[2] Flora Annie Steel, 'The Blue Monkey', in *From the Five Rivers*, London, 1912, p. 33.
[3] Ibid., p. 71.

resistance in his paper for several years, showed his lack of real spunk. Dr. Dillon explains:

> He barricaded himself in with his printing-press. Fact; jammed his fingers in so doing, and came to me in a blind funk for a professional certificate that the wound could not have been caused by any lethal weapon. As if anyone could ever have suspected him of taking part in raising a row, or even in settling one! His sort are simply negligible quantities.[1]

Steel especially stresses the idea of being caught between two worlds. The half-Westernized Dya Ram does not really know what is expected of him when he is in Western society in contrast to a Rajput prince who has remained unaffected by the West and thus retained his personal dignity. Gopâl, the coppersmith, had attended the Municipal School where

> the forty and odd ounces of grey matter in Gopâl's own skull were leavened with ideas foreign to those which had been transmitted to him through ages of slow heredity. A curious anomaly; one which has to be taken into account by the master builders of the Great Imperial Institute when they count the cost of progress.[2]

This leaves him between the new and the old. When he wants to marry a childless widow with whom he is in love, because his first wife has not been able to have a child, his wife is able to break it up with an appeal to tradition. Gopâl is forced to take a woman he doesn't love and thinks to himself: 'What a fool he had been! halting as it were between the new and the old. He had glossed over the secrecy by appealing to the customs of his forefathers, and now he hated the tie they imposed upon him.'[3]

The problem of mutual understanding, or its lack, between the two races is a theme which came to dominate the British image of India from the second decade of the twentieth century onwards. In this early period, however, this theme is only a minor one. Dr. Dillon remarks in regard to this problem: 'Understand! Of course you don't. I don't though I've been here two years. And what's more, I don't want to. . . . So long as we don't understand them . . . and they don't understand us, we jog along the same path amicably. . . . It is when we begin to

---

[1] Steel, *The Hosts of the Lord*, pp. 334–5.
[2] Steel, 'In the House of the Coppersmith', in *The Flower of Forgiveness*, vol. 2, p. 9.
[3] Ibid., vol. 2, p. 22.

have glimmerings that the deuce and all comes in.'[1] This is but another expression of that constant theme which runs through this period—everything works better so long as the races maintain their separateness and thus their racial and cultural integrity. To attempt to understand India and the Indians was to recognize that there was something worth understanding there. It also would have involved the necessity of the British, to some degree, immersing themselves in Indian culture with the concomitant danger of losing something of their personal heritage.

The reader of this literature constantly found references to the British saying that they could not understand India.

> You'll never plumb the Oriental mind,
> And if you did it isn't worth the toil.
> Think of a sleek French priest in Canada;
> Divide by twenty half-breeds; multiply
> By twice the Sphinx's silence. There's your East.
> And you're as wise as ever. So am I.[2]

This leads to and gives further weight to the distinctions between the races. They are not able to understand each other, but there is not necessarily anything wrong with this. Rather, it is a natural result of the differences which are thought innately to exist. That the Indians do not understand the British or what they are trying to do is evident from the misuse they make of those aspects of British civilization with which they come into contact.

Steel gives us a young girl, Hoshiaribi, who has been attending an English school for sixteen years. In this time she has learned very little. The only thing she can understand is that going to school is a rather pleasant life. As far as she is concerned, she is going to school for only one reason and that is because the English committee is paying her to do so. She thinks that all she has to do to earn the money is to attend classes. Thus she is very upset when the committee rules that since she has been in school so long it is time that her money be taken away and she start to teach for a living. Hoshiaribi

---

[1] Steel, *The Hosts of the Lord*, p. 1.
[2] Rudyard Kipling, 'One Viceroy Resigns', in *Departmental Ditties and Barrack Room Ballads*, p. 103.

complains: 'I have been here all my life. I like it. I don't want to go home and nurse the babies. I don't want to work. The committee paid me to learn, and I have learned. I will learn anything else they like. Why, then, should they take away my scholarship.'[1] This relationship between learning one's lessons and money is proved to her simple mind by the English teacher's statement: 'Do stick to your lessons, and remember why you come here. Think, just think, of the money that is being spent on your education.'[2]

Finally, Hoshiaribi does found a school, but after a while tires of it and leaves it to be run by her little servant Fâtma.

The organization of Mussamat Fâtma's school was excellent, its discipline first class. The cleanliness, too, of its primers, its pens, and its writing-boards was quite abnormal. Not because of abnormal neatness, but because none of these things were ever used. They were there because that was part of the game of school, and Fâtma's school was emphatically a school with the learning left out. To be sure, the pupils chanted their letters, and asserted the gospel that one and one make two all the world over; but, after that, education went down the by-path of learning how to sit still and do as you were bid. Yet somehow the wee girlies liked it well, and their busy mothers liked it better still. In that crowded quarter of evil repute it was something to have a *crèche*, where for a few hours the little ones with a tempting jewel or two were safe from the avarice of any passer-by. And then Fâtma's pupils gave no trouble at home. So the school throve, and though educationally, of course, it was a miserable sham, it gave great satisfaction to all concerned.[3]

This, then, was the result of the money spent to educate Hoshiaribi and showed how the Indians thought that it had been wisely spent even though the result was a far cry from what the committee was trying to do.

One of Kipling's most affectionately drawn Indian characters, Kim's Bengali friend, Hurree Chunder Mookerjee, is interested in collecting examples of native folklore in the hope that he will be accepted into the Royal Society. At the same time, however, and despite his ridicule of native superstitions, he is not above being frightened by a sorceress himself.

Hurry Bungsho Jabberjee in England is equally unable to

[1] Steel, 'At a Girls' School', in *From the Five Rivers*, p. 154.
[2] Ibid., p. 156.   [3] Ibid., p. 171.

understand the British civilization which he thinks he has properly learned while getting his M.A. On one occasion he goes to the Academy to see the paintings. 'There was also a picture of a Diptych, in two portions, with a background of gilt, but the figure of the Diptych himself very poorly represented as an anatomy.'[1] Another time he goes to a wedding where the bridegroom takes him in to see the gifts. Hurry sees the display through purely Indian eyes although as usual he thinks that he understands perfectly and refuses to think that it is necessary for him to ask any questions. He sees 'an apartment wherein was a kind of bazaar, or exhibition of clocks and lamps and stationery cases and knives and forks and other trinkets and gewgaws, none of which appeared to me at all different from similar objects in shop windows.'[2]

In another story by Steel, Bisram, a follower of Kali and a member of the Thugs, who is also the bearer to little Harry, actually gives his life in a vain attempt to save his charge's life from what he thinks is the malevolence of Kali. Harry's parents, and especially his mother, do not have the faintest idea of the mental turmoil that the Indian is going through and think that 'he is just like the rest of them—selfishly set out in what they are accustomed to'.[3] In very practical terms the same author gives us a pair of Englishmen talking about 'the indescribable dignity' of the Brahman.

> It is indescribable . . . because it is compounded of factors not only as wide as the poles as from you and me, but also from each other. Pride and twice-born trebly-distilled ancestry bringing a conviction of inherited worthiness; pride in hardly-acquired devotion giving birth to a sense of personal frailty. That is the Brahman whom we lump into a third-class railway carriage with the ruck of humanity, and then wonder.[4]

Much of this attitude is summed up in the phrase 'the inscrutable Orient'. It is thought to be an area which cannot fully be understood by the Westerner. This image sneaks into many mentions of the Indian people and country even when it is of no significance to the plot. When a case of theft occurs at a college,

[1] Guthrie, *Baboo Hurry Bungsho Jabberjee*, pp. 30–1.   [2] Ibid., p. 110.
[3] Steel, 'Little Henry and His Bearer', in *In the Guardianship of God*, p. 73.
[4] Steel, 'The Flower of Forgiveness', in *The Flower of Forgiveness*, vol. 1, p. 7.

Sherlock Holmes is called in and among the suspects, although
he is not found to be guilty, is an Indian, Daulat Rao. 'He is a
quiet, inscrutable fellow; as most of those Indians are.'[1] Mason's
Political Agent Ralston expresses a similar statement. 'It is
difficult, however long you stay in India, to get behind these
fellows' minds, to understand the thoughts and the motives
which move them. And the longer you stay, the more difficult
you realize it to be.'[2] Finally, Steel, who feels that she knows a
great deal more about India than most people, still ends by giving up any attempt to understand India—'In India . . . it is
foolish to try and settle which comes first, the owl or the egg.
You can't differentiate cause and effect when both are
incomprehensible.'[3]

The place in which the most fundamental and important
lack of British understanding of India, for these authors, occurs
is in the field of land policy. Kipling's 'Tods' Amendment'
which has been discussed above is based upon this problem.
Besides showing a criticism of action by men who are not
personally 'on the spot' this story shows a strong feeling that the
British or Indian Governments were making things harder for
the very people that they were trying to help. Steel takes up the
same theme in several stories. In ' "London" ' she shows a Jat
cultivator who has lost his land because of having the right
of alienation. He cannot understand how the British who, he
feels, are completely worthy of trust could have allowed this to
happen to him. He decides that it must be because the Queen
doesn't know what is going on and goes to London without any
success.[4] Along the same lines the Punjabi peasant Jaimul has
fallen into the debt of a usurer. Traditionally this would not
have been disastrous because the usurer could not get the land.
Under the British system, however, the Hindu money-lender
Anunt Râm is able to take control of the land with the tragic
result of Jaimul murdering the Hindu and then dying himself
by the bite of a snake attracted by the blood on his hands. The
conclusion of this affair is that the home Jaimul had worked so
hard to preserve and better is completely destroyed and his

[1] Doyle, 'The Adventures of the Three Students', in *The Return of Sherlock Holmes*,
p. 262.
[2] A. E. W. Mason, *The Broken Road*, p. 231.
[3] Steel, *On the Face of the Waters*, p. 272.
[4] Steel, " 'London' ", in *The Flower of Forgiveness*, vol. 2, p. 130–55.

family is left without anything—land or the head of the family.[1]
In an interesting dedication to 'Harvest' the same author
expresses similar sentiments.

> Respectfully dedicated to our lawmakers in India, who by giving to
> the soldier-peasants of the Punjab the novel right of alienating their
> ancestral holdings, are fast throwing the land, and with it the balance
> of power, into the hands of money-grabbers; thus reducing those who
> stood by us in our time of trouble to the position of serfs.[2]

The fascinating thing about this and other criticism of a
similar type, besides the fact that it is an expression, in part, of
the British image of peasant India as being the real India, is
that such criticism disappears later. When this same story, in a
revised form, was reissued in the 1920's the dedication was
dropped.[3] Part of this, no doubt, is due to the fact that the
problem of land alienation in the Punjab had been settled, but
it is also an expression of the feeling of relative security which
existed in the 1890s. This kind of criticism saying that the
Government did not understand the Indian situation and was
not following its trust to the letter was acceptable so long as it
was not a part of a general attack and so long as it would not
fall into the wrong, *i.e.* Indian, hands. Granted that it is only a
very specific criticism, but it, along with the criticism of the hill
station society, is interesting, coming from basically friendly
sources. In part, the mere fact that these people felt it was
possible for them to offer criticism concerning certain aspects of
the British in India is a sign of their confidence.

Once serious attacks have begun such 'innocent criticism' by
supporters of the Raj is no longer even to be thought of. Instead
it is necessary to support everything that the Raj does in India
and to ignore what cannot be supported. At the turn of the
century the British in India did not feel themselves to be
threatened politically by the Indians and therefore could afford
to be somewhat critical of specific aspects of their rule in India.

---

[1] Steel, 'Harvest', in ibid., vol. 1, *passim.*
[2] Ibid., vol. 1, p. 34.
[3] Compare the two versions of the story in ibid., and in *Indian Scene*, London,
1933, pp. 374–93.

The Era of Doubt
1910–1935

V

THE BRITISH SELF-IMAGE

The relative confidence in Western civilization felt by the late Victorian and Edwardian English was followed by doubt as to the worth of the whole system.[1] This doubt is the basis of the British image of India from 1910 to 1935. It is difficult to pinpoint the start of this feeling but it had roots even in the security of the turn of the century. It first became a dominant theme in the few years just preceding the final dissolution of this civilization in the horrors of World War I. Following the war the attack reached its height.

There were literary defenders of the old system who continued to write novels and stories highly reminiscent of those of Kipling or Steel, but they, too, were affected by the change. No longer was it possible for them blithely to write about the British mission to action, the suffering of the British in doing what they saw to be their duties, and the loyalty of the childlike Indians. These themes continue to be utilized in defence of the British position, but, unlike the earlier period, they are being consciously used. They are no longer stated in the straightforward way in which they first appeared, but are reiterated in a persistent attempt to prove a point against both the attackers and the self-doubt which affected the defenders.

Thus, in treating the novels of this period, it is necessary to deal with the more complex problem of different images which, although seemingly in direct contradiction to each other, are often actually reflections of similar beliefs. In addition to those writers who are clearly opponents or defenders of the Raj, there are many who are doubters. These writers are basically friendly to the continuation of British rule in India, but have serious doubts about the effectiveness of this rule.[2]

---

[1] See George Dangerfield, *The Strange Death of Liberal England, 1910–1914*, London, 1936, *passim*, for an excellent discussion of this point.

[2] See Howe, *Novels of Empire*, p. 19.

The growing doubt which many Englishmen were beginning to feel is seen in the description of the attitude of Oxford towards Indian students there. Whereas this attitude had been a favourable one in the early days of this century, it had changed and become 'less friendly, perhaps because it had known many more Indians and those not all of a commendable sort, perhaps because the Anglo-Saxon, growing ever more uneasy, felt his ascendancy threatened'.[1] There is, in this statement, the beginning of self-analysis and in this self-analysis the beginning of a lack of confidence.

An Indian youth asks his English friend for a book to read and at first the Englishman thinks of giving him some of Maugham's short stories. However, he rejects his choice fearing it will give the Indian the wrong idea of English civilization in the tropical East.[2] Similarly, Beck describes a meeting with a young Burmese student who shows an interest in the writings of Swinburne. The author feels that this could only cause trouble and instead suggests 'books of a milder vintage'.[3] For the first time the British feel themselves faced with the necessity of explaining and justifying their own civilization to the Indians. This, in itself, marks a major break with the earlier period.

The most striking new theme is that of attack on the institution of the Raj. Men such as Forster and Orwell who attacked the Raj did not do so basically because of what they felt the system was doing to the Indians, but rather because of what the situation of forcibly ruling over aliens was doing to the British. Whereas to the more confident English writers of the Late Victorian period rule of any kind, and absolute rule in particular, was good because it gave Englishmen the opportunity for self-development, these writers believed that such a position destroyed the British. The very act of authority tended to corrupt the holders of that authority.

For the first time serious attacks on the value of the whole of Western civilization are expressed in fiction dealing with India. There had been some criticism of this type, notably by Bain in his highly romantic stories about India, but it is only

[1] Edward Thompson, *An Indian Day*, London, 1927, p. 35.
[2] Dennis Kincaid, *Their Ways Divide*, London, 1936, pp. 133–4.
[3] L. Adams Beck, 'The Sorrow of the Queen: A Story in Burma', in *The Perfume of the Rainbow and Other Stories*, London, 1931, p. 173.

in this period and especially towards its end that these attacks emerge as a major theme.

L. H. Myers is very different from most of the writers who concerned themselves with India. His India was solely the creation of his imagination and his choice of the setting of sixteenth-century India was dictated only by his desire 'to carry the reader away from the machinery of a life that is familiar to him . . . to obtain an attention undisturbed by the social and economic problems of our day.'[1] He uses India to attack the West. In *Rajah Amar* he brings in a wandering Englishman named Smith who is visiting Asia to study the religions of the East. The rather long incident involving this man is clearly imposed upon the novel with little regard to the essentials of the plot.[2] Smith is shown to represent 'Western materialism' as derived from the Greeks, with its emphasis on reason, in opposition to Eastern intuition. This Englishman is clearly meant to represent the kind of man who was respected in the contemporary West. Thus, the following statement is an attack on the whole of Western society. 'It is well that people like Smith should exist, and it is perhaps inevitable that they should exaggerate their own importance; but it is also well that society should not give them even the importance they deserve. A world that honoured them would be a decaying one.'[3]

Orwell is more bitter as his hero, Flory, says that the civilization the English have brought to Burma cannot possibly improve that country because Western civilization in itself is degenerate.

'Of course I don't deny,' Flory said, 'that we modernize this country in certain ways. We can't help doing so. In fact, before we've finished we'll have wrecked the whole Burmese national culture. But we're not civilizing them, we're only rubbing our dirt on to them. Where's it going to lead, this uprush of modern progress, as you call it? Just to our own dear swinery of gramophones and billycock hats. Sometimes I think that in two hundred years all this—' he waved a foot towards the horizon—'all this will be gone—forests, villages, monasteries, pagodas all vanished. and instead, pink villas fifty yards

---

[1] L. H. Myers, *The Root and the Flower*, London, 1935, p. 9.
[2] G. H. Bantock, *L. H. Myers: A Critical Study*, London, 1956, p. 77.
[3] Myers, *The Root and the Flower*, p. 446.

apart; All over those hills, as far as you can see, villa after villa, with all the gramophones playing the same tune. And all the forests shaved flat—chewed into wood-pulp for the *News of the World* or sawn up into gramophone cases.[1]

Forster uses a wedding between two 'advanced' Muslims to attack Western values. He first describes, with ridicule, the mixture of the worst of East and West in the wedding ceremony and then, for contrast, the sight of a group of religious Muslims stepping aside to pray. Their impressive and touching prayers are interrupted by the gift which the British have brought to India—a gramophone blaring out 'I'd sooner be busy with my little Lizzie.'[2]

Writing a little later Edward John Thompson is even more pessimistic. To him, 'what the world takes for just weakness in our Government and imbecility in our film magnates and authors and Book Societies is merely senility. We've fallen into a drowse, the drowse of old age.'[3] When his leading character Alden stops at a small village he finds that:

> Here, too, civilization had pushed its all-conquering march. Gramophones ground out songs of an ear-piercing shrillness; on the walls were pictures of Indian cuties disporting themselves. Alden again wondered by what right our diehards block India's path to independence; she will soon be as fit for self-government as the democratic Western people.[4]

On his return to India the same character sarcastically believes that the world has finally been made one. 'The differences were dying, a communal dream united the countries and peoples.'[5] What is it that has brought about this unification? 'Hollywood in Indian Clothes: a marriage of East and West at last and indeed.'[6] When he meets a child selling chocolates in the street and saving the coupons in order to collect pictures of movie stars, Alden sees in this the victory of Western civilization over the East. 'Benares was yielding to Hollywood; Mecca was tumbling to the touch of the cuties. India was in the Modern Age at last; she had caught up with Progress. In India—mystic unchanging 'spiritual' India—a little boy was about to slay her

[1] George Orwell, *Burmese Days*, London, 1935, p. 45.
[2] E. M. Forster, 'Advance, India!' in *Abinger Harvest*, London, 1936, p. 302.
[3] Edward Thompson, *An End of the Hours*, London, 1938, p. 25.
[4] Ibid., p. 85.   [5] Ibid., p. 19.   [6] Ibid.

ancient cultures.'[1] Even so strong a supporter of the Raj as Maud Diver has doubts about Western civilization as it is brought to India. She continually refers to it as being totally materialistic, hence bad. In one incident she gives a picture not unlike Thompson's. Roy Sinclair comes upon a 'portly spectacled Hindu' selling picture post-cards and chanting, 'Obscene—obscene—.' He buys and destroys them with the remarks: 'Beastly stuff. English—American—German. *This* is the way we civilize the East.'[2]

In regard to British officials in India, a doubter like Thompson sees the difficulty of ruling: 'Is there anywhere, in the wide wide world, a raggeder job than the Englishman's in India.'[3] Even such an anti-Raj writer as Orwell can write: 'The life of the Anglo-Indian officials is not all jam. In comfortless camps, in sweltering offices, in gloomy dak bungalows smelling of dust and earth-oil, they earn, perhaps, the right to be a little disagreeable.'[4] However, the image of the Anglo-Indian official that appears throughout the novel is unsympathetic.

There is a prevalent idea that the men at the 'outposts of Empire' are at least able and hardworking. It is a delusion. Outside the scientific services—the Forest Department and the like—there is no particular need for a British official in India to do this job competently. Few of them work as hard or as intelligently as the postmaster of a provincial town in England. The real work of administration is done mainly by native subordinates; and the real backbone of the despotisms is not the officials but the Army. Given the Army, the officials and the business men can rub along safely enough even if they are fools. And most of them *are* fools. A dull, decent people, cherishing and fortifying their dullness behind a quarter of a million bayonets.[5]

That even Orwell could be somewhat sympathetic shows that among the writers of the anti-Raj camp there was still some feeling, however slight, of respect for what they saw the British doing. One of the most poignant sides to the opponents of imperialism is that they are not totally without respect for the Empire. This is particularly seen in the case of Orwell, who is

[1] Edward Thompson, *An End of the Hours*, p. 29.
[2] Maud Diver, *The Singer Passes: An Indian Tapestry*, Edinburgh and London, 1934, p. 273.
[3] Edward Thompson, *A Farewell to India*, London, 1931, p. 283.
[4] Orwell, *Burmese Days*, p. 37.   [5] Ibid., pp. 74-5.

G

often thought of as having been one of the strongest attackers of the Empire. This does not come out so strongly in the *Burmese Days*, but it does in some of his other writings. It has been noted that 'there was a Kiplingesque side to his character which made him romanticize the Raj and its mystique'.[1] However, this is only a minor point and is nothing more than a very slight qualification of the harsh picture these writers painted. If anything, their mild respect probably made their attack all the more severe in an attempt to cover this up.

In a moving autobiographical passage Orwell gets at the heart of what he feels is the most rotten side of the imperial picture.

All over India there are Englishmen who secretly loathe the system of which they are part; and just occasionally, when they are quite certain of being in the right company, their hidden bitterness over-flows. I remember a night I spent on the train with a man in the Educational Service, a stranger to myself whose name I never discovered. It was too hot to sleep and we spent the night in talking. Half an hour's cautious questioning decided each of us that the other was 'safe;' and then for hours, while the train jolted slowly through the pitch-black night, sitting up in our bunks with bottles of beer handy, we damned the British Empire—damned it from the inside, intelligently and intimately. It did us both good. But we had been speaking forbidden things, and in the haggard morning light, when the train crawled into Mandalay, we parted as guiltily as any adulterous couple.[2]

The wielding of authority has made it impossible for the British to be true to their own principles. Even if the civilization which they represented were worthwhile, and writers of this type seriously doubted that, the self-destruction that they saw as being an inevitable part of the structure of imperialism made the empire a bad thing. In short, absolute authority brings out the worst in those who possess it.

Britain was judged a failure in her mission in India by many

---

[1] See particularly George Orwell's essay, 'Rudyard Kipling', in *Critical Essays*, London, 1946, *passim*, where he expresses sympathy and approval for Kipling's willingness to accept responsibility. On this point see Tom Hopkinson, *George Orwell*, London, 1953, p. 14 and p. 28; Christopher Hollis, *A Study of George Orwell: The Man and His Works*, London, 1956, *passim*; and especially Richard Cook, 'Rudyard Kipling and George Orwell', *Modern Fiction Studies*, 7, Summer 1961, *passim*.

[2] George Orwell, *The Road to Wigan Pier*, London, 1937, pp. 176-7.

of the writers of the 1920s and 1930s. This was not so muc because the British had failed to bring law, order, or educatio to the Indians—they had—but because of the attitude with which this had been done. When, in *A Passage to India*, Ronny Moore explains to his mother that the British are in India to do justice and keep the peace, she is annoyed by his manner rather than by the sentiments.

His words without his voice might have impressed her, but when she heard the self-satisfied lilt of them, when she saw the mouth moving so complacently and competently beneath the little red nose, she felt quite illogically, that this was not the last word on India. One touch of regret—not the canny substitute but the true regret from the heart—would have made him a different man, and the British Empire a different institution.[1]

As Forster says elsewhere of the Anglo-Indian attitude:

The great blunder of the past is neither political nor economic nor education, but social; that he was associated with a system that supported rudeness in railway carriages, and is paying the penalty. . . . Never in history did ill-breeding contribute so much towards the dissolution of an Empire.[2]

The whole reason for the lack of sympathy with which Candler's Riley views the Imperial idea 'was that he believed Empires were the nurseries of cads'.[3] In a similar, if somewhat more sympathetic way, Thompson's Alden says that the average sahib is a fine person.

You can rely on the average sahib to do his job till he drops. . . . I could worship the ordinary sahib for his decency and genuineness! Only, only only . . . when our *actions* are so decent and so honourable, why—why—*why*—do we always talk as if we were half cad, half imbecile?[4]

Hilda agrees with him and thinks:

As Alden maintained, every one of his countrymen was an able man at his job; the slackers or the bunglers in the Civil Service, or the police, or any other service, could almost be counted on one

[1] E. M. Forster, *A Passage to India*, London, 1924, p. 49.
[2] E. M. Forster, 'Reflections in India: I—Too Late?' *The Nation and the Athenaeum*, XXX, 21 January 1922, pp. 614–15.
[3] Edmund Candler, *Abdication*, London, 1922, p. 201.
[4] Thompson, *An Indian Day*, p. 180.

hand. But intellectually the community was third-rate, and its mind was fed on starch and sawdust. . . . Administering the myriads evenly and firmly—administering them with an utter lack of perception of what was in the minds of a subject populace and with an unshakable conviction that he was in the place of God and could not err—if you like, doing his magnificent work like a damned fool—but has the world ever seen such glorious damned fools?[1]

The earlier authors believed that the most effective type of British character for dealing with India was the strong man who possessed the physical and mental virtues of the warrior. He most likely would be found in the army. The new attackers and doubters saw these very same men in a much harsher light. They thought the army was the backbone of British rule in India, a bad thing in and of itself. It was bad because it supported a living system which they abhorred. In addition the military machine, in their eyes, had proved itself destructive in the recent carnage of the trenches—a carnage which did not seem to have accomplished anything approximating the cost in lives. Finally, it was bad because there was no use in using force when one had doubts concerning the value of what was being forced.

In *Burmese Days* we are introduced to the British officer Verall who

had come out to India in a British cavalry regiment, and exchanged into the Indian Army because it was cheaper and left him greater freedom for polo. After two years his debts were so enormous that he entered the Burma Military Police, in which it was notoriously possible to save money; however, he detested Burma—it is no country for a horseman—and he had already applied to go back to his regiment. . . . He knew the society of those small Burma stations—a nasty, poodle-faking, horseless riffraff. He despised them.

They were not the only people whom Verall despised, however. His various contempts would take a long time to catalogue in detail. He despised the entire non-military population of India, a few famous polo players excepted. He despised the entire Army as well, except the cavalry. He despised all Indian regiments, infantry and cavalry alike. It was true that he himself belonged to a native regiment, but that was only for his own convenience. He took no interest in Indians, and his Urdu consisted mainly of swear-words, with all the verbs in the third person singular.[2]

[1] Thompson, *An Indian Day*, p. 207–8.   [2] Orwell, *Burmese Days*, pp. 122–3.

One can only imagine how differently Kipling would have described a similar officer even if he possessed all of these bad traits because Verall lived 'ascetically as a monk' and 'horsemanship and physical fitness were the only gods he knew'. Orwell delivers a blow to this man by making him absent from the scene the only time in the book when his army might have been useful.

To these military men killing Indians was a big game. Forster recounts that after the attempted assassination of Lord Harding in 1912 'several Englishmen—officials of high position, too —were anxious for the Tommies to be turned to fire at the crowd and seemed really sorry that the Viceroy had not been killed because then there would have been a better excuse for doing such a thing.'[1] The military in *A Passage to India* are forever in favour of calling out the troops over the slightest disturbance and the Superintendent of Police in *Burmese Days* mourns that the Burmese are afraid to riot.

> God, if they'd only break out and rebel properly for once! . . . But it'll be a bloody washout as usual. Always the same story with these rebellions—peter out almost before they've begun. Would you believe it, I've never fired my gun at a fellow yet, not even a dacoit. Eleven years of it, not counting the War, and never killed a man. Depressing![2]

Later, when a riot does occur but is put down without bloodshed, another Englishman complains: 'But why don't they use their rifles, the miserable sons of bitches? They could slaughter them in bloody heaps if they'd only open fire. Oh, God, to think of missing a chance like this!'[3]

The background to Thompson's *Night Falls on Siva's Hill* involves an attack on the military. This time it is not so much an attack on the bloodthirstiness of the military as on their general attitude. In the 1870s the promising young officer of the Miani Light Horse, John Carmichael Lyon, is forced to leave the military service to which he has devoted his life because he has fallen in love with a woman who is not considered socially acceptable by the members of the regiment. After the marriage they make life miserable for the newly married couple and in

---

[1] E. M. Forster, *The Hill of Devi*, London, 1953, p. 18.
[2] Orwell, *Burmese Days*, p. 122.   [3] Ibid., p. 275.

self-protection Lyon resigns. To Lyon nothing seems to work
out for him from this point onward. The liberal Commissioner,
Tom Felvus, thinks that it is not totally tragic that Lyon had
resigned from Miani because all the officers did was to sit
around and act like gods. 'It's bad enough being any sort of a
sahib out here', he thinks.[1] He doesn't say that apparently it is
even worse to be a soldier, but it is implicit in his attitude.

Instead of military heroes the only Englishmen who are
favourably represented by these anti-Raj authors are those of a
non-official variety; Forster's schoolmaster Fielding, Orwell's
businessman Flory, or Candler's journalist Riley. It is not so
much that these men are particularly successful in their action
in India, but rather that at least they attempt to understand the
country in which they have chosen to reside. They all possess the
same passive personality and are not able, nor do they try, to
dominate their environment. These somewhat unsuccessful
individuals are the closest thing that this school can imagine as
the British hero in India.

The hero of the supporters of the Raj is the same figure that
was met in the earlier writings.

The much-abused public school product *in excelsis*. No parade of
brains or force; revelling in understatement; but they've got guts,
those boys, and a fine sense of responsibility. . . . They're no thinkers,
but they're born improvisers and adminstrators. They've just
sauntered down the ages, impervious to darts of criticism or hate or
jealousy.[2]

For Mundy's Bill Brown 'duty was the only thing that mattered'
in his 'scheme of things'.[3] Tom Oliver, the namesake of Ollivant's adventure novel *Old For-Ever*, 'was one of the few men
who genuinely enjoy danger'[4] and who was made up of a
'core of Puritan steel that was the fundamental characteristic
of a soldier'.[5] Athelstan King, Mundy's King of the Khyber
Rifles, is a 'perfect' Anglo-Saxon hero in his bravery, independence, and resourcefulness. He is a man who acts only when he
is forced to in what is 'perhaps . . . the most dominant characteristic of the British race that it will not defend itself until it must'.[6]

[1] Edward Thompson, *Night Falls on Siva's Hill*, London, 1929, p. 253.
[2] Diver, *The Singer Passes*, p. 243.
[3] Talbot Mundy, 'Hookum Hai', in *Told in the East*, New York, 1920, p. 14.
[4] Alfred Ollivant, *Old For-Ever*, London, 1923, p. 162.   [5] Ibid., p. 18.
[6] Talbot Mundy, *King—of the Khyber Rifles*, London, 1917, p. 39.

When necessary he is willing and able to do whatever is needed. His name with its Anglo-Saxon ring means 'slow of resolution' and was chosen by Mundy to emphasize King's race and character. Maud Diver's Eldred Lenox is similar both in character and in the Anglo-Saxon sound of his name.[1] In all of her novels, and in those of Ethel M. Dell, this kind of character appears with great regularity. These are all men who do their job 'because their chosen work was their religion'.[2]

Even in an age given over to the marketable commodity, England can still breed men of this quality. Not often in her cities, where individual aspiration and character are cramped, warped, deadened by the brute force of money, the complex mechanism of modern life but in unconsidered corners of her Empire, in the vast spaces and comparative isolation, where old-fashioned patriotism takes the place of party politics, and where, alone, strong natures can grow up in their own way.

It is to the Desmonds and Merediths of an earlier day, that we are indebted for the sturdy loyalty of our Punjab and Frontier troops. India may have been won by the sword, but it has been held mainly by individual strength of purpose, capacity for sympathy, and devotion to the interests of those we govern. When we fail in these, and not till then will power pass out of our hands. . . . Perhaps only those who have had close dealings with the British officer in time of action or emergency realize, to the full, the effective qualities hidden under a careless or conventional exterior—the vital force, the pluck, endurance, and irrepressible spirit of enterprise, which it has been aptly said, make him, at his best, the most romantic figure of our modern time.[3]

These men are most likely found in, or are closely associated with, the army. They are still seen primarily as 'doers' rather than 'thinkers'. In this way they are in direct contrast to the ideal Briton in India as viewed by the anti-Raj writers.

Since the pro-Raj writers continued to insist that the British know what is right and wrong, they still have the right and obligation to rule.

We can hand over the reins of Government, if nothing else will satisfy India. But we can't hand over with it, a gift for sound and just administration. It's a talent only certain races possess; and even

---

[1] In Maud Diver, *The Great Amulet*, New York and London, 1914, *passim*.
[2] Diver, *The Singer Passes*, p. 426.   [3] Diver, *The Great Amulet*, pp. 252-4.

so, it's the fruit of long experience. We've built it up, out here, on a scale that no race could have attempted or achieved.[1]

This obligation again entails the necessity of using whatever means are available to further their power. Unlike the earlier period more emphasis is placed on the use of force. Sir Lakshman Singh, Diver's idea of the perfect Indian, explains that he believes India's welfare can only be improved with a continuation of British rule. The problem, as he and Diver see it, is that Britain is actually fomenting trouble by not continuing to act in a forceful way.

'In my belief—and I am sharing it with scores of men better than myself—no worse harm could befall to India than that Great Britain should cease to be paramount power. But only this—in order for being paramount she must be, in best sense, a *power*; not mere figure-head or rash experimentalist, shifting now to this foot, now to that. Even in your own Book is it not written if the trumpet give an uncertain sound, who shall prepare themselves for battle?'
'Who indeed?' the daughter of England assented ruefully. 'And of late years the sound has been less imperious, less inspiring than it should be if we are to hold our own.'
'Unhappily—yes. I cannot help but agree. It is not that I am disloyal, as you know. It is that we are troubled—we Indians, who believe in England's power—to see how such a great land is seeming to lose grasp on those noble ideals of straight-forward strength and courage that we learnt in the early days to couple with the name of the British Raj.'[2]

In one of the few mentions of the important Amritsar Incident, Diver well expresses the importance of this idea.

Organized revolt is amenable only to the ultimate argument of force. Nothing, now, would serve but strong action, and the compelling power of martial law. . . .
At Amritsar strong action had already been taken; and the sobering effect of it spread in widening circles, bringing relief to thousands of both races.[3]

---

[1] Diver, *The Singer Passes*, p. 504.
[2] Maud Diver, *Lilamani*, London, 1911, pp. 106–7.
[3] Maud Diver, *Far to Seek*, London, 1921, p. 385. The use of the term organized revolt, in my italics, shows how many of the British of this period tended to view the growth of nationalism in India as 'the prelude to another mutiny'. See Dennis Kincaid, *British Social Life in India*, p. 276. This harsh attitude shows a lack of

Later, Roy writes from Lahore.

> No more trouble here or Amritsar. . . . Martial law arrangements
> are being carried through to admiration . . . and in no time the poor
> deluded beggars in the city were shouting 'Martial law *ki jai*' as
> fervently as ever they shouted for Gandhi and Co. One of my fellows
> said to me: 'Our people don't understand this new talk of *Committee
> ki raj* and *Dyarchy raj*. Too many orders make confusion. But they
> understand *'Hukm ki raj.'* In fact, it's the general opinion that prompt
> action in the Punjab has fairly well steadied India—for the present
> at least.[1]

In the same way that Kipling's Tarvin defeated the Indian
princess, Mundy's King triumphs over Yasmini who wants to
open India to the hordes of the North. When King and Yasmini
embrace, he knows that he has won because, although she loves
him, he does not love her. He is devoted to something bigger
than personal happiness in his deep commitment to helping
India remain secure through British rule.[2]

These writers continue to present the image of an India
threatened from the north by Russia, Germany, or the barbarian tribes while the British play 'The Great Game'. 'For
whatever fresh experiments might emerge from conference and
reports, "the North safeguarded" must remain a categorical
imperative, for decades to come.'[3]

Sir Henry Forsyth is sent to the small independent state of
Hunza north of Kashmir to bring peace to the area. He is
described in glowing terms. 'For all his great brain, he was a
man of one idea; and that idea—'The North safeguarded.'
Mere men, himself included, were for him no more than pawns
in the great game to be played out between two empires, on
the chessboard of Central Asia.'[4] Eldred Lenox explains to the
woman he loves what he and the other British are doing in
India.

---

recognition by Diver of the way in which Amritsar affected many Indians. Tagore,
who she says she admires a great deal, was virtually shattered by both the action
and, even more, by the feeling in Britain that nothing wrong had happened. See
Rabindranath Tagore, *Letters to a Friend*, London, 1928, pp. 83–7 and 92.

[1] Diver, *Far to Seek*, p. 390. '*Ki jai*' means 'long live'; '*Committee ki raj*' means
'government by committee'; and '*Hukm ki raj*' means 'government by order'.

[2] Mundy, *King—of the Khyber Rifles*, p. 260.

[3] Diver, *The Singer Passes*, p. 190.   [4] Diver, *The Great Amulet*, p. 453.

'We keep *cave* along six hundred miles of heart-breaking border country.'

'In other words, you are watch-dogs guarding the gates of Empire?'

'That sounds far more imposing! We are also actively engaged in helping the Indian Government to cultivate friendly relations with the tribes at the point of the bayonet!'

'And don't the tribes respond?'

'Yes, vigorously, to the tune of bullets and cold steel; so that we keep things pretty lively between us.'[1]

An element of having fun is often involved in these military ventures. When in *The Elephant God* Dermot tells his subaltern about the possibility of an invasion from the north, the youth replies: 'By Jove, Major, that's great. Do you think there's anything in it? How ripping it'll be if they try to come in by this pass.'[2] Even if it was not fun, fighting and dying for the protection of the Frontier was felt to give meaning to a man's life. When a young soldier is killed in a small frontier skirmish, Beck's very spiritual and pro-Indian Vanna says:

I am not sorry for Harry, if you mean that. He knew—we all know—that he was on guard here holding the outposts against blood and treachery and terrible things—playing the Great Game. One never loses at that game if one plays it straight, and I am sure that at the last it was joy he felt and not fear. He has not lost. Did you notice in the church a niche before every soldier's seat to hold his loaded gun? And the tablets on the walls; 'Killed at Kabul River, aged 22.' —Killed on outpost duty.'—'Murdered by an Afghan fanatic.' This will be one memory more. Why be sorry?[3]

'The Great Game' is still largely being played against the Russians who are thought to be making use of the tribes north of the passes. In spite of the threat of Germany in the period around World War I that country was never viewed as being as great a threat to the Raj in India as was Russia. Writing in the 1920s and looking back to the 1870s, Diver notes: 'And now, as then, the shadow of the Bear, rampant, loomed large on the political horizon.'[4] The pro-British Alam Khan talks with

[1] Diver, *The Great Amulet*, p. 13.

[2] Gordon Casserly, *The Elephant God*, London, 1920, pp. 16–17.

[3] L. Adams Beck, 'The Interpreter: A Romance of the East', in *The Ninth Vibration and Other Stories*, London, 1928, pp. 83–4.

[4] Maud Diver, 'Light Marching Order', in *Siege Perilous and Other Stories*, London, 1924, p. 5.

Lance Dunbar about the politics of the Frontier. Lance complains that the future of the area depends on flying and that depends upon the weather.

Alam Khan shrugged his shoulders. 'Who knows! The mercy of Allah is on the Sahibs and all their works!' . . .
'But Russia—Russia!' the Khan added with darkening brows. 'The Bear is at work up yonder, and many of the tribesmen drink his vodka and listen to his smooth talk. And then what?'
Dunbar laid a finger on the hilt of his sword.
'That!' he said: the Khan nodded.[1]

Sometimes the tribes are acting on their own as they plot against the 'keepers of the passes' through which 'the North of Asia trickle down into India and back again when weather and the tribes permit.'[2] Why do they want to get into India? 'Object? What but to force the Khyber and burst through into India and loot? What but to plunder, now that English backs are turned the other way?'[3] The leader of one such plot, Yasmini, is equally blunt in describing what will happen when her minions sweep into India. 'They will lay waste India! They will butcher and plunder and burn!'[4] Finally, one of her followers says: 'There will be a *jihad* when she is ready, such an one as never yet was! India shall bleed for all the fat years she has lain unplundered! Not a throat of an unbeliever in the world shall be left unslit.'[5]

If anything, there is a greater emphasis on the idea of holding India in order to protect the frontier of civilization, in this period than in the preceding one. In some ways it is ironic because undoubtedly there was less of a real threat from the 'barbarian' tribes than in previous years. However, it is understandable since these writers felt a greater insecurity as to British rule in India and because of this were driven to strongly defend what they were doing in India. That it largely took the form of military protection from barbarism is highly significant.

Alfred Ollivant, more famed for his dog story, describes his novel, *Old For-Ever:* 'It is essentially a Frontier-story: its subject the clash between White Men and Brown, East and West,

---

[1] L. Adams Beck, *The House of Fulfilment*, London, 1927, p. 243.
[2] Mundy, *King—of the Khyber Rifles*, p. 82.   [3] Ibid., p. 106.
[4] Ibid., p. 246.   [5] Ibid., p. 169.

Civilization and Savagery.'[1] His hero, Tom Oliver, was a part of

the thin but efficient bulwark against the lean wolf-men roaming the hills in packs from the Malakand to Dera Ghazi Khan, and looking down with covetous eyes from their barbarian fastness on to the provocative plains, shining with water, . . . yellow with corn, and teeming with loot and women. Over those sleek, river-laced lands successive waves of wolf-men have surged out of the ravenous North, century after century, from the passes which gave the Sikhs the cholera in the days of Ranjit Singh; harrying, ravishing, and leaving their scars on the countryside.[2]

Only the white man had succeeded in pushing north themselves, where they

established themselves forthwith like a wire fence, barbed too, between the tribesmen and their prey. *Our side of the fence law, order and security*, said the audacious Feringhis. *Your side, go as you please*. And the white race succeeded under conditions which had baffled the Lion of the Punjab himself. . . . The dun mountains that lie across the gate of the North, for all their air of deadness, are always a-flicker and not seldom a-blaze. Those blazes are sudden as explosions. . . . A long-time smouldering, perhaps a faint eddy of smoke upon a ridge, then a sudden spurt of flame stabs the darkness, and fifty miles of Frontier is *up*.[3]

This stress on the protection of the Frontier entails an equally strong emphasis on the use of force and a glorification of war. The heroes of these stories are likely to be military men who glory in the use of warfare. Eldred Lenox describes his life: 'I'm a keen soldier, if that's what you're driving at; and I believe the world holds no finer school for character than active service.'[4] It is this characteristic which most attracts Quita to him because 'the man who has faced death and dealt it out to others appeals irresistibly to the fundamentally barbaric in women'. In Quita's case this fascination was added to by the artist's 'reverence for the men who "do things", as opposed to the men who record or express them'.[5]

Mundy expresses a similar sentiment, adding an attack on

---

[1] Ollivant, *Old For-Ever*, p. ix of Preface to American edition.
[2] Ibid., p. 13.　　　[3] Ibid., pp. 13–14.　　　[4] Diver, *The Great Amulet*, p. 13.
[5] Ibid., p. 315.

anyone who does not recognize that the use of force—not the use of words—is essential. In a chapter-heading poem he states:

> When the last evil jest has been made, and the rest
> Of the ink of hypocrisy spilt,
> When the awfully right have elected to fight
> Lest their own should discover their guilt;
> When the door has been shut on the 'if' and the 'but'
> And it's up to the men with the guns,
> On their knees in that day let diplomatists pray
> For forgiveness from prodigal sons.[1]

These largely military men and their women are willing to devote their lives and, even more, the lives of those they love, to the maintenance of British rule in India. They are shown to imagine that through their suffering, India is being saved from the potential ravages of those who are 'beyond the pale of civilization'. When, at the end of *Old For-Ever* Tom Oliver returns to his wife, following an excursion against a local disturbance, he finds that his only child has died. His wife, Marion, greets him and the first phrase that she utters tells the whole story of the devotion the defenders of the Raj believed existed: 'It was worth it, Tom.'[2] There is no questioning here. There is only an acceptance of the idea that the British must die in order to make good their 'obligations'. In fact, to die in carrying out this obligation is the fulfilment of one's life. Athelstan King is greeted by the gory sight of his brother's head when he goes to Yasmini's secret caves. When she realizes that, unlike the East, in the West a brother is not necessarily a rival whose death is desired, she promises to punish the man who took the head. King rebuffs her and tells her to leave the murderer alone. 'My brother died at the head of his men. He couldn't ask for more.'[3] Similarly an unnamed soldier who is fatally wounded in a campaign against the Afghans lies there 'cursing the accuracy of Afghan marksmen, but with never a word of complaint or impatience on his lips. In war, the touchstone of character.'[4]

Not all of those who made the Indian image in this period saw the British simply protecting India. In a good many of the

---

[1] Mundy, *King—of the Khyber Rifles*, p. 303.
[2] Ollivant, *Old For-Ever*, p. 267.
[3] Mundy, *King—of the Khyber Rifles*, p. 242.
[4] Diver, 'Light Marching Order', in *Siege Perilous*, p. 22.

novels and stories it is difficult to see what, if anything, the British are doing. It cannot even be said, as is true of the earlier period, that at least they were having fun in India. They may have had a good time once upon time, as when Alden thinks of his Indian past: 'How happy-making nearly all those memories were!'[1] The present, and even more the future, are not viewed in such happy terms. No matter, the Englishman, so long as he is there, will continue to 'get his job done, for this is the religion of the English'.[2] Whatever they think their job is, whether it be educating the Indians, defeating the plague, or serving as a political officer, they will stick to their jobs.

The Englishman may believe, as Alden does, that the British have done a good job in India.

Certainly India has been lucky. She has had close on two centuries administration by the most enlightened and benevolent nation on earth and millenniums of uplift dispensed by the most spiritual religion on earth. Yet her boundaries contain a seething wretchedness no other land can produce.[3]

Despite this the British no longer believe that they are really accomplishing anything. Alden finds: 'Not for the first time he had been manoeuvred into a position where whatever he did was wrong and misrepresented him. Fate was daily playing this trick on Englishmen now.'[4]

Vincent Hamar believes that the problems of ruling India have become so great that the job is not worth the effort that staying in India entails. He believes that the British time in India is about up.[5] John McCormick, the new principal of the College, says: 'The days of our pride are nearly finished and our race is about to come to judgement.'[6] He goes on to observe that the English know that they are fighting a losing battle and just want to get rid of the problem that is causing them so much trouble. 'England has given up empire *already*. She finished *within herself*, and wants only to linger out her days in coma. And of course everyone else knows this.'[7] This was written in 1938 and is perhaps not too surprising at that point in time.

---

[1] Thompson, *An End of the Hours*, p. 227.   [2] Thompson, *An Indian Day*, p. 287.
[3] Thompson, *An End of the Hours*, p. 238.
[4] Thompson, *A Farewell to India*, p. 160.
[5] Ibid., p. 280.   [6] Thompson, *An End of the Hours*, p. 125.
[7] Ibid., p. 127.

Four years before that, such a strong supporter of continued British rule in India as Maud Diver could at least occasionally express similarly pessimistic accounts of what the British were doing in India. When, in *The Singer Passes*, Roy Sinclair gets stuck in a traffic jam, he notes: 'We're really stuck. . . . We can't go forward. We won't go backwards. Rather like the English in India!'[1] Another character later says: 'We neither govern nor misgovern. We hang on like a lot of Micawbers, waiting for something to turn up—'[2] In 1931 Thompson was writing in the same vein. In fact, Diver's statements could well have been taken from the remarks of Robin Alden on what the British were doing in India. 'We neither govern nor misgovern We're just hanging on, hoping that the Last Trump will sound "Time!" and save us from the bother of making a decision.'[3] Kincaid's Hilton in *Durbar*, the local administrator, is a perfect example of this type of Englishman. All he wants is to go on leave to London and he is glad that nothing serious happens in his district about which he would have to file a report. Only a person convinced of his own stature and importance could be a successful colonial administrator. Without this trait, in the imperial sphere, all he could hope to do would be to hang on.

It is possible to go even further back to find this same sentiment being expressed. As early as 1922 Edmund Candler wrote a novel, *Abdication*, which expresses the idea that Britain has already abdicated her power and should recognize this fact by getting out of India.[4] Candler's hero, Brian Riley, who is very much like the author in both his life and views, continually reiterates this theme, pointing out that with the rise of racial tensions and Indian nationalist 'agitators' there is no place left in India for the British. In addition, Riley 'belonged to that growing class of young Englishmen who are incapable of seeing the point of an argument on their own side'. Even though the English can make a strong point for their position in India, Riley can see nothing of it.

Besides the feeling that the British are not accomplishing anything is a melancholy impression that once upon a time things were better. Writing of the 1900 period Thompson puts it nicely.

---

[1] Diver, *The Singer Passes*, p. 202.   [2] Ibid, p. 326.
[3] Thompson, *A Farewell to India*, p. 151.   [4] Candler, *Abdication*, p. 118.

The big political turmoils had not begun, Anglo-India seemed
safe and majestic as ever. But the old life was perishing, and it was
now that the changes came, and came rapidly, for all their quietness.
Indigo was nearly dead. . . . With its death a large part of British
dominion, as this used to be, was torn out. That dominion became a
more glaring alien thing than ever, official and military and regional,
cantonments and offices perched on frontiers or mountains or
segregated in cities, planter communities no longer scattered across
the interior but hugging the side and course of Himalayan valleys. . . .
This corner of dying Anglo-India had entered on its last phase.[1]

The supporters of the Raj occasionally express harsh criticism of the Anglo-Indian women, as when Beck refers to Simla
as 'a cannibal feast at best and seasoned with much sniggering
and chuckling'.[2] There 'the aggregated scandal of India—
meaning, of course, all that concerns the governing race—rises
like the smoke of an especially black and acrid nature to the
Simla heights'.[3] Even Casserly is not fond of Simla which is
described as 'a rotten place. . . . Too many brass hats and
women. They're the curse of India, each of them. And I'm sure
the women do the most harm.'[4] But because their growing lack
of confidence has made these writers less willing to criticize
anything in Anglo-Indian society, there is no detailed attack
such as that which Kipling had made. Maud Diver, who generally follows Kipling's lead, defends the Englishwoman in
India. Part of this may be due to her natural defence of her own
sex, but this image is too strong to be laid totally at the doorstep
of feminine prejudice.

The women who follow, soon or late, in the track of her victorious
arms, women of Honor Desmond's calibre—home-loving, home-
making, skilled in the lore of heart and spirit—have done fully as
much to establish, strengthen, and settle her scattered Empire as
shot, or steel, or the doubtful machinations of diplomacy.[5]

Mundy says the same thing:

But strong men are not the only makings of an Empire, nor yet the
only sufferers. Wherever the flag of England flies above a distant outpost or droops in the stagnant moisture of an Eastern swamp, there

[1] Thompson, *Night Falls on Siva's Hill*, p. 218.
[2] Beck, *The House of Fulfilment*, p. 9.
[3] Ibid., p. 1.   [4] Casserly, *The Elephant God*, p. 18.
[5] Diver, *The Great Amulet*, p. 68.

are the graves of England's women. . . . Man does the work, but he
is held to it and cheered on by the girl who loves him.[1]

Diver is just as favourable in her depiction of Anglo-Indian
society as a whole.

> For this is India: the land of the Good Samaritan, as those who
> have lived there longest know best. It has been well said that 'an
> Englishman's house in India is not his castle, but a thousand better
> things'—a casual ward, a convalescent home, a rest-house for the
> strayed traveller; and he himself is the steward of it merely.[2]

At the same time, it is true that she is critical of the overly
social attitude of the worst members of this society and does
depict people like this who are concerned only with 'pay,
promotion, prestige'. Yet, whenever the British are confronted
with a threat from Indians or others, all such criticism of Anglo-
Indian society disappears—even in the same novel where it had
appeared.

Ollivant's Marion Oliver is the personification of the type of
self-sacrificing woman who is oft-depicted by the pro-Raj
authors of this period. She refuses to leave her husband no
matter what the danger is and goes so far as to insist on accom-
panying him on his return to his cholera-infested camp. She
believes that the showing of confidence is a part of every Englishwoman's job in India. Old For-Ever's wife never thinks of
complaining no matter how difficult the situation; even the
death of her little son does not cause her to regret her decision.

Among those writers who either attack the Raj frontally or
feel that the British have failed in India, the Englishwoman in
India is dealt with very harshly. Forster obviously agrees with
his Muslim characters who say that whereas an Englishman
needs two years to 'learn' to despise all Indians, an Englishwoman needs only six months.[3] In the same manner, Candler's
Skene thinks of Englishwomen in India: 'God, how India does
spoil them. . . . You wouldn't think they were of the same breed.
I wonder if they'd get any of the virtues back if they were
transplanted.'[4] Even the pro-Raj writers like Casserly came to
the same conclusion often. This has been seen in the previously

[1] Talbot Mundy, 'For the Salt He Had Eaten', in *Told in the East*, p. 146.
[2] Diver, *The Great Amulet*, p. 397.   [3] Forster, *A Passage to India*, p. 9.
[4] Edmund Candler, *Siri Ram Revolutionist*, London, 1912, pp. 236-7.

quoted statement that it is the women who do the most harm in India.[1]

Almost without exception these women are shown to be totally lacking in sensitivity and intelligence. They are concerned only with the achievement of their own comfort. They damn the whole missionary enterprise 'by the fact that it had produced so few good, cheap servants'.[2] Miss Quested and Mrs. Moore run into the same thing when they first encounter the society of Englishwomen in India. Miss Quested innocently remarks that she wants to see Indians.

> She became the centre of an amused group of ladies. One said, 'Wanting to see Indians! How new that sounds!' A third, more serious, said, 'Let me explain. Natives don't respect one any more after meeting one, you see.'
>
> 'That occurs after so many meetings.'
>
> But the lady, entirely stupid and friendly, continued. 'What I mean is . . . I was a nurse in a Native State. One's only hope was to hold sternly aloof.'
>
> 'Even from one's patient?'
>
> 'Why, the kindest thing one can do to a native is to let him die,' said Mrs. Callendar.
>
> 'How if he went to heaven?' asked Mrs. Moore, with a gentle but crooked smile.
>
> 'He can go where he likes so long as he doesn't come near me. They give me the creeps.'
>
> 'As a matter of fact I have thought what you were saying about heaven, and that is why I am against Missionaries,' said the lady who had been a nurse. 'I am all for Chaplains, but all against Missionaries.'[3]

Later a Miss Derek who served as a companion to a Maharani described 'the entire peninsula as a comic opera'.

> 'If one couldn't see the laughable side of these people one 'l'd be done for,' said Miss Derek. Mrs. McBryde—it was she who had been the nurse—ceased not to exclaim, 'Oh, Nancy, how topping! Oh, Nancy, how killing! I wish I could look at things like that.' Mr. McBryde did not speak much; he seemed nice.[4]

The Political Agent's wife, Dorothy Hilton, in *Durbar*, by Kincaid, has found it virtually impossible to talk to Indian

---

[1] See above, p. 102.   [2] Thompson, *An Indian Day*, p. 61.
[3] Forster, *A Passage to India*, pp. 24–5.   [4] Ibid., p. 46.

women, but when she is forced to, she 'simulates the most *enormous* interest' in their children and clothes which she sees as 'horrid little brats' and 'tawdry, tinselly clothes'.[1] She thinks that all Indians are alike beneath their façade of differences and although they are happy, they are 'the dullest, dullest people'.[2] Mrs. Hilton tells a newly arrived English girl that she speaks Hindustani well enough to talk to the servants, but when she orders a drink from her own servant she uses English and calls him 'fathead'. Then she explains that actually she only knows words of abuse in Hindustani. 'After all, they're all you need, really'.[3]

Fanny's English girl-friend, Agatha, is the only one of the characters in Jesse's *The Lacquer Lady* who is racially prejudiced. When she finds Fanny looking into her locked box on the trip out to Burma, she attacks the Eurasian girl: 'It's easy to see you're not English! You've been prying in my things. What a dishonourable thing to do.'[4] Later, after she has married an Englishman, Fanny lords her new state over Agatha who consoles herself by thinking: 'Anyway I *am* white.'[5] Finally, she is disappointed on seeing the Burmese princesses because 'they looked all brown and insignificant. . . . Of course, you couldn't expect them to be really pretty like English people.'[6] Even without her racial prejudice, Agatha is the least sympathetic character in the novel.

Thompson sums up this whole attack by saying that the biggest mistake of the English in India is the way their women act.[7] The laying of the blame for the British failures in India on the Englishwoman there is a much more serious attack on them than anything that had been made by the Kiplings and Crokers of the preceding period. Their attack was a species of social criticism based almost entirely on woman's place in society. For writers like Forster, Thompson, Candler, and Kincaid, the criticism goes far deeper. The Englishwoman in India made it impossible for the English and Indian to meet each other as friends. As will be seen below, these men saw the problem between the races as social rather than political. Therefore, anyone who created social barriers between the races was

---

[1] Dennis Kincaid, *Durbar*, London, 1933, p. 108.   [2] Ibid., p. 182.
[3] Ibid., pp. 183–4.   [4] F. Tennyson Jesse, *The Lacquer Lady*, London, 1929, p. 5.
[5] Ibid., p. 86.   [6] Ibid., p. 118.   [7] Thompson, *A Farewell to India*, p. 116.

thought to be the real cause of the difficulties. It was the Englishwoman who was in large measure believed to be guilty of raising these barriers.

A theme which remains from the earlier period is a distrust of any authority which is not on-the-spot. In *Old For-Ever* a *bunniah*, Lala, is kidnapped by a frontier tribe. The Calcutta Government wires the local political agent, Ruddy Gore, asking him to find out how much the ransom is. He replies, rightly according to Ollivant, that to pay such a ransom would only be to encourage the Hill-men to kidnap more men. 'But what's Calcutta know or care about that Frontier—two thousand miles away. They tell me the very latest thing down there is to roll around all day in a victoria with india-rubber tyres to save the bumps. God help old England!'[1] He comes to the heart of this attitude in a discussion with Old For-Ever as he tells him not to let his son come out to India.

Don't let him sweat his soul out in this damn continent. India's never been a country for white women; and it's ceasing to be for white men. By 1900 if things go on as they're going now, there won't be a sahib from Landi Khana to Cape Comorin. India'll have relapsed into jungle with Kadir and his kind doling out justice and mercy. And they'll deserve all they'll get.

'Some of 'em,' interjected the soldier.

The two men strolled down the garden.

'Where are you going to get the men from to man the services under modern conditions?—Can't be done. No scope. No initiative. What room to-day would there be for a Nicholson on the Frontier! Why they'd break him in ten minutes. They want babus not Nicholsons. It's all centralization, centralization. No room for initiative, or authority. *Don't trust the man on the spot* is our modern policy. Somebody sitting on your head all the blessed time. Why I have to write to Calcutta for permission to wipe a drop of sweat off my nose during the monsoon.'

They had reached the road.

'I quite agree,' said Old For-ever. 'I've never been on an expedition yet but the show's been spoilt by some Political wet blanketing the soldiers all the time. And as to Nicholson!' He turned to meet the Chief's eye. 'Why I was with him when he rode through the Kohat Pass on the eve of the Mutiny with a chit in his pocket from John Lawrence forbidding him to do so, and another from Sidney Cotton

---

[1] Ollivant, *Old For-Ever*, p. 145.

ordering him to prepare to meet his God if he got through the Peshawar alive as it was his, Sidney's, intention to have him shot for insubordination.'[1]

Besides the idea of the importance of the man on the spot, the last paragraph of this quotation shows the view that, above all else, it was the military who filled the role the best. Although political agents such as Ruddy Gore are depicted favourably, there is still a feeling, among the defenders of the Raj, that the soldier is by nature more independent and, hence, the better man for the British in India. It is noticeable that there is a strong element of melancholy present in this quotation—even from a man who is one of the strongest defenders of the Raj and one who believes that British rule in India is a necessity.

Although Edmund Candler is not as simple a pro-Raj writer as most of the authors of that class, much of his writing fits into the same pattern. In *Siri Ram* he gives us the same kind of a visiting English parliamentarian as Kipling's Pagett. 'A Radical member of Parliament' named Dr. Byleman uses the rostrum of Parliament to attack the actions of Chauncey and Merivale in successfully ridding the village of Mehlagtha of cholera. These two men are perfect examples of the men on the spot. They acted without orders because they knew that prompt action was essential. At the time of the plague, Merivale had realized that all he would get from the Government was 'a good deal of grumbling and little thanks''.[2] However, he did not realize that it would go so far. With 'the bitterness, and meanness and ignorance of the Little England group in the House' Dr. Byleman complained that the two men had broken *purdah* and profaned the Indian houses. It didn't matter to him that Chauncey died of cholera contacted in the village, or that the two men had succeeded in their aim of stopping the spread of the disease. He wanted them to be removed from office. Led by his statement, the 'Radical press' screamed 'outrage' and 'violence' saying that it was an example of the 'high-handed insolence of Anglo-Indian officialdom'. This was all copied by the Indian press and believed by all of them because if it were not true, they thought, the British would not be saying it themselves. Thus, Dr. Byleman had 'knocked more nails into

[1] Ollivant, *Old For-Ever*, pp. 157–8.   [2] Candler, *Siri Ram*, p. 65.

the coffin of our prestige than anyone could count'.[1] These charges did harm to the British position everywhere, except in the village of Mehlagtha itself. There the people were thankful and when agitators came in to the area, the villagers could not be persuaded that they had been wronged—after all, their lives had been saved. The Home press in England is attacked for running articles such as, 'Can we hold India? Probably not', which are critical of the Raj, because all it succeeds in doing is to play into the hands of the agitators by making the people feel insecure. This, then, Candler tells his readers, causes the Indian people to think that the British have lost their power and a belief such as this encourages them to revolt.[2] Involved is the thought that a large degree of the trouble in India, whenever it occurs, is due to the loss, actual or believed, of British power and prestige.

When Dr. Byleman decides that for all of his constant criticism he needs some first-hand knowledge of India, in order to make his voice carry further, he takes a tour of India. He spends a month there in his attempt to become an expert. Of his total of four weeks in India, three of them are spent in Bengal—the same Bengal which is viewed by writers like Candler in such harsh terms as being the 'least Indian' part of India. As the final irony, the Indian nationalists succeed in getting one of the worst of their number, the Bengali Mohan Roy, to be taken as Byleman's secretary. Thus the Parliamentarian sees little of Candler's 'real India'—the India of the Frontier, the Punjab, and the loyal martial races. What he does see is completely distorted by being viewed from the Bengali nationalist's point of view—a point of view which the author feels is wrong.

In the harsh phrases used in describing the touring Parliamentarian, Candler sounds a great deal like Kipling, but there is a significant difference—one which shows something of the change which had transpired by the second decade of the new century. Whereas Kipling believes that the encounter with India may have had some effect in teaching Pagett, M.P., the truth about the country, Candler holds no such hope. He describes the result of the dispute over the proper way to handle the plague.

---

[1] Candler, *Siri Ram*, p. 124.   [2] Ibid., pp. 230–1.

Government, however, took the hint from the agitators. Nowadays methods are changed. There is no searching of houses or general disinfection or forced evacuation. Inoculation and health camps are the rule. Persuasion is discouraged, and the plague rages with little check. In the Punjab the villagers have learnt to evacuate for themselves. And perhaps the new system is as well. It would be impossible for anyone to do what Merivale and Chauncey did without their tact and sympathy and knowledge of the people. The breed that yap at Westminister—to use Hobb's phrase—would make the most unholy mess of it.[1]

The harshest statement of this image is created by Gordon Casserly in the person of Mr. Donald Macgregor, Labour Party Parliamentary-*wallah*, who had impressed the anti-British Indians with his hatred of England. The Indians recognize the power of Parliament and the men who serve in it. However, Casserly believes that the existence of this power is very unfortunate. One Indian explains: 'Thou knowest that any fool from their Parliament holds a whip over the back of the *Lat Sahib* and all the white men of this land.'[2] Although the M.P. bears an 'historic Highland name' he actually is a foreign Jew who has become a Scot and he 'hated the country of his adoption, as only these gentry do, and was ready to believe any lie against it and eager to do all in his power to injure it'.[3] 'The Hebrew Highlander' describes himself as 'a Pacifist and a socialist' and says that he does not 'hold with soldiers or with keeping coloured races enslaved'.[4] Even the Indians are amazed at his gullibility and his willingness to believe the worst possible lies against the British—lies that the slightest experience in India should have shown him to be false. Macgregor is perfectly willing to see the anti-British forces move into the open, even with the support of the tribes beyond the Frontier, but he does warn them not to 'kill the white women and children—at least, not openly. They might not like it in England, though personally, I don't care if you massacre every damned Britisher in the country.'[5]

In the case of Macgregor, it is made clear that his opposition is because he is not really an Englishman. This was only hinted

[1] Candler, *Siri Ram*, p. 126.
[2] Casserly, *The Elephant God*, p. 127. '*Lat Sahib*' means Viceroy.
[3] Ibid., pp. 131–2.   [4] Ibid., p. 130.   [5] Ibid., p. 133.

at with other such Parliamentarians. Byleman's name or the red colour of Cox's hair are perhaps earlier implications of this image. It is based on the idea that 'real Englishmen', by virtue of their Englishness, must support the Empire. For a slight variation of this theme of the 'radical' Englishman coming to India and being fooled into thinking that he understands the country, Thompson gives us the Tory Sir Spencer Tomlinson. When he meets the Indian Commissioner Deogharia he is so impressed with him that he thinks: 'The British Empire had justified its existence by producing even one such man' as Deogharia.[1] The Indian is actually a completely corrupt individual who acts only to improve his own position. Despite his veneer of Western civilization and his protestations of loyalty, he is trying to build a little empire of his own. If it means destroying his rivals, he does so. The local English judge attacks Deogharia in the presence of Tomlinson. The Tory is shocked and says that up to this point he had believed that attacks by white men on Indians were only made up by the Labour Press—' "And this mark you"—as he used to say . . ."to the whitest Indian that ever lived—the one man among them who's every bit a saheb." '[2] Not only is this incident another example of the image of the travelling Englishman in India not understanding the true situation there, but an important shift has taken place. Heretofore it had been the radical or liberal visitor who was lampooned, but now it is the conservative supporter of the Raj who is shown to be a fool.

The British self-image thus had developed new dimensions in the 1920s and 1930s. A great deal of the confidence which had marked it in the first period—even if that confidence was not without its limits—had disappeared. For those men who had completely lost the feeling that British civilization was the best in the world, the whole meaning of the Empire and everything that went with it was equally lost. Those who retained some of the older faith attempted to prove the rightness of the Empire by holding forth old ideas with a new vengeance. Finally, there were those who were in favour of the Empire, but saw that it was passing or, perhaps, had already passed, and who were wondering why this had happened and feeling a great deal of melancholy at the events they believed they were seeing.

[1] Thompson, *An Indian Day*, p. 230.   [2] Ibid., p. 227.

VI

THE INDIAN SCENE

In the new century the novels and stories of India show almost as marked a preoccupation with the same small part of the sub-continent as was seen in Chapter III. The settings are still almost entirely in North India and, even more particularly, the frontier regions of the Punjab or the Himalayan foothills. This is especially true of those authors who are most favourably disposed to the Raj. Among the other authors there is the beginning of a shift, with Thompson writing about Bengal, and Kincaid about the Bombay region. There are still only a few stories set in the cities of India.

For those who saw India in the older way, the reason for this is clear. It is merely a continuation of the image of India as a place for adventure and feats of arms. To men like Mundy, Wren, and Ollivant, India's main characteristic was still that it provided a place where the Englishman, interested in adventure, could find a field of action. This view of India as the home of mystery is nothing new, but it is interesting that those authors who were not full-fledged allies of the Raj did not see India in this way. True, men like Forster did see India itself as something of a mystery, but as a very different sort from the romantic mystery of Wren or Mundy. Even though Indian nationalists and anti-imperialistic Englishmen were making it more and more difficult for anyone to ignore the social and political side of India, these writers were able to continue to write the same old stories about the same old India. They might feel it necessary to introduce some discussion of politics into their novel, but John Eyton could still write a book like *Bulbulla* in which a young boy experiences all kinds of adventures in the Indian jungles. It is remarkably similar to Kipling's *Kim*, to which it was compared upon publication. Even Gordon Casserly's novel, *The Elephant God*, which is filled with violent attacks on Indian nationalists and British anti-imperialists, is still basically a story demonstrating the love of the author for *his* India—the India of the Terai Forests on the Himalayan foothills. In this India—the India of the jungles or mountains—it was still possible to write stories in which the predominant themes were the adventure, mystery, or romance of India. None of these things could be found in the cities of the sub-continent.

Even those authors who are more concerned with the social and political problems of India tend to keep their settings out of the Westernized cities. Neither the opponents nor the supporters of the Raj, in this period, show anything but dislike for the culturally hybrid cities. Unlike the imperialist authors who disliked seeing British civilization watered down, the anti-imperialist authors are more concerned with what they see as the bad effect of that civilization on India. While the latter do not limit the geographical locale or use the jungles and mountains to escape from problems confronting the British in India, neither do they demonstrate the same feeling of affection as the imperialist writers. Despite occasional sympathetic and even romantic descriptions of the beauties of the country, one is much more likely to find in their work pictures of the filth and squalor of India. Among the earlier writers one can find many discussions of the harshness of the climate, but in most of these cases such descriptions are counterbalanced by positive images elsewhere. Furthermore, in these older pictures it is the climate which is the only thing depicted in such harsh terms. In the case of the anti-imperialist authors, or those who see Anglo-Indian relations in terms of futility or melancholy, filth joins the pictures of the harsh Indian climate.

The description of an Indian train is filled with the disgust for squalor and filth that, for the first time, many of these authors felt towards India.

> People spat everywhere, urinated on the floor, waited in a queue for the single lavatory, which had never been cleaned, whose pipe had long ago been blocked and whose floor was ankle-deep in filth. An old bania seemed to be occupying the lavatory for an unconscionable time. They hammered on the door and, receiving no reply, burst the rusty lock to find the old man dead, having fallen in a fit and suffocated, his face among the excrement.[1]

[1] Dennis Kincaid, *Cactus Land*, London, 1934, pp. 54–5.

Along the same lines Kincaid also describes a village street in terms far different from the colourful way such a scene would probably have been depicted in the earlier period.

> Shopkeepers sprinkle rose-water in the dust before their houses. Slops are emptied from windows. Urine and human excrement trickle thinly from under wooden doorways. Piles of paper and rotting straw and stinking linen and fly-spotted faeces clutter every angle of the streets. Pink-manged mongrels nuzzle and roll and lift boil-scarred hind-legs above these reeking dumps. Green slime and trickling filth rope verminous clay walls.[1]

What is lacking from descriptions of this type is the old image of the glamorous East.

Forster's Fielding, in describing India to the newly-arrived Miss Quested and Mrs. Moore, introduces a new image of the area when he says: 'Aziz and I know well that India's a muddle.'[2] Something of this is also seen in Alden's plaintive statement that 'whatever he did was wrong and misrepresented him. Fate was daily playing this trick on Englishmen now.'[3] However, the idea of India as a muddle goes deeper than this. It is even more than the feeling that India is a land of mystery, but it is related to that old theme. The Indian girl, Gunevati, in Myers' novels represents the mysterious forces that he sees as being the heart of India. She is a part of the 'strange world of underground forces, subterranean modes of existence which permeate Myers' descriptions of India'.[4] This image is more particularly found in the mystery and ghost stories by people like Wren and Mundy where things happen that would be thought impossible in the West.

In a similar, but more pessimistic, vein is the idea that nothing can go right in India whether done by the English or the Indians. In his autobiographical account of his Indian experiences, *The Hill of Devi*, Forster gives a delightful but sad account of the muddle he sees as being India.

> I could never describe the muddle in this place. It is a wheel within a wheel. Pipes have been laid (for example) all down the flower border, and connected with the empty water tank, which stands on four legs and takes its share in spoiling our surroundings.

[1] Kincaid, *Durbar*, p. 175.   [2] Forster, *A Passage to India*, p. 67.
[3] Thompson, *A Farewell to India*, p. 160.   [4] Bantock, *L. H. Myers*, p. 49.

It is connected—in its turn—with an almost empty well, and if there was any water in the well it would be raised into the tank by an electric pump of insufficient power to raise the water. You are not at the end of the chain yet, for the electric pump is connected with the Electric House which is only on at night, when all its energies are required for the Palace lighting. So there we are, and there are the flowers dying.[1]

Almost identical is Kincaid's description of a party which is given by the local rajah for the European community. The whole affair is planned along the most elaborate lines with flowers being placed in front of each one's place. 'There was, however, no water in the vases and the flowers were already dead.'[2]

Things in India were simply never what they seemed. When Alden is unable to find out who has committed a crime, he is not surprised.

It's like that in India. People's lives go swirling along like rafts on a water in the monsoon. Something hits one like a water-kelpie's hand pushed out from the stream. It sinks. It's no good asking who did it, or what particular hole the kelpies have gone back to.[3]

Similarly, when Ronny and Adela see a bird they naturally, for Westerners, wonder what kind of a bird it is and want to identify it, but fail because 'nothing in India is identifiable, the mere asking of a question causes it to disappear or to merge in something else'.[4] Nothing is what it seems and the most enormous contradictions can be bound up in one thing. The description of Shahu's palace goes along these lines.

From a distance the palace was imposing. . . . Behind the façade lay the reception rooms, whose furnishing was a medley of the disordered tastes of three successive rulers. The grandfather's rocking chairs, beaded cushions and Louis-Philippe fauteuils still fraternally companioned the elaborate deck-chairs and arty garden-seats and musical-boxes of Shahu's father—while Shahu's contribution was a set of English smoking-room chairs, which the servants used to enjoy trundling to and fro on their squeaky castors, scarring deep canals in the incredibly valuable carpets. . . . On the walls a few masterpieces of Rajput art . . . were hung crookedly on loops of frayed and knotted

[1] Forster, *The Hill of Devi*, p. 77.   [2] Kincaid, *Durbar*, p. 97.
[3] Thompson, *A Farewell to India*, p. 122.   [4] Forster, *A Passage to India*, p. 84.

string beside old calendars and advertisements of Pompeian beauty-cream and Palmolive school-girls and sports photos from the *Daily Mirror*. . . . Wastes of empty rooms full of garbage and rotting woodwork alternated with rooms crowded to suffocation with servants, clients, hangers-on.[1]

The whole thing partakes of a tragi-comic element which is very common in the descriptions given by those writers who are not completely supporters of the existing British control in India. On the holiday of Dassera, Shahu's palace provides the perfect setting for a scene that is so ridiculous that it is laughable, but not funny.

The nobles and chieftains of the State arrived, sometimes with a trumpeter in the front seat of their car, tooting with melancholy and tuneless persistence, but loudly enough to emphasize the importance of his master. . . . Dismounting from their cars, the nobles stood about the courtyard in bunches, eyeing each other's jewels, chewing cloves, pan-leaves and betel-nuts, and ejecting streams of scarlet spittle upon the lovely carpets. The bands played indefatigably and deafeningly. A mad elephant confined somewhere in the recesses of the palace roared and trumpeted.[2]

India is simply not seen by these authors to be the majestic, romantic, adventurous place that it is by those who favour the maintenance of British rule. Part of this is perhaps derived from more acute observation, but a part of it would seem to be closely related to the generally pessimistic view they took of everything which related to India.

Among the defenders of the Raj the Indian people continued to be viewed in relatively minor roles. There are more Indians in their stories and occasionally, one even finds Indian characters painted with a certain depth that had been lacking. Still, the basic conception of the Indian people which these men hold is little different from the earlier period. The most significant difference is that they feel forced to discuss disloyal Indians, Indian nationalists, or at least, Indian nationalism in virtually every story. This is equally true of those writers who are less favourably disposed to the Raj. Another marked difference between the two periods is that, particularly among the anti-Raj writers, there are attempts being made to write about the Indian people as fully developed characters. In the earlier

---

[1] Kincaid, *Durbar*, p. 39.   [2] Ibid., p. 102.

period, only in the works of Steel was this the case, but in this period, it becomes a common attempt.

The 'good' Indian is seen by the pro-Raj writers to be above all else loyal to the British. There is a loyalty here that is thought be found only in India. Eldred Lenox's Pathan servant Zyarulla is described in glowing terms.

Zyarulla, entering soundlessly, set down the *chota hazri* on a small table at his master's elbow without betraying his surprise and concern by the flicker of an eyelash. Not even your immaculate family butler can excel, in dignity and true reserve, a bearer of the old school, whose Sahib stands only second to his God, and who would almost as soon think of defiling his caste as of entering another man's service. We have educated the grand old ideal of service out of our own land; and we are fast educating it out of India also; though it remains an open question whether the good wrought by over-civilization can honestly be said to counterbalance the evil—a question few Anglo-Indians will be found to answer in the affirmative.[1]

This loyalty is most often shown to be a reward to the English for their 'good policies' towards India—it is a way of saying 'Thank you'. Rup Singh, for example, is completely loyal to the British because, 'like most Orientals, he never forgets a good turn'.[2] The Rajput Juggut Khan has felt himself to be a friend of the British ever since Bill Brown cared for a wounded Indian boy at the cost of his own health. Although the Englishman tosses this episode off as being nothing any other man would not have done, the Rajput knows better saying: 'And you know that there were others there, of my own people, who might have done what you did, and did not.'[3] Another Rajput notes that he fights for the British because 'they have treated us with honour, as surely no other conquerors had done!'[4] This loyalty is a part of the character of certain Indian groups like Rajputs, Pathans, and Marathas. Nana Saheb assures the ruler of the princely state that he has nothing to worry about because the troops are bound to be loyal—'A Mahratha does not easily change his allegiance.'[5] Nana's loyalty, itself, is unquestionable, as he

[1] Diver, *The Great Amulet*, p. 116.

[2] L. Adams Beck, 'The Ninth Vibration', in *The Ninth Vibration*, p. 17.

[3] Mundy, 'Hookum Hai', in *Told in the East*, p. 28.

[4] Mundy, 'For the Salt He Had Eaten', in ibid., p. 132. This whole story, like many of Mundy's works, is an ode to loyalty.

[5] Kincaid, *Durbar*, p. 212.

explains: 'My ancestors have served this kingdom from the beginning of time. I have been Minister to three princes of Krishnagad. I shall serve you to the end.'[1]

Time and again the related themes of the timelessness of India and the fatalism that this is supposed to breed are reiterated—'ancient, unchanging India; utterly impervious to mere birds of passage from the West'.[2] Yasmini explains to King that the real gods of India 'are neither Hindu, nor Muhammadan, but are older by a thousand ages than either foolishness'.[3] The sub-continent was thought to be possessed with primeval forces which had always existed and would always exist. This image of timelessness not only implied a belief that Indians were fatalists, but that nothing could be done to change them. For the pro-Raj authors this offered an excuse for their opposition to reform and for the anti-Raj group it meant that reforms would not be effective.

Diver's Roy Sinclair worries that, because of his part Indian blood, he may have 'a less purposeful grip' on his chosen work than would be true if he were completely English in his biological heritage.[4] References to 'Asiatics with the phlegm of fatalism'[5] or 'the dread note of fatalism—the moral microbe of the East'[6] or 'her fatalistic mixed heritage of Eastern and Latin blood'[7] are so common as to be expected when the Indian people or the East in general is being referred to. This prevents the Indians from acting, whether it be to defend themselves from the plague in *Siri Ram*, or from false charges of the possession of magical powers which are levelled against an innocent man in order to gain his land. Am Singh 'knew that the charge was false; there was no magic in him; but unjust as it was, it was fate. Somehow, doubtless, he deserved it.'[8] When a townsman learns that his ruler, Shahu, is in danger, he first feels that out of loyalty he should warn the prince, but then sits back and does nothing because he believes that fate must work itself out.[9]

---

[1] Ibid., p. 161.   [2] Diver, *Far to Seek*, p. 159.
[3] Mundy, *King—of the Khyber Rifles*, p. 233.   [4] Diver, *The Singer Passes*, p. 6.
[5] Diver, *The Great Amulet*, p. 476.   [6] Ibid., p. 118.
[7] Jesse, *The Lacquer Lady*, p. 242.
[8] John Eyton, 'Poetic Justice', in *The Dancing Fakir and Other Stories*, London, 22, p. 46.
[9] Kincaid, *Durbar*, p. 178.

Fanny finds this same thing in the Royal Burmese Palace.

Time itself was oddly different here in the Palace, from time in the West. It went so much faster, though it seemed to stand still. Past hardly existed and the future not at all. . . . The immediate present was so intensely theirs in the Palace that no one wondered over the truth that there is no present, that it is perpetually becoming the past. There was such an illusion of time being static, everything was so changeless, dress, customs, outlook; the very buildings, though new, were so exactly what they had been as far as man could remember or history relate, that no one could notice how swiftly it was slipping away. Fanny's days were ordered as had been the days of Palace dwellers in Indo-China for hundreds of years, days that passed as they had passed in the days of Kublai Khan whose palace had been of just the same design as was this in Mandalay.[1]

When Leonard Woolf describes the ancient method of pearl fishing off the Ceylonese coast, he has his narrator remark: 'Unscientific? Yes, perhaps; but after all it's our camp, our fisher—just as it was in Solomon's time? At any rate, you see, it's the East.'[2] The whole thing is most nicely put when there is the question of who really rules India, the nationalists or the English and a character says: 'I've gathered the impression . . . that neither George nor the Mahatma is ruler here, but the Past is king.'[3]

Forster's Caves are very similar to the Cow's Mouth Shrine in Kipling's *The Naulahka*. Both authors see them in terms of total negation—containing 'nothing' both in the literal and figurative sense. They represent 'the sudden intrusion of timelessness, the horror of absolute vacuum in which human ambition, love, hate, even religion vanish as undifferentiated particles down an eternal drain'.[4] Similarly both authors make the encounter with the force of negation the 'structural centre and narrative climax' of the novels.[5] Here the similarity ends as each author has his characters react differently. As has been seen above, Kipling's Tarvin recognizes the strength inherent in the 'nothingness' found in the shrine and flees from it. He is not destroyed

[1] Jesse, *The Lacquer Lady*, pp. 229–30.
[2] Leonard Woolf, 'Pearls and Swine', in *Stories from the East*, p. 30.
[3] Thompson, *A Farewell to India*, p. 120.
[4] Cooperman, 'The Imperial Posture and The Shrine of Darkness', p. 9.
[5] Ibid., p. 10.

by the revelation which he has experienced, but rather is led to reaffirm his faith in progress and the value of Western civilization.[1] The reaction of Forster's characters is totally different and in this difference the changing British image of themselves in India is illustrated. Mrs. Moore is the most strongly affected of the visitors to the Caves. She embraces their negation, but in so doing gives up her own personality and the possibility of any effective action. Forster is not critical of her unwillingness to testify at the trial on the question of whether or not Aziz raped Miss Quested. To Mrs. Moore this no longer has any meaning and it is not surprising that she dies before returning to England, because as a meaningful individual she has been non-existent since her encounter with the Caves. The only major character to remain consistent throughout the novel is Fielding, and he is also the only one who does not visit the Caves. Whereas Kipling's novel ends with a continued belief in the value of action, Forster's is 'a statement of ironic relativeness in which no standard of action is justified at all'.[2] As Cooperman has written:

It is here, in the response to the immediate confrontation of metaphysical doubt, that basic differences between the poet of the empire and 20th century novelist emerge. The enormous gulf, however, separating their respective attitudes toward religion, empire and human action itself, must be seen not in terms of awareness, but rather in terms of moral will.[3]

The acceptance and, even more, the enjoyment of physical cruelty also continues to be seen as a fundamental part of the general Indian character. This is shown to be in direct contrast to the British attitude. Ruddy Gore describes to Old For-Ever the scene when one of the Pathan Kadir's wives came to him for protection. Kadir had cut one of her breasts off and she had fled to the city with her infant. In order to stay alive she has sought to become a prostitute—an occupation for which she hardly possessed the necessary physical charms. Finally she went to Ruddy Gore. When Kadir learned of this, he demanded that the Political Agent return her to him so that he could finish the

[1] See above, Chapter II, pp. 17–18.
[2] Cooperman, 'The Imperial Posture and The Shrine of Darkness', p. 12.
[3] Ibid., p. 11.

job. The reaction to this story by the two Englishmen is telling. 'The two sat in silence. The horror of physical cruelty, perhaps more marked in the men of their race than in any other, had laid hold upon them.'[1] Of all Indians it is still the Hindus, particularly, who are thought to enjoy the physically horrible side of life. In a story entitled 'The Gods of the East', Diver tells about a Brahman whose occupation entails serving as collateral for a pledge between two other people. If the pledge is broken the Brahman must kill himself, thus covering the pledge breaker with the shame of having caused the death of a Brahman. 'A grim occupation; but to your orthodox Hindu, custom renders all things possible and most things endurable.'[2] This is bad enough, but there is even more to this job.

Nor was even this enough to satisfy the Hindu's innate love of the horrible and the grim. Should a herald have reason to fear that the indelible disgrace of causing a Brahman's death might fail to over-awe the defaulter, he was constrained to take, instead, a life more sacred than his own—to kill, in open daylight, on the offender's doorsill, either his wife or his mother.[3]

It is finally his mother whom the herald kills.

When Hira Singh's Sikhs attack a group of Turks whom they have observed mistreating some Armenians, Hira Singh says:

I looked long for the Turk who had fouled the water, and for the other one who had lanced the child's body, but failed to identify either of them. I found two who looked like them, crawling out from under a heap of slain, and shot them through the head; but as to whether I slew the right ones or not I do not know.[4]

In fact, it is clear that he does not care. Prince Salim in the seventeenth century is depicted as liking to have innocent villagers murdered in front of him for his pleasure when he is drunk.[5] Similarly the Burmese king is described: 'Mindoon was not the blood-thirsty maniac that his brother Pagan Min and his father Tharawaddy, had been, but he was of the unstable race of Alompra, quick-tempered for all his genuine piety and kindliness.'[6]

[1] Ollivant, *Old For-Ever*, p. 155.
[2] Diver, 'The Gods of the East', in *Siege Perilous*, p. 63.   [3] Ibid., p. 58.
[4] Talbot Mundy, *Hira Singh's Tale*, London, 1918, p. 216.
[5] Dennis Kincaid, *Tropic Rome*, London, 1935, p. 232.
[6] Jesse, *The Lacquer Lady*, p. 26.

This trait comes out strongly in the massacre of the princes and the rest of the royal family which is carried out while the King and Queen watch a play, with the music being used to drown out the cries of the victims of the slaughter. The eighty princes, queens, and princesses are clubbed on the throat until they are dead.

A dozen of the Palace elephants were being driven back and forth. . . . For the outraged soil had refused the martyred flesh thrust into it, and had heaved up and disclosed it, thrust it forth in all its accusing misery, its pathos of broken limbs and limp dangling hands, and the elephants were being forced to trample earth and flesh down once again. The sensitive beasts, knowing that they were violating a law by placing their feet upon even the remains of humanity, their nostrils sickened by the escaping gases, were urged on by the attendants who cared nothing and encouraged the inferior animals with shouts and goads.[1]

Even 'inferior animals' are thus thought to possess more restraints on the drive to blood lust than their Burmese mahouts and owners.

The Indians are believed not only to put up with scenes like this, but actually to revel in the shedding of blood. A detailed description of a pig baiting is given with the crowd screaming in pleasure every time they see any blood. When the boar shows too much skill in killing the dogs which have been put on him, his leg is speared so it is useless and left 'hanging by a few bloody shreds of torn flesh. The boar spun round squealing and drove his tusk into the soft mud of the wall. The crowd howled with delight; they laughed, embraced one another, flung their turbans into the arena.'[2] Finally, thinking the boar to be dead, a native goes into the arena and kicks the body. The pig is not dead and 'ripped his leg from ankle to knee. . . . How the crowd laughed. It was the best joke they had ever enjoyed. They clapped each other's backs, they rolled about in ecstasies of mirth.'[3] Scenes such as these are doubtless related to the old image of the East as being filled with barbaric splendour. The fact that authors were willing, almost eager, to go into such detail is not an expression of their feeling towards the Indians, but is a part of the growing trend towards the depiction of

[1] Jesse, *The Lacquer Lady*, p. 170.   [2] Kincaid, *Cactus Land*, p. 74.
[3] Ibid, p. 76.

bloody scenes in all literature. Thus, it may well be true that this kind of writing tells us a great deal about the sensibilities of the West.

Another generalization which is carried over from the earlier period is the treatment of the Indians as children. *The Lacquer Lady* repeats this phrase so often that it is impossible for the reader to finish the novel without linking the words 'childlike' and 'Burmese' together—'the infantile yet subtle imagery'[1] of the Burmans; 'They're only children';[2] 'these large children';[3] and like children they are 'incorrigibly gay'.[4] Or, when Findlay realizes that both his wife and daughter have died because he had thought more of his mission to the Indians than of them, Alden explains to him that he had to act that way. He says that one cannot ignore the 'thousands of grown-up babies all around you'.[5] Just as has been pointed out in regard to Kipling, this image of the Indians as children had its ethically good side as well as having connotations of inferiority. They are thought to possess certain traits which have been lost to the more sophisticated British.

What is far more important, however, is that this attitude implied a continuation of the paternalistic ideal of the relationship between the English and Indians. Like children they are believed to be naturally dependent and most comfortable in this role. Tom Oliver's trusted aide, Subahdar Singh, asks the Englishman to get him a jumping-jack. He wants it because he thinks it is a kind of 'white man's god' having seen a memsahib showing it to her baby. He thought that the baby was being taught to pray to it. 'Old For-Ever nodded solemnly. It was a favourite saying with him that every Asiatic is a baby.'[6]

Even among those writers who are not defenders of the continued existence of the Raj, there is a tendency to treat the Indians as children. In these cases there is nothing as definite as the above statements. Rather it is that characters like Forster's Aziz are creatures of their emotions who are highly changeable in their nature. They are undependable because of this characteristic. They are likely to take affront at the most innocent remark and to react, like a child, in the most overly sensitive way.

---

[1] Jesse, *The Lacquer Lady*, p. 115.   [2] Ibid., p. 349.   [3] Ibid., p. 246.
[4] Ibid., p. 188.   [5] Thompson, *An Indian Day*, p. 244.
[6] Ollivant, *Old For-Ever*, p. 23.

The feminine nature of the East also remained a theme through the 1930s. For example, in *The Lacquer Lady*, the missionary Edward Protheroe 'felt that his Kingdom of Ava stood for feminine domination, for feminine guile and points of view in a way that was new to him'[1] and that there 'women seem to run the place far more than they do even at home. It seems . . . that the whole country is in the hands of women.'[2]

Interestingly, the over-all image of the Indian people given by the writers who are most opposed to the Raj is not particularly favourable. If anything, it was the authors who most strongly favoured the Raj that treated the Indian in the best light, provided, and this is a major provision, that they fit the image of the 'loyal native'. Although it is only in the more critical writers that one finds Indians who are no longer the simple naïve two-dimensional salaaming creatures of the earlier period and the continuing pro-Raj writers, the Indians they depict are filled with flaws. The over-riding concern of these authors with what they saw to be the failure of Britain in India or with British civilization in general caused them to see the whole Indian picture in dark colours.

Writers like Orwell who were violently opposed to the whole imperial situation did not turn to a sympathetic idealization of the natives over whom this 'evil system' ruled. Rather, they found themselves almost as exasperated by the natives as they were by the system. They do not particularly like the Indians or Burmans any more than they do the imperialists.[3] Orwell has given us a picture of a Burman, U Po Kyin, who is forever scheming against both the British and his fellow Burmese. He is totally despicable as a character who has grown fat, as if by consuming the bodies of those he has stepped on along the road to power. Much like him is Flory's native mistress, Ma Hla May, who wants only what she can get out of Flory. When he finally throws her out, she has no qualms about aiding to destroy him despite the good things he had done for her. Almost identical with U Po Kyin is Thompson's Commissioner Deogharia who not only succeeds in bankrupting a small local rajah to make

---

[1] Jesse, *The Lacquer Lady*, p. 41.   [2] Ibid., p. 45.
[3] See Lionel Trilling, 'George Orwell and the Politics of Truth', in *The Opposing Self: Nine Essays in Criticism*, London, 1955, p. 161; and Richard Voorhees, *The Paradox of George Orwell*, Lafayette, Indiana, 1961, p. 77.

him more dependent, but also gets one of the most sympathetic Indian characters transferred to a post where he 'shall die of drink or malaria' because he refuses to accept Deogharia's claims to superiority.[1] Even Forster's Aziz, who is the most fully developed of any Indian character, is far from idealized. Although the basis of his characterization is affection, he is shown to be completely unstable and many of the problems of the book are due to the weakness of his own character.

'You couldn't get away from the gods. They were in the very air of India.'[2] This kind of a statement could well have been made by one of the writers of the earlier period. Unlike that period, however, one finds the emphasis on the spirituality of India far more pronounced and also a great deal more favourable. It is not in the least bit uncommon to find writers like Thompson, Diver, or, especially, Beck making highly complimentary statements about what India has to offer the West in the way of teaching her the true meaning of spirituality. The most interesting thing here is not only that feelings such as this are found among writers who differ a great deal on every other subject, but that they place great limitations in their definition of what Indian spirituality is—it is Buddhism. Buddhism alone among the religions of India seems to have impressed the British. Even in Kipling's *Kim* we find a very favourable image of the religion and its practitioners being given. In fact, the lama depicted there is one of the few non-European characters in that period who is drawn 'in the round' rather than 'in the flat'.[3] This is so noticeable that Edmund Wilson believes 'that Kipling has been seriously influenced by the Buddhism he had imbibed with his first language in his boyhood'.[4] In the same way Perrin had referred to the Buddha as 'the greatest reformer, save One, that the world has ever known'.[5]

Although not as strongly anti-Hindu as these writers, Maud Diver still refers to the Middle Way as the only way of truth.[6] Similarly, Woolf writes that 'Buddhism seems to me superior to all other religions'.[7] Thompson's Alden carries this a step

---

[1] Thompson, *An Indian Day*, p. 265.   [2] Kincaid, *Their Ways Divide*, p. 271.
[3] Garratt, 'Indo-British Civilization', in Garratt, ed., *The Legacy of India*, p. 416.
[4] Edmund Wilson, 'The Kipling that Nobody Read', in Rutherford, ed., *Kipling's Mind and Art*, p. 57.
[5] Perrin, *Idolatry*, p. 101.   [6] Diver, *The Great Amulet*, p. 16.
[7] Leonard Woolf, *Growing*, p. 159.

further when he thinks that the only saving feature in Indian religiosity is that at least somewhere in their hearts they remember the story of the Buddha. 'India, he thought to himself, made the mistake of millenniums and shackled and ravaged herself for all future times, when she rejected the Buddha and chose the other way.'[1] As to specifically what Buddhism is to these people it is hard to tell. Beck has at least attempted to explain what she means. One of her Buddhist-influenced characters, Vanna, states

that the Buddhist philosophers are right when they teach that all forms of what we call matter are really but aggregates of spiritual units, and that life itself is a curtain hiding reality as the vast veil of day conceals from out of sight the countless orbs of space. So that purified man even while prisoned in the body, may enter into union with the Real and, according to attainment, see it as it is.[2]

On the whole, Westerners have been more impressed by Buddhism than Hinduism. When he visited Burma, Marco Polo remarked that if only Buddhism had come from God it would be the best religion in the world.[3] To most Westerners, Buddhism was a less alien way of worship than was Hinduism and, as usual, they favoured the familiar over the strange. The significant thing is that only in this second period does the favouritism towards Buddhism manifest itself to such a large degree.

This idealization of and great interest in Indian spiritualism in the form of Buddhism is obviously closely related to the lack of confidence which the British felt in their own Western and Christian culture. 'Concern for eastern ideas is, of course, one of the marks of the eclecticism of our age; with the decay of Christian dogmatic beliefs we have sought consolation in . . . comprehension of other religious approaches. This eclecticism points, perhaps, to one more aspect of our decaying moral order.'[4] At least the people of India are thought to 'believe, and we of the western world . . . have lost our faith' so that all we have is 'our own arid skepticism and the curse of a cruel materialism'.[5]

[1] Thompson, *An End of the Hours*, p. 232–3.
[2] Beck, 'The Interpreter', in *The Ninth Vibration*, p. 145.
[3] Guy Wint, *The British in Asia*, London, 1954, p. 84
[4] Bantock, *L. H. Myers*, p. 87.
[5] Beck, 'The Desolate City: A Story in Mahabalipuram', in *The Perfume of the Rainbow*, p. 278.

This is all far more closely related to pessimism about the West than to a true concern with the Indian people. Beck's Vanna who is continually shown as a perfect example of the best kind of Westerner learning about the East and who is deeply in love with India raves about the beauties of the country. Stephen remarks that that is all well, but that there is a lot of misery in the country. She shows a total lack of interest in that side of India as she says: 'Of course. We shall get to work one day. But look at the sunset. It opens like a mysterious flower.'[1]

It has been said that Kipling was the first Englishman to bring to the attention of the Home English that there were many Indias rather than a single nation. Among the defenders of the Raj one of the most noticeable points in this period is their growing emphasis on the divisions of India.

And how could all the Indias he had seen—not to mention the many he had not seen—be jumbled together under that one misleading name? That was the root fallacy of dreamers and 'reformers'. They spoke of her as one, when in truth she was many—bewilderingly many. Her semblance of unity sprang mainly from England's unparalleled achievement—her Pax Britannica.[2]

Mundy goes into great detail in describing the make-up of the Indian troops sailing to Europe during the First World War.

In that great fleet of ships we were men of many creeds and tongues—Sikh, Mohammedan, Dogra, Gurkha—the Dogra and Gurkha be both Hindu, though of different kinds—Jat, Punjabi, Guzerati, Pathan, Mahratta—who can recall how many! No one language could have sufficed to explain one thought to all of us—no, nor yet ten languages.[3]

In the same way Ollivant describes Old For-Ever's 'regiment of many races'.

They came swarming out of their tents like the rats from their holes at the call of the pied piper of Hamelin . . . bearded Sikhs, trans-frontier Pathans, cis-frontier Pathans, the dark Afridi type, the high-cheeked Hazara, the rosy-faced fellow of Afghan origin, the solid Jat, the merry-eyed Ghurkha, the Dôgra from the foothills in the northern Punjab.[4]

---

[1] Beck, 'The Interpreter', in *The Ninth Vibration*, p. 80.
[2] Diver, *Far to Seek*, p. 424.   [3] Mundy, *Hira Singh's Tale*, p. 10.
[4] Ollivant, *Old For-Ever*, p. 246.

Although the regiment works well as a unit under the leader-ship of the British, readers are not allowed to forget for a minute that there is a great deal of rivalry between its various parts. This was a feud 'which had its origins in racial antipathy'.[1] Only the British are able to control and utilize this rivalry so that each 'race' can best utilize its different 'racial virtues'.

Diver depicts the unity of the 'different Indias' under British rule with three Indian characters—a Pathan, a Sikh, and a Brahman—who are 'strongly united in the service of the new India; conjured by Army training, into brother officers and good friends—up to a point'.[2] That she feels this point is reached quickly is demonstrated a few pages later when the Brahman officer is supposed to keep scores in a shooting match between two companies—one Rajput and the other Pathan. They demand a '*pukka* British officer' because they believe that only he would be fair. This leaves the Brahman to wonder 'seriously how things would go, if ever there were no more white officers in the Indian Army?'[3] She also depicts the various Indian groups already talking about how they will rule India when the British have left, even if they have to destroy all other groups to gain power. Only the British are able to keep the communal riots from becoming even worse than they are. It is not only the army regiments and British neutrality which are seen to hold India together. In an echo of the earlier period, Diver writes: 'The whole heterogeneous mass drawn and held together by the universal love of hazard and sport, the spirit of competition without strife that is the corner-stone of British character and the British Empire.'[4] This growing emphasis on the lack of unity within India fits in with the British idea that they had to have some reason for being there. If there is no such thing as an 'Indian' person, then no group has any more rightful claim to ruling India than the British. 'India for the Indian nation is a fine rallying cry. . . . But a nation is not merely a geographical term; it implies a compact people, united and inspired by common aims and traditions. India, as you know, is not one people any more than Europe is one people.'[5] The various authors naturally expressed different opinions

---

[1] Ollivant, *Old For-Ever*, p. 27.
[2] Maud Diver, *The Dream Prevails*, London, 1938, p. 55.   [3] Ibid., p. 57.
[4] Diver, *Far to Seek*, p. 324.   [5] Candler, *Siri Ram*, pp. 97–8.

about these varied groups of Indians. Certain 'races', however, get a consistently good press. Punjabis are always well treated because they are 'a strong hardy stock, assertive of their own rights, men of the toughest fibre, innocent of nerves, with little or no physical fear'.[1] Of his troops Tom Oliver would always say: 'There's only one man in Asia who's reliable. . . . And that man's the Jat.'[2] The Pathans, like the Rajputs, have 'the free air' which is lacking among the south Indians.[3] The Gurkhas, because they are spirited, and the Sikhs, because they are loyal, also fall into the groups which are most admired by the British. In fact, it is loyalty and a love of adventure that mark all the groups which the British single out for the best treatment.

In opposition to those Indians they liked, Casserly's hero, Dermot, a typical supporter of the Raj

respected the men of those gallant warrior races that once had faced the British valiantly in battle and fought as loyally beside them since. But for the effeminate and cowardly peoples of India, that ever crawled to kiss the feet of each conqueror of the peninsula in turn and then stabbed him in the back if they could, he had the contempt that every member of the martial races of the land, every Sikh, Rajput, Gurkha, Punjabi had.[4]

As in the earlier period, the British image of the Indian people centred on the Muslim community. The basic preference for men of action continued among those writers who favoured the Raj—'the English are more successful in the North. They better understand the Moslem. And I think they like him better than the Hindu.'[5]

Again we find that even when a Muslim, almost always a Pathan, opposed the British, he still received a warm treatment. Saleem is a border raider who particularly attacks Hindu *bunniahs*. He is finally subdued by the British who have to protect the border from such lawlessness. Yet, it is clear that all of the sympathies of the author are with the outlaw. Finally, the British believe they have killed him, but at the end he is seen surviving to continue to plunder the merchants.[6] He

---

[1] Candler, *Siri Ram*.   [2] Ollivant, *Old For-Ever*, p. 19.
[3] Beck, 'The Desolate City', in *The Perfume of the Rainbow*, p. 271.
[4] Casserly, *The Elephant God*, p. 333.   [5] Diver, *The Singer Passes*, p. 503.
[6] Eyton, 'The Moods of Saleem', in *The Dancing Fakir*, *passim*.

is obviously the kind of man that the British respected. The same thing is true of the *mullah* in *Old For-Ever* who is killed as he attempts to slay Tom's wife. As the *mullah* dies, Tom offers to turn his face to Mecca as a gesture of respect. He does not believe that the Muslim actually meant to kill a defenceless woman—the kind of a thing a Hindu might be thought capable of—but rather that he thought she was a man in disguise. The *mullah* remains harsh to the end. He refuses to accept Tom's gesture because he is an infidel, but it is clear that both men have a deep respect for each other as men of action who are willing to accept the results of what they do.

It is not merely that Muslims continue to be well treated, but that they are the group which still is most commonly dealt with. In discussing *A Passage to India*, Nirad Chaudhuri points out that although the book, through its criticisms, was an effective weapon in destroying the support of the Raj, it missed the point in describing India. One of its major defects is in its choice of characters. The major Indian character, Aziz, and most of the supporting Indians are Muslims. Chaudhuri believes that Forster did this because 'he shares the liking the British in India had for the Muslims, and the corresponding dislike for the Hindus',[1] and 'makes no secret that he did not feel drawn towards the Hindus, and that he preferred the Muslims'.[2] As another critic has pointed out: 'The first two parts of the novel are Muslim and Forster gets inside his Muslim characters with ease, for the Muslim is completely our brother, an exaggeration of our best selves. The difficulty comes in the third part when he deals with the Hindus.'[3] Chaudhuri feels that in Forster's pictures of the Indians he was not merely reflecting the opinion of the British ruling class with which he had very poor relations and which he also attacked, but rather, that this uncomplimentary image was so widely shared as to be almost universal.[4] In his provocative manner this Indian author feels that his point is proven by the way in which he reads Forster's treatment of Dr. Godbole, the chief Hindu character. He thinks

[1] Nirad C. Chaudhuri, 'Passage To and From India', *Encounter*, II, June, 1954, p. 22.
[2] Chaudhuri, 'On Understanding the Hindus', p. 24.
[3] Laurence Brander, 'E. M. Forster and India', *A Review of English Literature*, III, October, 1962, p. 76.
[4] Chaudhuri, 'On Understanding the Hindus', p. 24.

that Forster's 'Godbole is not an exponent of Hinduism, he is a clown.'[1] He goes even further in stating that '*A Passage to India* presents all the Indians in it either as perverted, clownish, or queer characters.'[2] Most readers would disagree with the harshness of these criticisms. In this great novel the British image of an India in which Muslims played a disproportionate role and in which Indians shared many bad traits with the British is revealed.

It is the Hindu community which is still treated most harshly by both the friends and enemies of the Raj. They are disliked in part by the supporters of the Raj because in Hinduism they see a potent rival to continued British rule. However, this feeling goes even deeper. They are usually seen as either effete troublemaking *babus* who are unwilling to act on their own, but are anxious to cause others to get themselves in trouble; or as money-grubbing *bunniahs* who put their own welfare above anyone else's concern.

The *bunniah* who was attacked by Saleem 'had acquired great wealth by selling grain at famine prices across the border, and by lending out the capital so gained at exorbitant rates to the poor and needy. A fat, bearded old miser this——.'[3] Just like him is the man who is kidnapped by the Pathans in Ollivant's novel.

A blamed fool of a Hindu bunniah, one Lala, bought up a lot of stuff, Bokhara silk, Persian brocades, carpets, furs, turquoises, Russian pottery, from a Kizibash caravan as it came through the Tochi. He was one of the get-rich-quick boys, and instead of taking it down country at his leisure, like a fat man and a gentleman, he rushed it along the Frontier, and through the Pass, to get it to Peshawar before his blood brother, Chuni Ram, a little swine like unto himself and on the same ramp, could get through: for both of them had heard there were a couple of big buyers come up here from native states—as they do at this time of year. In Lala's well-oiled bosom blue funk and lust of gold fought a mighty battle; and lust of gold prevailed.[4]

Before the *bunniah* is returned to the British, the leader of the

---

[1] Chaudhuri, 'Passage To and From India,' p. 21.
[2] Chaudhuri, 'On Understanding the Hindus', p. 24.
[3] Eyton, 'The Moods of Saleem', in *The Dancing Fakir*, p. 54.
[4] Ollivant, *Old For-Ever*, p. 96.

Pathan group which kidnapped him tells the British that they took him for his own safety since he was travelling in very dangerous country and someone who was an enemy of the Raj was likely to kill him. He reports that they have given Lala every possible convenience and fed him well, 'but he is a Hindu, and there is no gratitude in such men, sahib'.[1] This is borne out when the *bunniah* enters the English camp.

On his forehead was a caste-mark, in his ears were heavy gold rings. He was pursy, aggressive, and aggrieved. Directly he saw the sahibs in the door he began his tale in a shrill excited scream—his doing, his darings, his losses, and above all, his tortures. . . . 'I am a British subject and I want compensation—much—very much of it. So will my wife. For I have lost my all—my caravan, my manhood, my izzat. My face has been blackened, and my name made a mock of before all men, so that all the boys in the bazaar will run after me and call me thou knowest what as I pass down the street. And that will be bad for business.'[2]

Taking advantage of every situation to get more money—this was how the British thought a large segment, if not all, of the Hindu community acted. Particularly to the Englishman who valued loyalty to what he felt were the higher moral abstractions of service and self-sacrifice, people like these were disgraceful. Quite often men of this type like Ramji Das, the *bunniah* in *Siri Ram*, are not only disliked because of their value system, but also because of their political beliefs. The British felt that it was because of the law and order which they had brought to India that men like Ramji Das had been able to become wealthy. Then, when they refused to support the British and switched to support of the rising Indian nationalist movement, the English supporters of the Raj felt that they were guilty of 'biting the hand that fed them'.[3]

The Hindus are also imagined to be lacking in a recognition of their 'duties' to the community. In short, they are thought to be lacking both in the interest of anything beyond their narrow lives and in a sense of responsibility. When, at the age of seven, Siri Ram is taken on his first trip from home, he sits quietly in the cart, not looking at the new surroundings through which he

[1] Ollivant, *Old For-Ever*, p. 228.   [2] Ibid., pp. 256–7.
[3] See also the *bunniah* in Percival Christopher Wren, 'White Ants', in *Odd—But Even So: Stories Stranger Than Fiction*, London, 1940, pp. 78–118, *passim*.

is being taken. Candler contrasts this with the great amount of of curiosity an English youth of the same age and circumstances would have shown to anything new.[1] The Hindus are thought to sink into themselves and be suspicious of their neighbours. Even a sense of paternal responsibility is found to be lacking. When Siri Ram's sister gets the plague her father abandons her to die, showing a fatalistic acceptance of the situation. In addition, he is not altogether unhappy to see Shiv Das die because then he will not have to spend money on her wedding.[2] The author makes it clear that he feels this action shows the Indian father putting his own interests over those of his daughter.

Almost without exception the nationalist movement is identified with the Hindu community. In Eyton's 'The Dancing Fakir' a small village is being torn apart by communal tensions and in order to prevent them from breaking out in violence, the British have banned a Hindu procession from a street on which a mosque is located. This antagonizes the Hindus, and their feeling is made even stronger by the presence in the town of a friend of Gandhi's named Bapu Gopi Nath. He first urges the crowd to attack a liquor shop in order to work them into an even greater frenzy. 'Then later—one could not miss the words; they were like a clarion call—'Hotel'—'Club'—'Blood of the English dogs!'[3] The crowd moves off to the unprotected club where the defenceless English women are playing tennis. 'Bapu Gopi Nath slipped off quietly to the car placed at his disposal by the All-Indian Non-co-operation Society, and was soon far away. After all, he was not a man of action.'[4] The reader of a story such as this was probably angered by the bloody words put in the mouth of the Hindu nationalist. If this were not enough to create a harsh image of the nationalist movement, his refusal to accept the responsibilities for his action was bound to make it even worse.

The image of Hinduism as a religion is mixed. One does find a few favourable comments about it as in the series of novels by Diver dealing with the bringing together of East and West. Lilamani marries Sir Nevil Sinclair and goes to England where she continues practising her Hindu rites. These are sympathetically described, but in the second of the four novels stretching in

[1] Candler, *Siri Ram*, p. 26.   [2] Ibid., p. 106.
[3] Eyton, 'The Dancing Fakir', in *The Dancing Fakir*, p. 7.   [4] Ibid., p. 8.

publication from 1911 to 1938 she converts to Christianity and even this favourable account disappears. The Brahman Prime Minister, Nana Saheb, in Kincaid's *Durbar* is treated kindly in terms of his religiosity. 'He must perform religiously every action in his life, whether being born or dying or sleeping with his wife.'[1] Despite this there is something harsh about what otherwise is shown to be a valuable set of beliefs. The reason that Nana Saheb is anxious to keep British rule in force is that he feels that without it, the control of the Hindu hierarchy, and especially the Brahmans like himself, would be weakened. Here Hindu conservatism demonstrates itself as he is totally committed to the maintenance of autocratic princely rule and regrets the changes from 'wonderful days of old' when such things as *suttee* were allowed.

Unlike Buddhism which is presented in highly idealized forms, Hinduism is shown in its more popularized forms. There is a common identification of a large part of Hinduism with the worship of Kali.[2] It is this bloodthirsty side of the religion which is most often used as a short-hand way of describing Hinduism. The *gosain* or head of the shrine to Krishna is shown partaking in rites that are nothing short of disgusting, with eunuchs licking up his spit and drinking the water in which they have washed his feet.[3] To Alden, any Englishman who finds himself becoming an anti-imperialist can cure himself of this by a trip to Madura where he would visit the 'mess which was swum up from man's most primitive levels' which is the Hindu temple there.[4] Ideas like *ahimsa* which might be presented favourably by men like Thompson are either ignored or said not to be a meaningful part of Hinduism—'*ahimsa* went out ages ago—if it ever was in'.[5] Instead we are given detailed pictures of Hindu social customs like child-marriage and *suttee* in their worst forms. Mundy, who constantly depicts all religious persons in harsh terms, saves his strongest contempt for the Hindus. He describes a fakir in repulsive terms:

His eyes were his only organs that really lived still, and they expressed the steely hate and cruelty, the mad fanaticism, the greedy

---

[1] Kincaid, *Durbar*, p. 137.
[2] See for example Edward Thompson, *Krishna Kumari*, London, 1924, p. 61.
[3] Kincaid, *Durbar*, p. 137.   [4] Thompson, *An End of the Hours*, p. 181.
[5] Ibid., p. 159.

self-love—self-immolating for the sake of self—that is the thorough-going fakir's stock in trade.[1]

The same attitude is taken by Philip Mason in his description of the holy city of Hardwar.

Wickedness clings to the skirt of holiness, for what is holy becomes lost in superstition, and at once those arise who are eager to make a profit. There are charlatans among the priests, there are evil-eyed fakirs, and there is every kind of imposter among the hundreds of beggars. And it is because the place is holy and blessed by nature that it is also the home of pimps and panders, smugglers of the intoxicating hemp drugs, vendors of cocaine, cattle-thieves, kidnappers and gamblers.[2]

Of all the Hindus, again the Bengali stands out as the most important group. For the first time he occasionally gets a kindly notice. Thompson writes that 'every Bengali is a born nurse, and compassion comes naturally to the race'[3] and sees it as 'a race of poets'.[4] Generally, however, the Bengali is still the most castigated of all Indians. As a 'race' they are thought to be less hardy and robust than the people of the north, but there is more than that wrong with them.

The swami in Candler's *Siri Ram* is 'a Bengali Lingauyat' and is 'bloodthirsty'. His goal is 'to introduce the Bengali system into the Punjab' and hence to destroy the good relations that the author believes prevail there.[5] The whole plot of *The Elephant God* is filled with attacks on the Bengalis. The hero, Dermot, knows that something is wrong on the border when he discovers that many Bengalis had been crossing into Bhutan. This, he felt, was a very strange thing for 'members of this timorous race' to go into such dangerous territory.[6] Besides this, Dermot 'was always suspicious of the Hindu'[7] and Casserly implies that this is the best way to behave in India. The leading figure in the conspiracy which he finds is a Bengali Brahman, the English educated and highly Anglicized Chunnerbutty. His participation in the anti-English movement is even more despicable than would normally be the case, since he is supposed to be a friend

---

[1] Mundy, 'Hookum Hai', in *Told in the East*, p. 8.
[2] Philip Mason, *Call the Next Witness*, London, 1945, p. 33.
[3] Thompson, *An Indian Day*, p. 171. [4] Thompson, *A Farewell to India*, p. 183.
[5] Candler, *Siri Ram*, p. 17. [6] Casserly, *The Elephant God*, p. 62.
[7] Ibid., p. 152.

of the Dalehams, on whose tea estate he is an engineer. When Dermot sees him in this position he is immediately and, it turns out, properly worried. The existence of Bengali Brahmins serving as coolies in the area further concerns him because 'their race furnishes the extremist and disloyal elements in India'.[1] Chunnerbutty may be a completely immoral, untrustworthy, and generally evil man, but Casserly does give him credit for having a subtle mind. However, this is not a virtue to the Englishman, like Casserly, who values 'doers' rather than 'thinkers'.

The Indian woman is still believed to be a particularly passionate being, who is single-mindedly devoted to whomever she loves—particularly if her loved one is an Englishman. Even if the Englishman does not feel too strongly towards her, he cannot avoid the strength of her devotion—'When an Englishman encounters Oriental passion, in its pristine simplicity and strength, he is compelled to take it seriously, first or last.'[2]

Leonard Woolf has written a pitiable story of what happens when this passion is unleashed. In a Colombo brothel the Englishman Reynolds falls in love with a prostitute. They begin to live together, but despite their love a meaningful relationship is impossible. 'He couldn't speak to her and she couldn't speak to him, she couldn't understand him. He was a civilized cultivated intelligent nervous little man and she—she was an animal, dumb and stupid and beautiful.'[3] Hers was

the love of dogs and women, at any rate of those slow, big-eyed women of the East. . . . But it wasn't what he wanted, it was that, I expect, more than anything which got on his nerves.

She used to follow him about the bungalow like a dog. He wanted to talk to her about his novel and she only understood how to pound and cook rice. It exasperated him, made him unkind, cruel. And when he looked into her patient, mysterious eyes he saw behind them what he had fallen in love with, what he knew didn't exist.[4]

In a futile attempt to recapture Reynolds, Celestinahami takes to wearing English clothes. This, of course, fails, and the Englishman leaves Ceylon while the broken-hearted girl drowns

[1] Casserly, *The Elephant God*, p. 111.
[2] Diver, 'Sunia: Daughter of the Hills,' in *Siege Perilous*, p. 156.
[3] Woolf, 'A Tale Told by Moonlight', in *Stories From the East*, p. 17.
[4] Ibid., pp. 17–18.

K

herself in her alien finery. Similarly, Diver's Sunia throws herself in front of a snake and receives the deadly bite meant for the Englishman she loves.

In all the stories of this type, whether by supporters or opponents of British rule in India, there is the continued belief that nothing but evil can come from the relationship between an Englishman and an Indian woman because of the enormous differences between their ways of life.

Eurasians are shown only rarely. Those who attack the Raj, like Orwell and Forster, or those who are somewhat ambivalent to its existence, such as Thompson and the later Candler, almost never mention their existence. Among those authors who can broadly be placed in the category of supporters of the British in India there is the same attack on this community as was seen before. Diver gives us the de Somerez family who 'considered themselves pure Dutch', but actually 'belonged to that mixed race known . . . as "half-castes". They had enough money to make a brave outward show, which was all they desired; and their life behind the scenes was of the scrambling, slatternly order dear to their kind.'[1] Elsewhere, a group of Eurasians in a restaurant are shown with their physically unattractive girls dressed in loud clothes 'saying "damn" and "Oh, my God" (pronounced Gudd), every sentence to show how jolly English they were'.[2]

An interesting description is that of the foreman of a nationalist newspaper. 'The man had a drop of white blood in him which may have explained his debauched habits. He was extraordinarily competent.'[3] Although this character makes only this one appearance, his treatment is a telling one. Unlike the way in which such a man would have been treated earlier where, like Michele d'Cruz, his good traits would have been credited to that 'drop of white blood' and his bad traits, such as drinking, to his Indian blood, both here are attributed to his 'white blood'—the former implicitly and the latter explicitly.

The most typical statement, in the sense that it sounds like something that was written earlier, is made by Ollivant. Marion Oliver has shot and critically wounded the *mullah* of Dargai after he has killed two young British soldiers. The Eurasian

[1] Diver, 'Requital', in *Siege Perilous*, p. 235.   [2] Kincaid, *Cactus Land*, p. 301.
[3] Candler, *Siri Ram*, p. 227.

doctor, Jigger Jackson, is called to help the *mullah* as he lies dying. Instead of helping his enemy who, despite his acts of bloodthirsty murder, is admirable because of his strength of character and purpose, the Eurasian starts to curse him. Marion and Old For-Ever are shocked and tell him to stop, but Jackson refuses, saying that he doesn't care what they say. ' "You ought to!" snapped Old For-Ever. "Shut up! We're English— some of us." ' To this the *mullah* adds: 'O, Accursed, that trots like a camel, thou art a sahib even as is said among my people. . . . But *thou*, Black Face and Badzat, art the son of a pariah bitch by a jackal that died of the foaming madness.'[1] Tom and Marion do not have to add anything to this because they completely agree with the *mullah*.

One novel, written during this period, foretells future developments in the image held of the Eurasians. In the next period this group of Indians and their problems comes to play a central role. *The Lacquer Lady* by F. Tennyson Jesse is the story of the British annexation of Upper Burma. Its leading character is Francesca (Fanny) Moroni, the daughter of an Italian father and a half-English, half-Burmese mother. The novel opens with her at school in Brighton and shortly thereafter she returns to Mandalay, where as a chief lady-in-waiting at the Burmese court, she becomes involved in the court intrigues leading up to the actual annexation.

Fanny—child of no man's land, of Tom Tiddler's ground, where all felt at liberty to pick up gold and silver—knew no tug of loyalty that was not purely personal. Why indeed, should she? . . . She was half Italian, but Italy was to her but a name, and what had been her father's pride was to her but a phrase. To be a European was to her only a snobbish satisfaction, nothing more.[2]

When she arrives at Rangoon and has her first glimpse of the Shwe Dagon, 'Christian as she was, at sight of that, some deep sense of inheritance in Fanny told her that she had come home.'[3] Despite her education, it was the Burmese part of her character that had remained predominant. The same was true of her half-caste mother who, on Fanny's first visit to the Royal Palace, is excited and pleased by being able to see 'the Lord White

[1] Ollivant, *Old For-Ever*, p. 31. The opening phrase is what the Pathans call Tom.
[2] Jesse, *The Lacquer Lady*, p. 159.   [3] Ibid., p. 15.

Elephant' being fed. 'In that moment, when she saw what was taking place, Fanny realized with a sudden vivid shock of surprise that her mother had remained always a Burman, that her English blood and Catholic upbringing had had no real effect at all.'[1] These Eurasians are depicted as not having been deeply touched by the West, but also are shown to have absorbed enough of the West to make it impossible for them to live as simple Burmans. Fanny is neither totally of the East or West. Wherever she is, she feels dragged to the other place— in England all she can think of is how romantic it would be to return to Burma and the glamour of the royal court, while in Burma she often regrets having ever left the safety and orderliness of England. While 'Fanny's soul was at home in the Palace' and 'her body was at home in the Burmese dress'[2] and while she is dazzled by 'knowing "real" Queens in a "real Palace" ',[3] she also believes that the pretensions of the Court of Ava are childish. Before coming out to Burma her friend Agatha had told Fanny the story of an English girl who killed her half-brother and then confessed after a spiritual conversion. Fanny thinks she was foolish to confess when no one knew, because in Burma it is normal for a king to kill his brothers. What the murderess should have done was to kill everyone, so that 'there would have been nobody left to mind and then she would have been all right'.[4] Yet, when the Burmese King, Thibaw, initiates a bloody massacre of all of his rivals, Fanny 'naturally' flees to the foreign settlement just outside the city 'where lived people with some relation to what at that time was uppermost in Fanny —her kinship with a world where life was regarded as sacred'.[5] The result of experiencing this massacre is that 'everything that was European in Fanny was in turmoil'.[6]

The final description of Fanny is given after she has married an Indian merchant after having first been married to an English river-boat captain. 'Fanny gave the effect of complete dullness. She had missed the impersonal philosophy of the East, the violence of the Latin, the capacity for self-deception of the Anglo-Saxon.'[7] In short, she had ended up by getting the least interesting qualities of all the races of which she was part. As a review of Candler's *Abdication* noted about that book: 'Racial

---

[1] Jesse, *The Lacquer Lady*, p. 55.   [2] Ibid., p. 260.   [3] Ibid., p. 121.
[4] Ibid., p. xxii.   [5] Ibid., p. 167.   [6] Ibid., p. 168.   [7] Ibid., p. 341.

arrogance is going. . . . Racial consciousness must also go.'[1] Clearly, this is a part of the change. No longer do writers hold forth the idea of racial superiority in the same way that they had once done, but at the same time they cannot get away from a racial consciousness which gives to each race certain values which are quite different from those of other races.

Another minor group, the Christian Indians, are treated in a similar way to the Eurasians. Despite their conversion, or rather because of it, they are shown to possess nothing but bad traits. In an historical novel set in seventeenth-century Goa, we see some converts walking with 'bowed heads and meek straggling steps' followed, for contrast, by a gypsy woman who strides along freely.[2] The older Indian Christian families there are even worse than the new converts as they 'were lackadaisical and cynical or at best resigned'.[3] Many of these converts act as servants for the British, 'but Christian servants are the worst of any, for they have lost all self-respect in the beginning, having been born outcasts'.[4] Even the missionary Findlay has no use for the Christian community which surrounds his home. As far as he was concerned, all that conversion did was to make the Indians worthless for anything except sitting around and waiting to be supported.[5] This continual depiction by writers of all political creeds of the Indian Christians as weak and debased creatures is a reflection of their own lack of commitment. Whereas in the early nineteenth century it was held that a convert became a better person through his adoption of Christianity, in the 1930s just the opposite was the belief. Christianity, like the rest of Western civilization, had failed in the eyes of many Britons.

The intellectually, rather than religiously, Westernized Indian continues to be treated harshly. In one of her short stories, Diver describes the Ceylonese Andrew de Silva who has reached 'the amphibian stage of evolution' in the most unflattering terms. Although he prides himself on how Westernized he is and thinks that because of this he should be accepted by the British in every way, including as a mate, the end result of friendliness towards him is that one night he breaks into and

---

[1] 'An Indian Jigsaw', *Nation and Athenaeum*, 31, 22 April 1922, p. 126.
[2] Kincaid, *Tropic Rome*, p. 175.   [3] Ibid., p. 21.
[4] Ethil Savi, *By Torchlight*, London, 1931, p. 148.
[5] Thompson, *An Indian Day*, p. 87.

robs the house of those who had befriended him.[1] The lesson to be learned from this story, so Diver would have her readers believe, is that you cannot trust a cultural half-breed.

Even the 'brilliant exception' to this role, Sir Lakshman Singh, who Diver depicts in the highest possible terms, has personality drawbacks because of his Westernization. He was 'a less satisfactory working force in the great native state he served, than men of half his ability whose hearts and minds were not torn between opposing interests and beliefs'.[2] At another point she goes even further, to proclaim that 'too much Anglicizing of India, instead of drawing us nearer, seems rather to widen the gulf'.[3] In a criticism of this type the author demonstrates a feeling that the British could only get along with Indians who remained 'simple'. The Western educated Indian is thus more than the comical figure of the earlier period. Now, in addition to the comic side, there is a tragic one which makes the whole question of such education even more debatable. It makes the Indians unhappy: 'England-returned—no hope anywhere: no true country now; no true belief; no true home; everything divided in two.'[4]

Candler feels that a Western education does make the recipient 'a better man in the end' although he may not be as lovable as 'the untutored produce of sunburnt clay'.[5] He thinks the the main thing that the Indian learns from an English education is a sense of responsibility. Yet, the picture that he and others give is one which does not do much towards creating a favourable impression of the Westernized Indian. His novels contain nothing but bad examples of Indian students. When a class is given the assignment of writing an essay on the subject of 'New King-Emperor and Gracious Consort', one student writes a five-page essay repeating the same line, 'God Bless Our royal Cupple', over and over again with varying capitalization.

So much for the 'loyalty' which through so many decades an official system of education had strenuously inculcated on a subject race. It ended in a phrase which an unhappy half-wit juggled and tossed over several pages, varying his capital letters and trying to see if he could plump out a whole essay with it.[6]

[1] Diver, 'As Others See Us', in *Siege Perilous, passim.*
[2] Diver, *Awakening*, pp. 278–9.   [3] Diver, *Far to Seek*, p. 192.
[4] Ibid., p. 251.   [5] Candler, *Siri Ram*, p. 83
[6] Thompson, *An End of the Hours*, p. 206.

In his novels set in Bombay, Kincaid introduces a new Westernized group to the English reader. The Parsees of that area are shown continually speaking of England as Home, taking their holidays in Europe, and knowing nothing whatsoever of India. Besides a few week-end trips to Poona, they have never been outside Bombay. This, and their speech, filled with words like 'Cheerio", is all a part of their goal of appearing English. Yet, they are shown to be very shallow and vulgar people.[1]

Western civilization certainly had done nothing to improve any of these people and the author obviously prefers the Indian who has remained with his own culture. This is again not so much a statement that the Indians are incapable of absorbing the 'superior' Western civilization, but that it will do nothing for them. Since many of the authors felt that Western civilization was itself a dying force, this is understandable. Beck has one of her characters ask what the Indian peoples 'have to gain from such a civilization as ours'.[2] The conclusion to all of this is the statement: 'For each country its own ways of life and work are best.'[3] 'Better all of us keep to our own ethos, Findlay's mind noted in passing: they have a decent one of their own, but this hybrid mess that they pick up, thinking it is ours!'[4]

Particularly in the 1920s a new group of Indians begins to emerge in the image of the Indian people—the loyal Indian prince. Although he never becomes a major element in the literary imagination, the new focus is interesting. Up to this point, on the rare occasions when he had been depicted, the Indian prince was shown in negative terms as 'proof' that direct British rule was beneficial. Instead, the more politically conscious writers in the period after the First World War were laying stress on their loyalty. Part of this is due to the support which the independent princes gave to Britain, and part of it is due to the recognition that the princes were one of the last bulwarks of British rule. Diver continually makes reference to the aristocratic nature of the Indian society which can only be properly recognized through a federation of princes rather than any 'democratic' government.

[1] Kincaid, *Their Ways Divide*, pp. 121–4.
[2] Beck, 'The Interpreter', in *The Ninth Vibration*, p. 126.
[3] Diver, *The Dream Prevails*, p. 82.   [4] Thompson, *An Indian Day*, p. 144.

As a rule the Indian reigning princes of today—especially those educated at the splendid Rajkumar College, or Princes' School—are an honour to their high lineage and the races from which they spring. In peace they devote themselves to the welfare of their subjects, and in war many of them have fought gallantly for the Empire and all have given their treasures or their troops loyally and generously to their King-Emperor.[1]

One of the most noticeable things of this period is the emergence of Indian nationalists as major characters. Prior to Candler's *Siri Ram*, which was written in 1912, there was virtually no mention of the nationalist movement. From that point on, however, the nationalists begin to appear quite often. Particularly in the 1930s it is impossible to get away from this problem. With rare exceptions, they are shown in an unfriendly light. It seems to make little difference whether the author favours or opposes the Raj, as to how he depicts Indian nationalists. They are not thought to be motivated by devotion to the betterment of India, but are either concerned with themselves, have been personally humiliated by the British, or are the dupes of others. A constant theme is that the nationalist troubles really are not being caused by the Indian people, but by a few leaders who are interested only in their personal advancement. The people should be given every chance because 'they've been artificially worked up. It's the men behind—pulling the strings —who are to blame—'.[2]

Siri Ram is a very weak young man who, above all else, wants to become famous. His vanity causes him to spend his time admiring himself in a hand mirror. The youth is momentarily attracted to the Arya Samaj, but does not stay with this group because there is too much discipline and hard work involved without the recompense of the fame he is avidly seeking. He is highly flattered when, after returning from a term in jail for being the scapegoat editor of a nationalist newspaper, he is chosen to kill Merivale.

The Englishman Skene says that the problem with the Indian nationalists is that they lack courage, and this perfectly describes Siri Ram. When he becomes involved in the movement he thinks that it would be a good thing if he became a political deportee so that he could *live* in comfort.[3] He is afraid to die,

---

[1] Casserly, *The Elephant God*, pp. 122–3.   [2] Diver, *Far to Seek*, p. 361.
[3] Candler, *Siri Ram*, p. 143.

and this unwillingness to sacrifice himself for what he is supposed to believe in is another sign of weakness in the eyes of the
author. He finally kills himself just before he can be executed
because he is afraid of being laughed at.

Tragically, Siri Ram is shown as merely being made use of by
others who are completely despicable. Dr. Hari Chand publicly
stands as a moderate in his appeals for work among the
depressed of India. Actually, he did not mind sacrifice if there
were no bloodshed. 'He objected to the idea of weapons or
wounds on either side, but poison was a compromise.'[1] The
'moderate' is prepared to poison all Englishmen. Another
nationalist leader, Swami Narashima, has become a nationalist
because of an incident when he was a student at Cambridge.
There 'a country bumpkin in cap and gown' had bumped him
and called the Swami 'a damned nigger'.[2] From this one occurrence he decided that all Englishmen were monsters and in
order to have them all killed, he was even willing to sacrifice
other nationalists like Siri Ram.

Ten years after writing *Siri Ram*, Candler continued his
attack on the nationalists in *Abdication*. There Siri Ram's
friend, Banarsi Das, is an even more tragic figure, showing 'the
miscarriage of our good intentions'.[3] He is continually seeking
after acceptance into a group which will give him a sense of
personal pride. Banarsi Das joins up with a Muslim nationalist
group for a while, but he is unable to stick with them because he
is a coward. The leading nationalist character in the book, the
editor Barkatullah, is exceptionally clever, but is interested only
in his own welfare. He took up a collection among the local
Muslim community for the welfare of the Turkish widows of
the First World War. He kept the money, but because he always
sounded like a good nationalist, no one criticizes him for it.

Dyan Singh is attracted to the nationalist movement because
he has been rejected by an English girl who does not love him.
He thinks that it is because he is an Indian and therefore turns
against all English. He is saved from his 'error' by the recognition that the nationalists are not really interested in what is
good for India.[4] This emphasis on personal humiliation as being
one of the major reasons for anti-British sentiment is a part of

---

[1] Candler, *Siri Ram*, p. 296. [2] Ibid., p. 139.
[3] Candler, *Abdication*, p. 169. [4] Diver, *Far to Seek*, *passim*.

the idea that what the Indians really wanted was to be friends with the British.

At meetings of the District Council, in another novel, all the Indian members want is to use the opportunity to make protests. Alden does not see anything wrong with this, but he does think that they should do a little work and concern themselves with things like sanitation and community welfare. ' "What work, when beloved Motherland is perishing?" asked an owl-faced lawyer reproachfully.'[1] In another case, the District Meeting wants to obtain money for flags and other nationalist paraphernalia to be used in a Congress celebration. Alden offers money if a rich *babu*, who talks like a nationalist, will also contribute. The *babu* finds his money is worth more to him than his 'principles' and refuses, pleading a lack of funds.[2] The Parsee community is also described as supporting nationalism only because it thinks that it will benefit economically from independence.[3] Likewise, an Indian inn-keeper is shown who, at the start of the novel, is pro-Congress, but at the end has become a violent imperialist. The reason for the switch has nothing to do with a change of principles, but is simply due to the fact that the Congress has begun to agitate for prohibition, so independence will hurt his business.[4] Diver sees 'Congress caring little for real social improvement. More exciting to lie down in front of trains or shout "Boycott British", than to wash up dispensary bottles or teach in school.'[5]

Kincaid's nationalists, like Ragya, are also involved in the movement for personal economic motives. Ragya hates the British because he cannot get a job. The nationalists are also shown to possess very weak characters. A Mr. Wamanrao shows his sympathies by having a teapot decorated with Congress flags.[6] He also shows something more about himself when he takes it out of a cupboard whose door is decorated with pictures of nude women. The man who finally kills Edward Holme is so complete a coward that he had taken part in the murder of his school principal with two other boys by shooting him in the back.

Although 'it would have been equally true—or untrue—to

<hr>

[1] Thompson, *A Farewell to India*, p. 159.   [2] Ibid., p. 243.
[3] Ibid., pp. 257–8.   [4] Kincaid, *Cactus Land*, p. 300.
[5] Diver, *The Singer Passes*, pp. 346–7.   [6] Kincaid, *Their Ways Divide*, p. 258.

say that Nannhe Singh's nationalism was wholly selfish', the description given of the man would tend to make any reader dislike him and his motives.

Nannhe Singh was a hater. It was written in his face, which was neither a healthy brown nor the clear pale colour that sometimes survives among the high-caste Indians, but a livid yellow. It was a bitter face, but full of purpose, and the purpose was hatred. He had a sufficiency of enemies outside the family group, but they were not enough for him. Ambition drove him to politics. He became a nationalist, he was bound to. It was the paying side in district politics, at least for a Hindu; it gave him something to hate; and it was based also on a genuine desire to see his country entirely in the hands of his countrymen.[1]

The treatment given to Nannhe Singh is particularly interesting for two reasons. Firstly, there is little need for the description of this individual since he never occurs again. Secondly, he makes a telling comparison with another minor character in the same book, Khan Bahadur Mohammad Altaf Khan, who is the leader of the local pro-Government forces and, in contrast to Nannhe Singh, is described as 'a man of character and enter-prise' who 'believed that he was much better off under the British than he could be under any national Government'.[2]

We have already met Eyton's Bapu Gopi Nath who is willing to stir up the people and then flee from the scene to avoid punishment. Similarly, he depicts a 'merry little man' who writes anti-British propaganda for profit. He does not seem to care much what he writes or even to believe it. However, it so affects one of the impressionable students to whom it is sold that he tries to kill an Englishman. He is captured and ends up in jail where he becomes a real rebel while the 'merry little man' goes on writing his propaganda.[3] An identical character is Wren's Mr. Mohandas Lala Misra, B.A., LL.B., pleader and politician who spends his time addressing student meetings. He stirs them up to attack the British so that he had led

not a few of such young men to a shameful death upon the gallows for cold-blooded and cowardly murder.

From the point of view of Mr. Misra, it was a good game, paying and safe, for it brought him to the notice of the disinterested patriots

---

[1] Philip Mason, *Call the Next Witness*, pp. 20–1.   [2] Ibid., p. 178.
[3] Eyton, 'The Seed', in *The Dancing Fakir, passim.*

who will soon be the rulers of India; and, in the way in which he played it, he ran no risk of punishment from the guardians of the *Pax Britannica*.[1]

Aliz Mirza Habibullah, like Swami Narashima, became a nationalist because of an attack on him while a student in in England. It was because of this and because of an unhappy family life that he turned against England and not because of any devotion to higher principles. He is strongly attracted to the use of violence, seemingly for its own sake.[2] Similarly, many of the nationalists depicted by Thompson are interested in the movement only because it gives them an excuse and an outlet for their urges to violence. Savi gives them credit for desiring more than violence, but not much more. She imagines that all they are interested in gaining is control of India so they can confiscate the land owned by white men, even if they have to trump up an excuse like the Bolsheviks.[3] An old lawyer explains that when the Indians get Dominion status, they will take his little plot of land away from him and really make money by exploiting the peasants as a sahib is now unable to do.[4]

While technically not nationalists in that they were not working for a unified independent India, these authors also depict a large group of anti-British Indian religious leaders. It is the *gosain* in *Durbar*, the *mullahs* in *The Great Amulet* and *Old For-Ever*, the Brahmans in *Their Ways Divide*, the fakir in 'Hookum Hai', and the High Priest of Khawani's temple in 'For the Salt He Had Eaten' who are the 'archringleaders of all the treachery'. Shawani's temple is

the place where every one must go who needed favours of the priests, the central hub of treason and intrigue, where every plot was hatched and every rumour had its origin—the ultimate, mazy, greedy, undisgorging goal of every bribe and every blackmail-wrung rupee.[5]

Besides seeking personal power, these men, like many nationalists, are depicted as being reactionaries. What they are interested in is a return to the old pre-British order in which they were able to dominate India.

[1] Wren, 'White Ants', in *Odd Stories*, p. 89.
[2] Wilfrid David, *Monsoon*, London, 1933, *passim*.
[3] Savi, *By Torchlight*, p. 111.   [4] Ibid., p. 4.
[5] Mundy, 'For the Salt He Had Eaten', in *Told in the East*, p. 178.

The most famous nationalist leader, Gandhi, is not particularly well treated. One of the major criticisms of him, as of many nationalists, is that he is so conservative he does not recognize the needs of modern life. To Diver he is associated with voodoo magic because Gandhi does not think that an English doctor should be called when a young Indian child is in danger of his life.[1] Also, with her strongly pro-Raj outlook, she feels that he is in the pay of rich supporters—'Wealthy Indian mill-owners were financing Gandhi's Civil Disobedience campaign, where excitable mobs could be hired from paid agents, prepared to supply a riot or a budding revolution to order.'[2] She is equally harsh in her evaluation of Nehru who is described as 'the fiery Communist, Moscow-bred'.[3]

Even Thompson who, in the 1940s, came to be a correspondent of Gandhi's and a supporter of the Congress, offers serious doubts about the man in his novels. He is somewhat friendlier towards Gandhi in his earlier novels, but by 1931 he is writing 'that Mr. Gandhi was living by instinct and passion, and not by reason any longer'.[4] This is particularly because of Gandhi's growing attack on everything that was Western. When Alden sees him:

He was troubled, as a man who loved and honoured this frail human wisp, by the undertone of weariness, as from a will whose resources are exhausted though the driving fire remains that must urge it on to self-destruction. Behind the speaker were the forces of ruin, which he was serving, though aware of them, and anxious to escape them.[5]

Linked with this and with the growing British emphasis on the lack of unity within India, is the idea that the nationalists were not facing the reality of the Indian situation. When they have arguments between Hindus and Muslims, and this is pointed out to them as a reason why they should not have independence, they reply by pointing to the Durham Report. 'The

---

[1] Diver, *The Dream Prevails*, p. 342. See also *Letters of an Indian Judge to an English Gentlewoman*, London, 1934, where the Indian judge recounts how his daughter has died of appendicitis because his wife refused to allow a Western doctor to operate on her. The reason for her refusal was that Gandhi had said: 'European Doctors are the worst of all.' Yet, when Gandhi had appendicitis, he called on a Western doctor and was saved. See pp. 101–3.

[2] Diver, *The Singer Passes*, p. 59.   [3] Ibid., p. 174.
[4] Thompson, *A Farewell to India*, p. 141.   [5] Ibid., p. 144.

thing that matters . . . is not that they're *like* Canada on paper, but that they *are* going to cut one another's throats.'[1] Likewise in *Monsoon* the nationalist, Ali Mirza Habibullah, who thinks that India is a unified nation just ripe for independence, is shown to find that this is not the case. He goes with the Englishman Fence to observe some communal rioting and while a Congress volunteer shouts: 'Nor Hindus, nor Mussulmans, but Indians all!' in true Gandhian phraseology, the Hindu crowd spots the Muslim Habibullah.

> The voice was love, unheeded. The Hindus wouldn't hear of Gandhi today. There in the car was a Mussulman alive before their eyes. True, he wore a Gandhi cap and a *khaddar* shirt. True, these were symbols of the nation's cause, badges of *Swaraj*. *Khaddar! Swaraj!* Gandhi—in a cell in far Yerowda! What was all that beside the frantic issue of the day—the glorious triumph of Hinduism over Islam! . . . And the Mussulman in the car stood in the way of that triumph. . . . The Hindus yearned to reach Ali. They yearned for a short cut to heaven.[2]

He is only saved from being killed through the intervention of the British. Diver uses a similar occurrence to demonstrate the lack of Indian unity and the ability of the British to stop the trouble, and, in addition, the 'hypocrisy' of the Indian nationalists. Two British policemen are described as putting down a riot 'while Gandhi was accusing their kind of stirring up strife for racial ends'.[3]

When Thompson describes Nehru's tour of South India, he says that although Nehru succeeded in winning the Hindus of the area over to the nationalist cause, the Muslims continued to stand aloof. 'And it was more certain than ever that in the womb of the old India, struggling to be born, were two nations tugging and fighting for mastery even before birth.'[4]

All of this is despite the fact that writers like Thompson do recognize that there is some justice on the nationalist side. When Nixon catches a group of trouble-making *swarajists*, he explains:

> I've got to smash these chaps, of course, and they're devils out for bloodshed. But you know, you can't wonder that any kid with any spunk prefers their game to being a tame clerk and saying '*Achchha*,

[1] Thompson, *A Farewell to India*, p. 77.   [2] David, *Monsoon*, p. 257.
[3] Diver, *The Singer Passes*, p. 207.   [4] Thompson, *An End of the Hours*, p. 175.

saheb' for the rest of his days. And think of it, Hamar! Imagine yourself a young Indian. And you know every inch of this land, and you feel you can fool these sahibs and tie them up in its jungles and have them in a fit all the time, because they don't know things, don't know *anything*. You'd want to take a hand in the movement![1]

He, and a good many other English, believe that the Indians have much to complain of, but in his pessimism he does not believe that the nationalists have the right answer. This seeing of both sides and finding them wanting is a part of the total pessimism of this period.

[1] Thompson, *An Indian Day*, p. 199.

VII

ANGLO-INDIAN RELATIONS

The change in the British image of India is reflected to a large degree in the fact that the problem of whether it was possible for the British and Indians to understand each other became a major theme. Many British writers believed that the problem of *personal* relations was *the* problem. They felt that the motivating factor for most Indians was their desire to be accepted by the British as personal friends. At the very beginning of *A Passage to India*, Forster introduces this as a major issue with a group of Muslims discussing the problem of whether or not it is possible for Indians and English to be friends.

'I only contend that it is possible in England,' replied Hamidullah, who had been to that country long ago, before the big rush, and had received a cordial welcome at Cambridge.

'It is impossible here. Aziz! The red-nosed boy has again insulted me in Court. I do not blame him. He was told that he ought to insult me. Until lately he was quite a nice boy, but the others have got hold of him.'

'Yes, they have no chance here, that is my point. They come out intending to be gentlemen, and are told it will not do. . . . They all become exactly the same, not worse, not better. I give any Englishman two years. . . . And I give any Englishwoman six months.'[1]

The placement of this scene so early in the book, before the plot proper has begun to be developed, shows how important Forster considered this issue to be.

Along the same lines, Kincaid gives us the young Brahman, Kaka, who has decided to become a policeman. His friends and family wonder why a Brahman should desire such a strange occupation. The reason is that it will give him a chance to work with the British. He says that he is going to be sent to a British regiment for six weeks' training. There, he has been told, 'the

[1] Forster, *A Passage to India*, pp. 8-10.

officers are awfully hospitable. Make you feel at home at once. Just like brothers.'[1] It is impossible for Kaka to gain English friends this way, but it is this friendship that he is seeking.

Candler's Riley believes that the basic problem is the lack of contact and communication between the English and Indians— 'If only they met us and knew us, he argued, it would be all right.'[2] Even Maud Diver who falls into the strongly pro-Raj camp sees the problem in much the same way. John Lynch, the Deputy Inspector General of Police, recognizes that what the young Indian officers need above all else is 'that extra touch of friendliness too seldom proffered by the white Brahmins and Kshattryas of British India'.[3] Her Roy Sinclair was

confirmed in his belief that the true solvents of the Indian complex were personal and spiritual; that one could hardly overestimate the influence for good of every English man or woman who accepted and returned the singular kindness and courtesy of Indians, even the bitterest opponents of British rule.[4]

Later he says: 'It's a matter of common sense . . . that if we want to stay on, in this changing India, we must be friends with Indians.'[5] One of her Indian characters goes even further:

Your so-called reforms do not interest the masses or touch their imagination. But the boot of the low-class European touches their backs and their pride and hardens their hearts. That is only human nature. In the East a few gold grains of courtesy touch the heart more than a handsome *Khillat* of political hotch-potch.[6]

This emphasis on personal relations—the social problem—as being the heart of Anglo-Indian relations meant that all writers saw little need for political reforms. Aziz explains this to Fielding who agrees with him.

'Mr. Fielding, no one can ever realize how much kindness we Indians need, we do not even realize it ourselves. But we know when it has been given. We do not forget, though we may seem to. Kindness, more kindness, and even after that more kindness. I assure you it is the only hope.' His voice seemed to arise from a dream. Altering it, yet still deep below his normal surface, he said, 'We can't build up India except on what we feel. What is the use of

---

[1] Kincaid, *Their Ways Divide*, p. 85.   [2] Candler, *Abdication*, p. 8.
[3] Diver, *The Dream Prevails*, p. 16.   [4] Diver, *The Singer Passes*, p. 306.
[5] Ibid., p. 374.
[6] Diver, *Far to Seek*, pp. 251–2. A *'khillat'* is a dress of honour.

L

all these reforms, and Conciliation Committees for Mohurram, and shall we cut the tazia short or shall we carry it another route, and Council of Notables and official parties where the English sneer at our skins?'

'It's beginning at the wrong end, isn't it? I know, but institutions and government don't.'[1]

In all her novels and stories Diver attacks any attempt at political reform. In an early story she depicts an Englishwoman who has come out to Ceylon filled with ideas of rapid reform. She thinks that the Anglo-Indian community is completely wrong in its opposition to reform. Before the end of the story, however, she has learned that she is wrong. The Anglo-Indian heroine, Molly, explains the results of the reformer's discouragement: 'Well, at any rate . . . we have the consolation of knowing that we helped to rid the world of one reformer-in-a-hurry. And they are the real stumbling blocks on the path of normal progress.'[2] At the heart of this belief that reforms are of no value is the feeling that they cannot be used to change the Indians. Riley is impressed by the frankness of the Montagu-Chelmsford Report, but is disturbed by its pious hope. 'As if by an Act of Parliament the three hundred millions could be made European-hearted.'[3]

In keeping with the basically pessimistic and defeatist attitude of the British of this period, the authors believed that the possibilities of building a sound personal relationship were very slight. In the earlier period one finds only occasional concern with the problems of friendship between the races. In 1894 Steel wrote that racial feelings enter into the picture no matter what anyone tries to do about it and 'make real social intercourse between the upper classes of the two races an impossibility'.[4] With this the writers of the 1920s and 1930s would agree; but whereas in the 1890s she added an emphatic and optimistic post-script—'*at present*', her successors would have written '*never*'.

---

[1] Forster, *A Passage to India*, p. 115.

[2] Diver, 'As Others See Us', in *Siege Perilous*, p. 275. Charles Freer Andrews wrote a memorandum dealing with the 1921 railway strike in India. In it he laid greatest stress on 'the need for direct human contact and personal friendliness between managers and men'. Benarsidas Chaturvedi and Marjorie Sykes, *Charles Freer Andrews: A Narrative*, London, 1949, p. 119.

[3] Candler, *Abdication*, p. 121.   [4] Steel, *The Potter's Thumb*, vol. 2, p. 110.

Adela Quested is not very sensitive, but she does have an honest desire to meet and to understand Indians. She accompanies Aziz on the trip to the Marabar Caves which forms the turning point of the plot. As they stand outside one of the caves, she asks what seems to be an innocent question—'Have you one wife or more than one?' Aziz is horrified at having his personal life questioned and does not understand that the question was born of a desire to learn about India. Because he is so disgusted with the question, he leaves Adela, thinking: 'Damn the English even at their best.'[1] While he is gone she goes into one of the caves where the assault, imagined or actual, occurs and the possibility of friendship disappears.

Roy Sinclair, in Diver's *The Singer Passes*, thinks that he has found a friend in the Rajput Suránj.

And friends they were—up to a point. Only when it came to argument or a matter of principle, differences crept in to prove the colour of their minds as diverse as their skins. It was a fact overlooked by those who saw race prejudice as mere odium attaching to colour. Here was he, unhampered by prejudice, throwing in his lot with Indians, liking them the better for it in many ways; and yet—just when one felt most confident, they would let one down in some disappointing fashion. With the best will on earth he could not fully accept that given assurance from Suránj as he would have accepted it from Jerry or Derek or Lance. Too well he knew that, for Indians, truth was apt to be a matter of convenience rather than principles:— a difference in the grain.[2]

Similarly in *Burmese Days*, Flory, who wants to understand the Asians, takes Elizabeth into a Chinese merchant's shop. She is horrified at the bound feet of the women, the serving of tea without milk, and virtually everything else that the Chinese do. To her, anyone that is so different from her must be a savage. The situation is not helped by the fact that the women of the Chinese house do not understand the Englishwoman any better than she understands them. There is nothing they desire more than that Elizabeth should undress and show them her corset. They all find it impossible to bridge the gulf of a different set of values. Everybody ends up being insulted despite the good will, or at least the lack of any bad will, motivating either side.

The Englishmen in Thompson's novels like the Indian Neogyi

---

[1] Forster, *A Passage to India*, p. 153.   [2] Diver, *The Singer Passes*, p. 259.

and he likes them. However, at a meeting chaired by Neogyi, Alden laughs at something Findlay says—a normal occurrence —but Neogyi thinks that he is being laughed at. Later Neogyi 'thought resentfully of the way Alden had openly laughed. . . . That was the way the friendliest Englishman treated an Indian who served his Raj! He could guess how the others felt, under their self-control.'[1]

The relations between Aziz and Fielding in Forster's *A Passage to India* are justly famed, but Dennis Kincaid gives an almost identical account in the ill-fated friendship between Naru and Edward Holme in *Their Ways Divide*. They have met as children and played together. Although Edward is immediately sent back to England for his education, Naru remembers the one occasion when it seemed that he had an English friend. When Edward left India, after the one meeting with Naru, the Indian youth had wanted to go to the station to say good-bye, but his father was afraid that the English would think that he was presuming on them: 'English people were queer like that; friendly one day and cold the next.'[2]

After Edward has returned to India he and Naru become friendly, but the Indian demands too much from their relationship. Naru expects Edward to be willing to devote all of his time to keeping him company. Even when Edward is able to spend time with Naru the result is not what the Indian desires. He wants Edward continually to be telling him how much their friendship means to him and he makes demands on the Englishman that Edward, or anyone else for that matter, would be unable to fulfil. In one case, shortly after his return from England, Edward is asked by Naru what he should do about getting married. Edward honestly is taken aback by this request because he feels that he does not know Naru well enough to make any recommendations about so personal a problem. Just as he does not understand the depth of the emotion which drove the Indian to ask such a question of his friend, so Naru does not understand why Edward will not give him an answer if he is truly his friend.[3] On another occasion Edward returns from a tiring tour of duty. He finds Naru waiting for him on his doorstep. All the Englishman wants to do is to take a bath and get

---

[1] Thompson, *An Indian Day*, p. 96. [2] Kincaid, *Their Ways Divide*, p. 25.
[3] Ibid., p. 136.

unpacked, but by this time he realizes that Naru is easily insulted. Still, his obligations to himself and to his work make it necessary for Edward to tell the Indian that he will not be able to visit him for a few days. Again Naru is hurt and again the possibilities of a good personal relationship become more remote.[1]

With the relationship between these two basically good individuals already in danger of failing because of mutual misunderstandings, the whole thing comes to a head when Edward returns from a trip to England with a wife. Naru feels that he has been betrayed. Edward's wife, Rachel, is a sensitive woman who, in London, had said that she was particularly interested in Indians. She also realized that the Indians she was used to seeing in England were not being seen at their best as they tried to put a show on for the English. Rachel wants to meet the Indians on their own grounds where they can be themselves and not feel it necessary to act a role.

On her arrival in India, Rachel looks forward to meeting Naru, of whom Edward had told her a great deal. Unfortunately, they find they cannot communicate. When Naru explains that Untouchables really have a different religion from the Brahmans and that it is only unscrupulous men who are agitating them to demand temple entry, it sounds to Rachel just like the Tory argument that the workers are happy and all the trouble is being caused by socialist agitators. She tries to recover from this disagreement by talking about movies and she mentions Eisenstein. Naru jumps at this seemingly innocent topic and says that he likes historical adventure films with a lot of excitement. Rachel is again taken aback by his remarks and Naru feels that she must dislike him and think him stupid.[2]

The final break comes when Edward actually makes an attempt to show his friendship for Naru. He writes the Indian a letter saying: 'You must come and stay with us some time.' This, too, like so much else in their relationship, seems to be friendly or at least innocent, but Naru reads the letter differently. To him it means that Edward and Rachel do not want him to visit them and that they are using the letter as a polite excuse. Once Naru no longer feels that Edward is his friend, he feels no compunction about writing to ask him for a job. Earlier, he had

[1] Kincaid, *Their Ways Divide*, pp. 164–6. [2] Ibid., p. 249.

shown a great deal of personal sensitivity in refusing to do this, but that was when he believed they were friends. The result is a polite letter back from Edward explaining that there is nothing that he can do about providing employment for Naru or, for that matter, for anyone. To Naru and his father this is final proof that Edward is not a friend of his. Because of this, Naru rejects all Englishmen and becomes involved in the Indian nationalist movement. Again the social problem—the key problem—is insoluble.

The inability to form such a friendly relationship is thought to be due to a lack of understanding. Unlike the first period, here more emphasis is placed on the British failure in this area than on the Indian side. Thompson describes two Indians who are totally different in their characters—Kamalakanta Neogyi, the District Collector, who is a fine individual with great loyalty to Britain, and Deogharia, the Commissioner, who is completely ruthless and without principles. The Commissioner's continual persecution of Neogyi goes unrecognized by the British. When Neogyi complains to Findlay, he is told: 'We've evolved a method of selecting you which picks out all your swabs and sets them over you.'[1] The British cannot recognize the loyalty of Neogyi or the crookedness of Deogharia and it is the latter who is continually rewarded. The irony is carried to its logical conclusion with Deogharia getting rid of Neogyi by having him sent to a very backward and unhealthy district where it is more than likely he will die of malaria while the Commissioner becomes K.C.I.E.

A similar contrast is drawn by Orwell between two characters in *Burmese Days*, the Burman U Po Kyin and the Indian Dr. Veraswami. The former is concerned only with gaining personal power and when this means scheming against the British, that is exactly what he does. The Indian, in direct contrast, is loyal to the British to the point of servility. However, at the end of the novel it is U Po Kyin who has become the first Asian to be elected to the local British club, a Deputy Commissioner, and an honoured figure at the durbar while Veraswami has been reduced in rank.

Thompson thinks that there is something elemental in India which makes a meeting between the races impossible. He calls

[1] Thompson, *An Indian Day*, p. 147.

these forces *bhuts* or ghosts. 'It's the *bhuts* that have worked madness in men's brains; and it doesn't depend now on whether we can coax Gandhi or the Nehrus into some sanity, but on whether the *bhuts* have got beyond all human conciliation.'[1] In *Durbar*, Kincaid includes a number of incidents based on this idea. At a party Phyllis, who is honestly interested in the Indians tries to talk with the Rajah's wife, Usha. Because of her high position and also because she had been educated in a Western manner, the Englishwoman feels that 'surely she must be clever and intelligent, in spite of being a Hindu'.[2] So she eagerly enters into the conversation. However, Usha has a more important problem on her mind than engaging in social talk with a stranger. She knows, although the English do not, that there is a serious assassination plot against her husband planned for that day. Therefore she finds it impossible to keep up her end of the conversation, and Phyllis, knowing nothing of Usha's problem, comes to a harsh conclusion about her, 'I suppose she doesn't really think at all. Just a parrot-chatter of English.'[3]

In a similar social situation Nana Saheb, who is worried about the possibilities of a coup against the Rajah, receives a note saying that the troops are going to remain loyal. This occurs when he is with the British Resident, Mr. Hilton, who is a good man, but not very intelligent. He realizes that the Brahman prime minister is upset and asks him what is wrong. Not wanting the British to know about the trouble, Nana Saheb explains that the message was only about his sick son. Hilton thinks: 'These Indians get so worked up over nothing at all. Nervy, jumpy creatures. Plenty of brains but no stamina.'[4] Finally, when the coup is attempted and successfully put down, Hilton does not even know what had happened and is satisfied with Nana's explanation that the shots the English had heard were a result of a small Congress demonstration and a part of the celebration of a holy day.[5]

The Indians are thought not to understand the English and what they are doing any more than the English understand them. Through great skill, an English girl has succeeded in saving a village from the heavy debt which threatened it, by getting the *zemindar* to pay a part of the debt and getting the

[1] Thompson, *A Farewell to India*, p. 279.   [2] Kincaid, *Durbar*, p. 199.
[3] Ibid., p. 201.   [4] Ibid., p. 208.   [5] Ibid., p. 274.

rest of it reduced. 'The experiment had not been encouraging.'[1]
It was thought, by the villagers, that their 'saviour' was lining
her own pocket. They could not understand any other reason
for her action and learned nothing from what had transpired.
No sooner had she succeeded in ridding them of the debt, than
they wanted to start borrowing all over again. They could see
no reason either to cultivate their land or to repay their debt.
It is not so much that they are imagined to be ungrateful, but
merely that they were not able to understand what the whole
transaction had been about.

This lack of understanding is believed to go very deep into the
national or racial souls of the British and Indians. Even Beck,
who comes close to the Orientalist point of view that 'between
the ordinary man of the West and his brother-man in the East
there exists not a barrier insurmountable but a common
humanity that craves for realization',[2] refers to 'the gay surface
fraternity of East and West' which is easily 'broken asunder,
revealing abysses of unbridgeable differences beneath'.[3] The
missionary Edward Protheroe, observing the funeral of the
Burmese king, is fascinated by the vivid colours of the scene, but
at the same time repelled by the ideas behind what is going on
—'How could any Western mind apprehend it?'[4] There is
simply something about India which the Westerner cannot
fathom.

Although there has been a great deal of dispute as to the
meaning of the Marabar Caves in Forster's novel, Virginia
Woolf has proposed a very satisfactory answer: 'The Marabar
Caves should appear to us not real caves, but it may be, the
soul of India.'[5] The inability of Europeans like Adela Quested
to understand the Caves, or like Fielding even to go into them,
demonstrates their failure to understand the soul of India. The
Caves also partake of the element of irrationality. 'Objectively,
it poses Western rationality against Eastern mysticism; time
against eternity; the conscious against the unconscious.'[6] A
part of this feeling is related to the older image of India as a part

[1] Thompson, *Night Falls on Siva's Hill*, p. 191.
[2] A. J. Arberry, *British Orientalists*, London, 1943, p. 47.
[3] Beck, *The House of Fulfilment*, p. 253.   [4] Jesse, *The Lacquer Lady*, p. 116.
[5] Virginia Woolf, *The Death of the Moth and Other Essays*, London, 1947, p. 108.
[6] Louise Daumier, 'What Happened in the Caves? Reflections on *A Passage
to India*', *Modern Fiction Studies*, 7, Autumn 1961, p. 270.

of the mysterious East where the things happen which would be impossible according to Western thought.

In the 1920s and 1930s there is an added implication that there are deep philosophical divisions between the East and West which inevitably make it impossible for them to understand each other. John Findlay in Thompson's *An End of the Hours* explains why it is that the West cannot grasp the Buddha and his giving up of his earthly life despite the obligations he had to his family.

East and West start their whole philosophy of life and existence on different bases. *We* think of the individual, *they* of the process. . . . Individuality is to us the peak and purpose of the whole cosmic process. But it *isn't* to these fellows! To them the individual is merely part of the phenomena . . .[1]

Diver adds to the old masculine-feminine contrast an element of conflict. 'But there's a deal of the man and woman element in West and East. Whichever way the West swings, the East would tend to swing away from it.'[2] To Forster, too, there is a basic difference between the two areas.

To the Westerner, be he artist or merchant, a flower is usually a flower, an elephant is an elephant, and a diamond a diamond; objects to the Westerner remain real and separable; they can be understood and described, they can be possessed or sold. . . . To the Indian nothing is real and nothing is separable: elephants and flowers and diamonds all blend and are part of the veil of illusion which severs unhappy mortals from truth.[3]

Similarly, in Myers' description of a meeting between Rajah Amar and Smith, the Indian finds that it is impossible for him to explain the Indian point of view to the Englishman. He finds that 'contact with the Western mind . . . had a disturbing effect'[4] on him. 'It shows me too well how, from every other angle except that at which we Indians stand, my present intention soon to withdraw from the world must appear selfish, and this moment singularly ill-chosen.'[5]

---

[1] Thompson, *An End of the Hours*, p.137. Note the author's use of italics to emphasize the words 'we' and 'they'.

[2] Diver, *The Singer Passes*, p. 246.

[3] E. M. Forster, Foreword to *Flowers and Elephants* by Constance Sitwell, London, 1927, pp. 7–8.

[4] Myers, *The Root and the Flower*, p. 445.   [5] Ibid.

An attitude shared by all the writers of this period is that
Westernization had been a failure in India. 'The *object* of
assimilation is an act of faith and a double act of faith. It
means that we believe both in the *possibility* and in the *value* of
assimilation.'[1] In keeping with this idea, there is a difference
between this period and the former one. For the earlier writers
assimilation or Westernization was of doubtful value because
they felt that the Indians were not capable of becoming
Westernized. In this period the same feeling continues to be
expressed by some of the writers who favour the continuation of
the Raj. Most of the authors, however, lack faith in assimilation
because of the way they view Western civilization. They
seriously doubt that it would be valuable to those who do
become assimilated.

The whole problem is far too serious for these men to give us
the humorous pictures that Guthrie described at the turn of the
century. The inability of Westernization to affect the Indian in
a basic way was a part of their feeling that civilization was not as
strong as it had once seemed and that there was no place for the
English in India. If they could not succeed in Westernizing
India then one of the reasons that was often cited for their being
there was invalid. Attempts to Westernize India were generally
regarded as futile endeavours. This was bound to strengthen the
pessimistic attitude towards reforms.

Tropic Rome, a novel by Dennis Kincaid set in seventeenth-
century Goa, would seem to have little relevance to this problem,
but the heart of the story revolves around the failure of the
Portuguese to have any effect on the Indians. It is the story of the
decline of what had been a great power in the face of an India
which is unchangeable. That such a story was written in the
1930s is undoubtedly related to the feeling among many Britons
that their days, too, were numbered and their effect was likewise
going to be drowned by the tide of the Indian past. Although the
Indians have been converted to Christianity, this conversion has
never affected them in any basic way. They sprinkle on Holy
Water as if it were Ganges water and the priest cannot convince
them of the difference. Once they have mastered the art of
crossing themselves, they do it all the time thinking it might 'be
of service against tree-spirits, necromancers and bats'.[2]

---

[1] Maunier, *The Sociology of Colonies*, p. 185.   [2] Kincaid, *Tropic Rome*, p. 6.

Gil, the leading Portuguese character in the novel, the son of a landowner just outside of Goa, stumbles on a small village where the natives say that their landholder has gone away. Gil thinks that it is more likely that he has been killed by the villagers and thrown down the well as an offering to the well-goddess. It is clear that all of the superficially Christian elements that had never taken root in the village are being erased. This is symbolized in the way in which the features of a statue of the Virgin placed over a Hindu shrine have been washed away, leaving her looking like a blind woman.

Gil's mother, *Dona* Tarejo, is part Indian, although she has always made the most strenuous attempts to emphasize her Western aspects. After the death of his father, he finds that she is becoming more and more Indianized. She begins to eat native foods and to grow fatter and fatter. At the same time she dismisses her Portuguese priest and, although she nominally remains Christian, begins to worship in a more and more Hindu way. Gil finds his mother placing offerings of champak flowers in front of the image of the Madonna in her room whereas before roses had always been used. He thinks: 'She shouldn't use champaks. They are used by the Hindus for their images.'[1] Even after her death, Gil, who is concerned with this development, is unable to stop the growing Indianization of his household. He brings the seductive Indian girl Gauri into the house and it is soon filled with Indian sounds and Indian smells along with her Indian friends and relatives. When he orders them out of the house, they return. It is clear at the end of the novel that Gauri has attained her goal and that Gil and the West have been defeated by India.

The end result of an attempt to introduce a steel steam ploughshare is described by Diver in similar terms. On its first outing the plough became so deeply embedded in the soil that it could not be loosed. When it finally was freed, it was put in a deserted temple where a priest splashed the blade with red and now charged admission to the peasants who worshipped it as a phallic symbol of Siva to insure the fertility of the soil.[2]

Although Candler believes that, despite its drawbacks, a Western education does improve the Indians by giving them a

[1] Kincaid. *Tropic Rome*, p. 103.   [2] Diver, *The Singer Passes*, p. 292.

greater sense of responsibility, he is not very optimistic. Skene, a teacher, is talking with Merivale about Western education in India.

'How long do you think we could hang on to the country,' he said, 'if we stayed here and bred and reared our children in it?'
'Four generations perhaps.'
'Human tissue couldn't stand more. It never has or will.'
'Not with education?' Dean suggested, looking across at Skene with friendly irony. The conversation had become general.
'No, not with education.'
'Here's an educationist who does not believe in education,' Hobbs broke in.
'Oh yes, I do. It must come, and it all helps, but it can't change the battery.'
'It can't give fibre, you mean,' Merivale suggested. 'That only comes from the soil.'
'Exactly.'[1]

At the end of *A Passage to India*, Aziz has gone to a native state where he is still practising medicine. However, he has begun to do his job according to traditional Indian methods, rather than in accordance with the modern Western ones he had been trained in and had used previously. Similarly, Godbole has opened a school in a native state, but he does not care that it has completely ceased to function although his original purpose was to modernize and Westernize the Indian people.

Casserly's Chunnerbutty professes to be completely Anglicized as he sneers at the customs and beliefs of his countrymen. Yet at the ritual slaying of a bull in honour of Kali, while the Europeans he has modelled himself after are sickened by the sight, the Anglicized Indian is entranced.

Noreen shuddered at Chunnerbutty's fiendish and bestial expression, as he leaned forward in the howdah, his face working convulsively, his eyes straining to lose no detail of the repulsive sight. He was enjoying it, like the excited, enthralled mobs of Indians of all ages around, who pressed forward. . . . Chunnerbutty, in whom old racial instincts were rekindled, had scarcely been able to restrain himself from climbing down and joining the frenzied rush on the bull.[2]

[1] Candler, *Siri Ram*, p. 274.
[2] Casserly, *The Elephant God*, pp. 314–15.

Even so staunch a supporter of the Raj as John Eyton shares this pessimism. 'The Pool' which, significantly, is the last story in one of his collections, starts with a flashback of 300 years at which time a Hindu temple is being built. It is destroyed by the Muslim invaders and in the present an Englishman, Colonel Brown, has built a cottage near by. He is upset by the continued reverence which the Hindus of the neighbourhood show for the site and becomes even angrier when a priest takes up residence there. The climax is reached with the rebuilding of the temple in a construction job that seemingly takes place overnight. There is nothing that Colonel Brown can do about it.

With the reader's indulgence, the author begs leave to draw a picture dating some three hundred years hence. . . . Colonel Brown is long forgotten. The Englishman, and his Government, and his rights, and his laws have faded away as a ripple dies on water—as a wind stirs in the trees and is gone. But on the back of the dark pool a little white temple stands, and still the pilgrims come . . . for such is India.[1]

Involved in all this there is also a feeling that, no matter how bad things may have been, the British 'improvements' were not worth the cost. Leonard Woolf's novel of the primitive Ceylonese people living in an unchanging jungle presents this theme. In *The Village in the Jungle* the people want only to be allowed to live their lives in a close relationship with nature, no matter how harsh it might seem to a Western educated person. To some degree this sounds like the kind of a comment that might have been made by Perrin. There is this difference: Woolf does not idealize the existence of his jungle dwellers. He recognizes the difficulties and horrors of these people, but nevertheless believes that for them it is the best way of life. Partially this is due to his own doubt of Western civilization and partly it is due to acceptance of the peasant's own values. Despite the desires of the people who live in the jungle village, Western civilization does interfere through the government land policy and the person of the half-breed Fernando. Together they destroy the primitive, but not unsatisfying system, and leave the village destroyed with the main characters dead.

Diver devotes much of the space in her long novels to attacks

[1] Eyton, 'The Pool', in *The Dancing Fakir*, p. 178.

on introducing democracy into India. As far as she is concerned, democracy and the institutions that go with it are 'the
political diseases of the West'.[1] They are not necessarily valuable for the West, and for India, which she sees as being a
naturally aristocratic society, they would be absolutely harmful.
Thus we see that the use of Western civilization can be attacked
both by people who are opposed to the Raj and by those who
favour it.

Edward Protheroe in Jesse's novel about Burma, *The Lacquer
Lady*, realizes that the conquest of the country by the British is
better for the physical welfare of the Burmese,

> but wasn't there something else, something intangible but perhaps
> more important than physical or even moral welfare? Naturally it
> was better for famines and fevers and leprosy to be dealt with pro-
> perly, naturally it was better to be decently governed, not to be
> squeezed dry. . . . But—but—[2]

And finally when the King and Queen leave Burma for their
exile,

> They went on board, and with them went a certain simplicity and
> arrogance, a lovely unconsciousness of others which soon will be
> found nowhere on the face of the globe, not even amongst the birds
> of its furthermost islands.[3]

Not only was the introduction of Western civilization and
government seen in this negative way, but the result of Anglo-
Indian relations as seen by a good many Englishmen was
negligible and likely to end in disaster. Candler, Kincaid, and
David give similar conclusions. Merivale has successfully put
down the plague in Siri Ram's village and in addition, saved the
life of his sister. As he prepares to leave India for a well-earned
vacation in England, he is still concerning himself with the well-
being of the Indians. At that instant he is killed by Siri Ram.

Dorion Fence, the hero of David's *Monsoon* and a newspaper
correspondent in India, is very interested in learning about the
country and its people. Although he feels that it is best for
India if Britain retains her control, he is a supporter of the liberal
point of view and a potential friend of the Indian nationalists.
Fence opposes his cousin, Alan Markham, who is against any

---

[1] See for example Diver, *The Dream Prevails*, p. 183.
[2] Jesse, *The Lacquer Lady*, p. 360.   [3] Ibid., p. 323.

concessions to the Indians. Markham believes that only through the use of force can the situation be put right. He had absolutely no principles and when his business is boycotted by the Indians, he secretly resorts to selling aphrodisiacs pretending they are virility drugs. At the end of the novel he is giving a speech urging harsh treatment of the Indian nationalists. At the same instant, Fence is killed by some nationalists who mistake him for his cousin. That the friend of India should die at Indian hands while the enemy that they sought to kill lives on is all a part of the ironic and futile way in which Anglo-Indian relations were viewed. The friendship of Naru and Edward Holme, described by Kincaid, ends in similarly futile violence. After their re-lationship has broken off, Naru has become involved in the Indian nationalist movement. Without his knowing it, the anti-British plot in which Naru is taking part includes the murder of Edward. He is feared by the nationalists because of the good work that he is doing—good work which might defeat the anti-British forces by bringing the two races closer together. When, at the last moment, Naru discovers who the victim is to be, he shoots himself while his accomplice succeeds in killing Edward as he wondered what ever became of 'dear Naru'.

If Orwell's Flory is not killed by a native friend, nevertheless, he is killed by the problems of Burma—problems that he finds impossible to solve—and the betrayal of his native mistress. Granted that not all his problems have to do with the imperial relationship, but still they are a contributing factor to the forces which drive him to suicide.

Not death, but something equally as futile, is all that Thompson has to offer as his addition to the solution of the problem of Anglo-Indian relations. Alden tells the wise *sadhu* that the difficulty of getting the two sides together is because the Indians do not complain about the things which are actually wrong, like their personal humiliation, but rather they harp on make-believe ills.

But the whole thing is the damndest dishonesty the world has ever seen—the Indian screaming about the injustice of our growing tea and jute, where nothing grew before, and the British diehard puffing about our great gifts to the country.[1]

[1] Thompson, *A Farewell to India*, pp. 242–3.

Again the problem is seen entirely in terms of personal relations
—one which political reforms could do little to solve. If only
both sides were sane, Alden thinks that there could have been
better relations and a solution to the problem. He announces,
on the eve of his return to England, that he had hoped to go
home in 1932 in order to see Gandhi granted his Doctorate of
Laws at Oxford. At the height of the nationalist disputes,
naturally everyone laughs at this 'impossible' statement. ' "All
the same", he said, "it ought to have happened, if, first of all, *we*
had been sane; and then, if *he* had been sane." '[1] Alden feels that
even with the snobbery of the Empire, India is better off within
it because outside of it is only chaos. He hopes to find the
answer of how this is to be accomplished from the *sadhu*.

'Is there going to be peace, Sadhuji?' asked Alden presently.
'Not till England and India come face to face.'
'You mean?'
'He means,' said Findlay, 'not while the non-violent humbug talks
to the look-what-we-have-done-for-India humbug.'
'Then there'll be a chance when the unbragging India comes face
to face with the unbragging England?'
'Yes. If one Indian can judge.'
'It's going to be hard for England,' said Findlay softly. 'She has
too many ghosts behind her eyes.'
'What do you mean, John?'
'I mean that you can't see straight, with so many *bhuts* trying to
use your one set of retina and visual nerves. You have the ghosts of
the American Revolution, of Ireland, of South Africa, all crowding
in upon one vision. God help her when she comes to that council-
table. For she wants to be decent and honest and fair.'[2]

The *bhuts* or ghosts that Thompson fills his books with infect not
only the British, but also the Indians. They are not only memories of the past, but are also a name for the elemental forces
within India which seem to make any sane relationship between
the races impossible.

Percival Christopher Wren, who is best known for his tales of
the French Foreign Legion, has set several novels and collections of stories in the East. He continually remarks that 'never
the twain shall meet' when he refers to race relations. Although
not taking place in India, but in Malaya, one of his short stories

[1] Thompson, *A Farewell to India*, p. 291.   [2] Ibid., p. 93.

best expresses this theme. An Englishman and a Malayan girl
have married, but because they are of different races 'fate' will
not allow them to find happiness. Wren makes use of Kipling's
'The Ballad of East and West', with changes to prove his point.

> It has been remarked, East is East and West is West, and never
> the twain shall meet.
> Nevertheless, in defiance of this Law, they do occasionally meet.
> Perhaps it is because the meeting is in defiance of the Law that it is
> usually disastrous. Whether it is a Law of God, of man or of Nature,
> is not stated, but it would appear that all three endorse the rule.
> There have been many meetings of East and West, but rarely a
> fortunate one.[1]

This is the way in which the story opens and it closes with the
line: 'East is East and West is West and there is danger whenever the twain shall meet.'[2] Wren sees absolutely no chance for a
good relationship between individuals of different races—even
though they are in love or are 'strong men'.

To Forster, the struggle of one man to achieve intimacy with
another exists in all places, but it is even more evident in India
where racial, imperial, and communal division seem to make
personal relationships just about impossible.[3]

> The author's interest is in the clash of human beings, the struggle
> which any one individual must endure if he is to achieve intimacy
> with any other. The fundamental personal difference is again
> deliberately heightened by an external circumstance—the difference
> of race.[4]

This idea is the heart of the plot—the friendship of Aziz and
Fielding—and leads up to the last great passage in the novel
which sums up his answer to the possibility of good relations
between the two races. The two friends ride together.

> All the way back to Mau they wrangled about politics. . . . Aziz
> in an awful rage danced this way and that, not knowing what to do,
> and cried, 'Down with the English anyhow. That's certain. Clear
> out, you fellows, double quick. . . . We shall drive every blasted

---

[1] Wren, 'The Pahwang', in *Odd Stories*, p. 135.   [2] Ibid., p. 153.
[3] Gertrude White, '*A Passage to India*: Analysis and Reëvaluation', *PMLA*,
LXVIII, September 1953, pp. 644–5.
[4] Peter Burra, 'The Novels of E. M. Forster', *The Nineteenth Century and After*,
CXVI, November 1934, p. 589. Forster personally selected this essay to serve as the
foreword for the Everyman Edition of *A Passage to India*.

M

Englishman into the sea, and then'—he rode against him furiously—
'and then,' he concluded, half kissing him, 'you and I shall be
friends.'

'Why can't we be friends now?' said the other holding him
affectionately. 'It's what I want. It's what you want.'

But the horses didn't want it—they swerved apart; the earth
didn't want it, sending up rocks through which riders must pass
single file; the temples, the tank, the jail, the palace, the birds, the
carrion, the Guest House, that came into view as they issued from
the gap and saw Mau beneath: they didn't want it, they said in their
hundred voices, 'No, not yet,' and the sky said, 'No, not here.'[1]

What Malcolm Cowley has called 'E. M. Forster's Answer'—
the answer that nothing can be done[2]—is as applicable to this
whole generation of writers as it is to the one individual.
Merely asking the question was something new and the pessimism with which it was answered certainly marked a change
from the confidence of the earlier period—a period in which
the question itself seemed unnecessary and this kind of answer
would have seemed wrong.

Older solutions were offered by those writers who were more
sympathetic to the Raj. The continuing image of the Indians
as children naturally meant that for many Englishmen the
paternal relationship remained the best one. This also meant
that the use of force continued to be looked upon as an essential.

Stacy Burlestone was by nature essentially and fundamentally a
kindly man; but long residence in the East and a wide experience of
Orientals had led him to the conclusion, right or wrong, that, to the
Eastern mind, kindness and weakness are synonymous terms. . . . He
knew that the Indian's mental attitude towards the kindly and easy
European is inevitably tinged with contempt; and that his transla-
tion of 'kind' is a word indistinguishable from 'soft'.[3]

The crucial point in his hero's attitude towards Indians for
Ollivant is his belief that 'every Asiatic is a baby'. ' "And if we
ever forget that we shall lose India," he would add. And perhaps part of the almost supernatural hold he had on his own
men in particular, and on the Indian generally, was due in no

[1] Forster, *A Passage to India*, pp. 323–5.
[2] Malcolm Cowley, 'E. M. Forster's Answer', *New Republic*, 109, 29 November
1943, p. 750.
[3] Percival Christopher Wren, *The Dark Woman*, Philadelphia, 1943, p. 228.

small measure to his recognition of that capital fact.'[1] The entire
novel is an ode to this kind of a relationship. The Englishman
continually calls the Indian troops 'sons', 'babies', or 'my
children' and they respond. Tom Oliver sees his role clearly
and without embarrassment so that he can say: 'The God-on-
Olympus business is the white man's role.'[2] On one occasion
Ollivant gets so carried away with this theme that he describes
the rapturous greetings his troops give to Oliver in biblical
terms: 'Even so must the disciples have looked upon their lost
Master when first they found Him after the Resurrection.'[3]

This image rested not only on the British idea that they were
leaders, but also on the belief that the Indians viewed themselves
as children. The Subahdar-Major describes the scene in the
army camp when cholera has struck.

> Then towards dawn the men came to us, a great company of them
> though as you knowest, sahib, it is against the Queen's Regulations
> for sepoys to come to their officers in crowds, but see thou!—these
> were no longer soldiers: they were little children lost as night in the
> great bazaar and crying for their parents. And they stood before
> Pollok Sahib and wailed and made obeisance and cried out together
> —*Send for the Colonel Sahib! He will take this torment from us. He will not
> let this thing be. It will not pass till he returns. But when he comes it will fly
> away for fear because of his great anger when he sees the evil it has wrought
> his children.*[4]

When a District Commissioner is dying, the leaders of the
frontier area gather around him.

> 'Oh, Sahib . . . Father of the District . . . this is an evil thing that
> hath befallen,' the oldest among them wailed, in deep-toned
> lamentation. 'How will it be with us who have so long been ruled by
> your wisdom, when the light of your Honour's countenance is
> withdrawn?'[5]

Finally, along the same line, Dermot is described as 'having no
unjust prejudice against the natives of the land in which so
much of his life was passed. Like every officer in the Indian
Army he loved his sepoys and regarded them as his children.'[6]
It is particularly in the army that this relationship is seen to

---

[1] Ollivant, *Old For-Ever*, p. 23.   [2] Ibid., p. 213.   [3] Ibid., p. 113.
[4] Ibid., p. 121.   [5] Diver, *The Great Amulet*, p. 392.
[6] Casserly, *The Elephant God*, p. 344.

continue. 'Only the Indian Army revealed no appreciable change in the old friendly relation between British officers and their men: the one enduring bond between East and West.'[1]

The Punjabis that Candler describes in such glowing terms are still 'helpless as cattle when there was no one to lead them'.[2] It is clear that he means that only with an *English* leader can they be properly led. The Sikhs of *Hira Singh's Tale* find themselves in trouble when their last British officer is killed. As he dies the Indians swarm around him trying to listen to his last words 'for we loved Colonel Kirby as sons love their father'.[3] With Kirby gone, the Sikhs are forced to rely upon themselves to produce a leader, but because of internal disunity and an unwillingness to trust each other they find this very difficult. 'Given a British commanding officer—just one British officer— even a little young one—one would have been enough—it would have been hard to find better backing for him'.[4] The Sikhs could respect the British officers because of their fairness and because they are free from the drives to loot and murder that Hira Singh thinks are basic to the Sikh character.

Even an author like Thompson who is not simply a supporter of the existing Raj does not scorn the paternal relationship. Nicky, a young and wise girl, loves and understands the India that she meets in 'her jungle'.

> Her mind was steeped in the land with a passion that was often utter, unspeaking ecstasy; she loved the people. . . . But she accepted them as dependents; in their jungle scheme of things they had their place as she had hers. . . . But she would have been very surprised by an obstinate questioning of her will.[5]

'As warden of these marches where jungle and civilization met, she felt a happy pride. She had rights over both—a master and queen to the one, swift, decided, graciously masterful—a ranger to the other.'[6] Thompson sees nothing wrong with this attitude of his heroine. In her jungle where the simple life of the past had not changed as much as elsewhere, such a relationship is thought possibly to be of merit.

The mystically spiritual writings of such persons as Beck or Thompson might, on the surface, seem to offer another solution

---

[1] Diver, *The Singer Passes*, p. 457.   [2] Candler, *Siri Ram*, p. 70.
[3] Mundy, *Hira Singh's Tale*, p. 46.   [4] Ibid., p. 182.
[5] Thompson, *Night Falls on Siva's Hill*, p. 38.   [6] Ibid., p. 132.

through the blending, spiritually, of the races. As John dies, he holds hands with both Alden and the *sadhu* and says that he has learned 'that love is not tied to any race or country, but lives indestructibly between those who have lost their very *selves*— have lost everything that made them separate from others'.[1] Similarly, Beck can write that 'below the differences on surface, are not humanity and purpose the same everywhere?'[2]

Thompson's Englishman and Indians, however, do not seem to be able to reach that level of love which takes one race out of itself and makes the differences meaningless—at least not while they are living and meeting each other in close contact. When Beck's Stephen decides that, having tasted the rarified atmosphere of the Ninth Vibration, he should stay in the Himalayas to learn even more, Vanna objects:

> No. Indeed I will say frankly that it would be lowering yourself to live a lotus-eating life among my people. It is a life with which you have no tie. A westerner who lives like that steps down; he loses his birth-right just as an Oriental does who Europeanises himself. He cannot live your life nor you his.[3]

If cultural assimilation is thought to be difficult, the solution of intermarriage is equally frowned upon. Writing in 1911 Mrs. Diver seems to be offering this as a solution. Lilamani Singh and Sir Nevil Sinclair are able to overcome all of the difficulties inherent in a marriage between the races. They even succeed in triumphing over what the author believes are the most serious barriers—a difference in religion and the danger of their mixed-blood offspring. The races are thought to be totally different, but complementary. Through her 'Eastern soul' with its well-developed elements of mysticism and sensitivity, Lilamani is able to kindle her English husband's artistic talent. There is a continual play on the contrast between East and West with the former being thought to be spiritual, passive, and fatalistic while the latter is practical and assertive. The secret of their success is that they both remain true to their 'racial characteristics'.[4] Still, it is Lilamani who converts to Christianity in order

---

[1] Thompson, *An End of the Hours*, p. 283.
[2] Beck, *The House of Fulfilment*, p. 153.
[3] Beck, 'The Interpreter', in *The Ninth Vibration*, p. 119.
[4] Diver, *Awakening*, p. 170.

to be more closely united to her husband and it is in England that the couple must remain in order to avoid further 'the lure of the East'.

The son of this marriage, Roy, is a highly idealized type representing the best of both cultures in himself. Still, Diver shies away from any further intermarriage. Roy is loved by his cousin Arúna, but they cannot marry. The reason for this is that it would emphasize Roy's 'Indianess', whereas it is his 'English blood' which 'should' be dominant.[1] This comes out particularly in a situation where Roy almost commits suicide because 'the fatalistic strain in his blood' thought it was the only solution for his unhappiness. He is saved by his 'Western blood' which cries out: 'Don't fret your heart out, Roy. Carry on.'[2] Throughout two more long novels, Roy seeks to find the bridge that will bind India and England together, but assimilation does not appear to be the answer. 'Each must honestly will to understand the other, each holding fast the essence of individuality, while respecting in the other those baffling qualities that strengthen this union and make it vital to the welfare of both.'[3]

The fact that the original idea of intermarriage which she proposed was not meant as a real solution is seen in the last of the quartet of novels on this subject. It either was to be reserved for very special individuals or, more likely, what was permissible in 1911 became less and less so as the years progressed, showing the increasing anxiety with which the defenders of the Raj were filled. Roy himself comes to say: 'I'm proud of my share of India. But I think on principle, it's a great mistake.'[4] In this last novel the English girl, Chrystal Adair, and the Pathan, Sher Afzul Khan, fall in love. Roy, the *successful* product of such a mixed marriage, persuades them that such a marriage is impossible because of the great differences between the races. Chrystal is convinced, despite her true affection for the Pathan, by Roy's playing on her racial prejudices. He tells her that although her decision will hurt Afzul, it is better than hurting her English suitor, Dixon Verney, 'a good man of your own race'.[5] She finally writes to the Pathan, saying that it is not racial pride or prejudice which caused her to act in this way, but the claims against them which 'our people and our race, have.'[6]

---

[1] Diver, *Far To Seek*, p, 426.   [2] Ibid.   [3] Ibid., p. 93.
[4] Ibid., p. 351.   [5] Diver, *The Dream Prevails*, p. 379.   [6] Ibid., p. 391.

Later she does admit that her decision was the right one for the good of the race.

Noreen Daleham, who is quite friendly with the Bengali Chunnerbutty and fairly liberal in her racial views,

was gradually realizing the existence of the 'colour bar,' illiberal as she considered it to be. But it will always exist, dormant perhaps but none the less alive in the bosoms of the white peoples. It is Nature herself who has planted it there, in order to preserve the separation of the races she has ordained.[1]

Similarly, in *Siri Ram*, Dean is talking with someone about racial prejudice:

'Talking about colour prejudice. Don't you think it is rather a misnomer? I mean the whole thing is chemical. You might as well talk of the prejudice of acids and alkaloids.'
'Simple as litmus paper.'[2]

This growing need to justify racial feelings is something new. Earlier there was little need to explain or to justify such feelings because they were more easily accepted. It is clear that the image of Indian inferiority remained an integral part of this attitude. When Brenda Lethorne discovers that Rod has Indian blood, he expects her to ask him why he isn't black. She is not concerned with the colour prejudice, but is surprised that he is so English. She says that the surprising thing is not his colour, but the fact that he does not show 'a trace of despotism, or the Oriental temperament'. If she ever loved an Indian she avers that she would marry him. 'But I don't think I could love any Indian I have seen. The type does not appeal to me.'[3] This is an explanation which seems to partake less of racialism than the others, but in fact it is little different. It served to accomplish the same thing, the separation of the races. In no way, whether for cultural or racial reasons, did the English see intermarriage as a solution to the problem of Anglo-Indian relations. These supporters of the Raj could offer nothing more than a defence of the old paternal methods seasoned liberally with the use of force.

A feeling which has been common throughout the entire British relationship with India is that although Britain may be

---

[1] Casserly, *The Elephant God*, p. 228.   [2] Candler, *Siri Ram*, pp. 219–20.
[3] Savi, *By Torchlight*, p. 123.

the ruler she cannot act entirely independently. There are ties
between the two peoples which force the British to recognize
their lack of a free hand in dealing with India. Phrases such as
Indians knowing all about the British 'although we little
suspect it'[1] or that 'in the East every blade of grass can hear'[2]
or that the servants know everything about their masters 'even
the things we think we've kept as secret as the graves, even the
things we don't know ourselves'[3] are not uncommon.

The rulers are often forced to act in certain ways, not because
they want to, but because they have to set an example for the
Indians.[4] Even more, there is a growing feeling in this period
that the Indians are capable of manipulating their rulers
through a superior understanding of what makes the English
function. A group of rajahs want to get the British Commissioner
to do something that he does not want to do. They know that he
would not take a direct bribe, but that he would accept money
for a hospital he wanted to build and this would make him feel
as indebted to them as would an actual bribe. U Po Kyin, in
Orwell's novel, succeeds, throughout the whole book, in manipulating the English as if they are puppets. He is successful in
getting whatever he wants and the British never know they are
being used. It is believed that it is not always necessary for the
Indians to consciously try to control the Europeans. They are
able to accomplish their control merely by the force of their
numbers. The strongest statement of this theme comes from
George Orwell. He describes a situation where the local police
officer is called out by the Burmese to shoot an elephant which
had gone wild. He realizes that the elephant had only had an
attack of 'must' and was now harmless. Hence there was no
reason to shoot him, but by that time a crowd of Burmans had
formed.

And suddenly I realized that I should have to shoot the elephant
after all. The people expected it of me and I had got to do it. . . .
And it was at this moment, as I stood there with the rifle in my hands,
and I first grasped the hollowness, the futility of the white man's
dominion in the East. Here was I, the white man with his gun

---

[1] Savi, *By Torchlight*, p. 123.   [2] Ollivant, *Old For-Ever*, p. 36.
[3] Thompson, *Night Falls on Siva's Hill*, p. 208.
[4] See for example Kincaid, *Tropic Rome*, p. 31, where Gil is forced to go to church,
although he does not want to, because he must impress the Indians.

standing in front of the unarmed native crowd—seemingly the leading actor of the piece; but in reality I was only an absurd puppet
pushed to and fro by the will of those yellow faces behind me. I
perceived in this moment that when the white man turns tyrant it is
his own freedom that he destroys. He becomes a sort of hollow,
posing dummy, the conventionalized figure of a sahib. For it is the
condition of his rule that he shall spend his life in trying to impress
the 'natives', and so in every crisis he has got to do what the 'natives'
expect of him. He wears a mask, and his face grows to fit it. I had got
to shoot the elephant. I had committed myself to doing it when I
sent for the rifle. A sahib has got to act like a sahib; he has got to
appear resolute, to know his own mind and do definite things. To
come all that way, and then to trail feebly away, having done
nothing—no, that was impossible. The crowd would laugh at me.
And my whole life, every white man's life in the East, was one long
struggle not to be laughed at.[1]

Therefore, he shoots the elephant and does not even do a neat
job as he butchers the beast.

This description makes an interesting contrast to a short story
by Kipling entitled 'Naboth' and termed by the author 'an
allegory of Empire'.[2] In it an Englishman befriends a starving
Indian who, taking advantage of his hospitality and protection,
sets himself up as a storekeeper on the grounds of his home. Due
to this he grows to be very prosperous. Although in his growing
wealth he impinges on the freedom of his 'protector', there is
nothing which the Englishman can do about the situation. He
has taken the responsibility for the Indian on his shoulders and
therefore is forced to live under his burden. Finally, someone is
killed because of the actions of the Indian on the Englishman's
property. This causes the Englishman, who is in part responsible for the death since the Indian was under his protection, to
drive the Indian off his land. It is not difficult throughout this
story to realize that Kipling was not writing merely about two
individuals—but about the two peoples.

There is a similarity here in that the 'ruler' finds himself
having to act in certain ways although he does not want to.
There is, however, a great difference. Kipling's Englishman
does find the strength to get rid of the Indian and assert his

---

[1] George Orwell, 'Shooting an Elephant', in *Shooting an Elephant and Other Essays*,
London, 1950, pp. 6–7.
[2] Kipling, 'Naboth', in *Life's Handicap*, 317–20, *passim*.

independence, whereas Orwell's Englishman is driven all the
way to commit an action he detests. The earlier period was
marked by at least enough self-confidence to feel that the
'rulers' could only be pushed so far and then they would assert
their power. By the 1930s the serious doubts which infected all
aspects of the British image of India had also made them see
themselves as being unable to control their own destinies. In all
their views the anti-Raj writers or those who felt that Britain
had been a failure in India had little in the way of anything
positive to say. The supporters of the Raj could only continue to
hold forth the old solutions while the opponents held forth no
solutions at all. A feeling of melancholy for an empire which, if
it were not yet dead, was on the verge of dying, was beginning
to fill the British image of India.

The Era of Melancholy
1935–1960

VIII

EPILOGUE

By the mid-1930s the British image of India and of their life in
that country had taken on a new colour. This change is not
marked so much by new themes as by the growth of an intro-
spective feeling of melancholy. This emotion had been expressed
by a few writers earlier, but in this period it came to be shared
by most writers. No longer did writers concerned with India
feel that they had to take a partisan stand either in favour of
or in opposition to the existence of the British Empire in India.
They tended to believe that the Empire was already dead.
Therefore there was no reason to continue to attack it. Most of
the authors, in fact, were favourably disposed to the historical
Empire and this looking backward on what they thought had
been better days added further depth to their melancholy
attitude. In the Era of Doubt there were virtually no historical
novels. The authors of that period were far too concerned with
the problems of the present to write about the past. In the post-
1935 period historical novels reappear, as literary men look
backwards rather than forwards.

The dedication of Masters' first novel, *Nightrunners of Bengal*,
to 'The Sepoy of India, 1695–1945' demonstrates this retrospec-
tive attitude. Mary Margaret Kaye looks back with pride on the
long relationship of her family with India. She dedicated her
novel of the Indian Mutiny to

Sir John William Kaye who wrote a history of the Indian Mutiny,
Major Edward Kaye who commanded a battery at the Siege of
Delhi, my grandfather, William Kaye of the Indian Civil Service,
my father, Sir Cecil Kaye, my brother, Colonel William Kaye, and
to all other men and women of my family and of so many other
British families who served, lived in and loved India.[1]

In one of the best novels of this period, Christine Weston's

[1] Mary Margaret Kaye, *Shadow of the Moon*, London, 1955, Dedication.

Indigo, the change from the preceding period is marked. Its theme is similar to that of Kincaid's *Their Ways Divide* or Forster's *A Passage to India* with its stress on the difficulty of friendship between the races. Unlike these works, however, the more recent novel tends to look backward towards what the author believes was a happier time. This attitude is partially seen in the title of the book since the indigo industry evokes memories of the turn of the century when that crop was still important.[1] In this novel the young Indian Hardyal finds that his friendship with the Europeans was not strong enough to conquer the lack of understanding brought about by racial divisions. He blames the First World War for making such a friendship impossible.

But now the great war had swamped individual concepts, it made personal considerations appear as mean and slight, it thrust past glories into a background lighted only a little by nostalgia; it imposed distance, like a no-man's-land of dreams between generation and generation.[2]

The old problem of the British in India—where was Home—became one of the leading themes. Unlike their predecessors, the more recent writers were not concerned with British isolation from England, but rather with their isolation from *both* England and India. Both Eurasians (as will be seen below) and British characters are shown being torn between two worlds, viewing their personal position in India with marked despondency. Now that they were faced with a new India the British found that they could not remain there. At the same time they did not want to go back to England. An Indian servant says of his master: 'My master is often sad. It is hard . . . for a man to live always between two worlds.'[3]

Another novel, Jon Godden's *The Peacock,* is completely devoted to this problem.

Eric Cathcart's father and grandfather and great-grandfather had been Indian Army officers as, until a year ago, when India had become independent, he had been. As a child living in the cantonments of Indian towns and later in schools and homes in an England

---

[1] For an earlier expression of this same idea concerning the indigo industry see Thompson, *Night Falls on Siva's Hill, passim.*
[2] Christine Weston, *Indigo,* London, 1944, p. 299.
[3] William Buchan, *Kumari,* London, 1955, p. 92.

which for a long time had been a strange country to him, he had
never imagined that he could be anything else. He followed a tradition and a pattern that was once thought as good as a pattern could
be but which is now seen as out of date and a little absurd. . . . He
was honest, conventional, narrow and proud, as his kind are supposed to be. He took himself and his work seriously and was as vain
and careful of his regiment as he was of his magnificent body.[1]

The end of the Second World War found Eric destroyed both
physically and emotionally. In what is a symbolic as well as an
actual destruction of his personality he lost his leg. In addition,
'The shock of emerging from over two years of hospital and
convalescent homes in India and England to find his regiment
disbanded, himself and his brother officers unwanted and his
army as he knew it, a thing of the past, was even greater.'[2] After
having tried and failed to adjust to life in England, Eric returned
to India although he realized that he had no future there. Of
the small group of Englishmen and Englishwomen who join
him for a hunting expedition in the jungle, everyone but the
half-Italian Kay understands Eric's need to remain there. Since
he is not wholly English by blood he thinks Eric should go somewhere else and make a new life. Eric says that that is impossible.

'But you see, there *is* nowhere else. I came back to that every time.
There's nowhere else for me.'
'What complete rubbish! Do you mean to stay here, in the jungle,
for the rest of your life? There's the rest of this considerable country
for a start. There are other countries. There's all the world.'
'Not for me. I don't see myself anywhere else.' Eric said slowly,
almost dreamily. 'There's no future for me anywhere. No future.'[3]

When Eric and Kay stop at the local rest-house they read the
list of visitors dating continuously from 1888.

Kay was turning the yellowed pages curiously. 'This record goes
back for years,' she said. 'The first name, one Robinson, is dated
1888. He was a Forest Officer too, it seems. Three months on end he
spent here. What was he doing? Building the place?'
'Down with malaria, more likely. They mostly were in those days,
poor devils. But they had the best of it. Their world lasted their time.'

---

[1] Jon Godden, *The Peacock*, London, 1950, pp. 24-5.   [2] Ibid., pp. 25-6.
[3] Ibid., pp. 195-6.

'This old place won't last much longer, anyway,' Kay said cheerfully. 'Time it went. It has served its purpose.'
'Perhaps. But what will they put in its place?'[1]

This rest-house is clearly meant to be taken as more than an actual building. When Kay notes 'cheerfully' that it is about to fall down having served its purpose, and Eric responds with the question as to what will be put in its place, the ex-soldier is no longer talking about the rest-house, but rather about what it symbolizes—the British Empire in India.

Finally, Eric solves his problem in the only way which seems open to him by committing suicide. Unlike the writers in the Era of Confidence, Jon Godden is sympathetic to such an act. Eric is buried in India and in that way he has found the only place where he belongs. Again it is only the half-Italian Kay who thinks that it is wrong to leave his body in the country which Eric regarded as home. In fact, Kay is not going back to England where he had been raised, but is returning to his father's country—Italy. Kay is also disturbed by the reappearance of Eric's dog at the end of the novel. The dog had disappeared following his owner's death and was presumed to be dead himself. Kay thinks that it would have been better if he had not come back at all because he is so old. One of the English characters sums up the whole feeling of dejection with which the British viewed themselves in India. 'Unfortunately death doesn't always arrive at the appropriate moment. The old have a way of lingering on long after it would have been better for themselves and everyone else if they had gone.'[2] Much of this feeling is found in the handling of the Eurasians who, of all the Indian peoples, receive the most extensive attention in this period. It is this theme—Eurasian life and personality—which is one of the major distinguishing features of fiction produced in this period. In contrast to the way in which they were generally depicted earlier, since the late 1930s the Eurasians have been presented rather sympathetically.

Jesse's *The Lacquer Lady* is one of the earlier novels of this class. She found many successors. Rumer Godden's *The Lady and the Unicorn*, John Masters' *Bhowani Junction*, and Jon Godden's *The City and the Wave* are all novels which deal with

---

[1] Jon Godden, *The Peacock*, p. 193.   [2] Ibid., p. 229.

the Eurasian community. In addition, there are many minor Eurasian characters in other novels. These people are not idealized and often are shown to have the same weak characters and vulgar personalities the earlier authors gave them. In contrast to writers such as Ollivant, Kipling, and Diver, however, there is an attempt made to understand them.

The life of Rumer Godden's Lemarchant family is described in terms that are similar to those a Maud Diver might have used.

The distemper had mildewed on the walls and a leg had come off the couch, which Boy had propped up with a brick. There was another brick to hold open the partition door into the bedroom. There was wire-netting over the windows to keep out thieves, and it was rusty and sagging. . . . Someone had left the skins of the eaten fruit on the dish so that the room reeked of bananas. It was auntie's habit to leave the cloth on the table because the wood was marked from hot plates: after the first meal it was usually soiled, especially where father sat. In the cracks of the basket chairs dust had collected, no scrubbing could get it out; and the curtains that shut off the pantry and windows did not match. . . . The garden was untidy, the flowers beginning to seed, and there was a congregation of crows worshipping a dead rat they had dropped on the grass.[1]

The father is concerned only with money—something he is unable to earn because he does not like to work; the aunt is always making a futile show attempting to prove she comes of a 'good family'; one of the sisters has become a prostitute; and they are all embarrassed by the youngest daughter's dark skin. No one in the family is willing to do any manual labour because that kind of work is thought to be worthy only of servants. They would rather see their home collapse around them than to attempt to *work* out a solution for their problems. All of them think that it is far more important to try to prove that they come of a fine old European family than to try to improve their present position. In fact, they spend most of their time looking backwards.

From this type of a description it would be easy for the author to go on to attack the Eurasians as being despicable people because of their 'race'. However, this is not what Rumer Godden, or anyone else, does. She believes that all of their weaknesses are explained by their inability to find a place of

---

[1] Rumer Godden, *The Lady and the Unicorn*, London, 1956, p. 43.

N

their own. The theme of the difficulty of existing in a never-never-land between two cultures had only been touched on before whereas here it has become a major theme.

It was like digging in sand, you could not get to the bottom of their contradictions, their cross purposes. It was their blood, the contempt of one part for another; the contempt of the Britisher for the native he rules, a contempt that runs like cold pure metal through the easy tissues of the native indolence and shiftlessness, pleasant dishonesty and shiftlessness, pleasant dishonesty and inconsequence; and the resentment of the Indian under that domination, his fight for freedom that is alien to his element of content, of settlement and culture if he could but find peace.

Peace. There could be no peace for these people who must always be against the winning side, no matter which side wins, carrying in themselves their certainty of defeat. For them a place would always have to be made, they could call no place their own.[1]

H. E. Bates introduces several minor Eurasian characters in his novels. Dr. Baretta, the woman doctor in *The Scarlet Sword*, continues to work and even cares for the Pathan attackers who have killed her husband, raped, and despised her because of her mixed blood. She possesses compassion and ability in direct contrast to the way Ollivant earlier depicted Dr. Jigger Jackson in *Old For-Ever*.[2]

John Sibly's half-Burmese nurse Nina Figuerdo is serving on a hospital ship evacuating British soldiers down the Irrawaddy before the invading Japanese. It is hard to find anything likeable about her as she refuses to do anything to help the men. She spends most of her time sitting in her cabin smoking the cigarettes which even the worst medical cases are unable to get. Nina only turns up when there is 'something pleasant to be served out; particularly . . . if it had been provided by the efforts of others'.[3] In all of this she is constantly contrasted with the English nurse on the same boat who is a completely unselfish person. However, even Nina Figuerdo is shown to have some justification for her attitude. She may, in fact, be oversensitive, but when one realizes the conflicts within her own soul everything she does is understandable. Sibly may not

---

[1] Rumer Godden, *The Lady and the Unicorn*, London, 1956, p. 14.
[2] See p. 137.
[3] John Sibly, *You'll Walk to Mandalay*, Garden City, 1961, p. 45.

present her as a very high-minded person, but by pointing out this conflict he does show sympathy for her position.

The Eurasians are imagined to be basically concerned with their place in an imperial world that was falling apart. British sympathy with this group—something which is completely new—is probably associated with the feeling of the British in India about themselves. They, too, were finding a conflict between their constant reiteration that England was home, their love for India, and their growing realization that they had a place in neither country. This problem is the heart of John Masters' *Bhowani Junction*. The Eurasian heroine, Victoria Jones, has suitors who represent all sides of her character— an Englishman, an Indian, and a Eurasian. The Eurasian, Patrick Taylor, is inept in whatever he tries to do and is not above having an affair with Victoria's sister. Victoria rejects him at first because all he can offer her is a continuation of the kind of meaningless life she is trying to escape. It is a life which is concerned with the wearing of *topis* (sun helmets), hating Indians, and talking about 'home'. In an attempt to find an identity, Victoria allows Taylor's Indian assistant, Ranjit Kasel, to court her. She goes so far as to wear a sari and finally consents to marry him according to the rites of the Sikh religion. In a very tense scene which takes place in a Sikh temple, Victoria is on the verge of completely denying her family, her background, and herself by taking a new name. She finds, however, that it is impossible to reject everything.

She finally makes a last try to find an escape from the ambivalence of her Eurasian background by having an affair with the English officer, Rodney Savage. At one point Rodney asks her to tell him about the time when she wore a sari.

She said slowly, 'It was going to be like a magic carpet. It was going to take me away from all the squabbling, and the topis that have to have waterproof covers on, and the betel-nut stains that Mater tries to hide.'

. . . She said sadly, 'It worked. The sari carried me away all right. But the place it took me to turned out to be foreign and frightening, and full of strangers.'[1]

Despite his hopes of winning her, Rodney finds that even their ties of love are not enough. Victoria finally decides that she

[1] John Masters, *Bhowani Junction*, London, 1954, p. 273.

must remain true to herself and marry Patrick Taylor although he is the least likeable of her trio of suitors.

This idea of the Eurasians as summing up within themselves the crucial problem of their day is expressed most succinctly by Sibly. He writes that Nina Figuerdo 'was clearly terrified of the Burmese. Her mixed blood seemed involved in the conflict of races which was approaching.'[1] In addition, this group of people by constantly looking backwards to a past which seemed better did not seem to be unlike the British in India themselves. As presented by the British authors of this period, the Eurasians sum up the melancholy feeling with which the British looked at India.

A Eurasian sub-inspector goes into a small South Indian village where he is faced with the problem of self-identity. Although he is a strong supporter of the British Government and an opponent of Indian nationalism who feels himself superior to the peasants, he cannot help but be impressed by the simple dignity of a people who are securely a part of India.

> The Eurasian sighed. So many civilizations, the sediment of count-less ages, underlay the smooth calm level of Hinduism's deep river. The Muslim Moguls had stirred the surface for a while and had then been largely absorbed into the vast silt bed of the stream, not as Hindus, but Indians. How long before Christian Eurasians like himself would mingle with the eternal flow of the River Mother? he wondered.[2]

In a most despondent statement, a Eurasian tells his Eurasian bride-to-be how he had fought during the Second World War without any thought of where he belonged. After the war, however,

> we were left here to sink or swim. Many of our people are well-to-do and proud and as respected as anyone in the city, but for many others of us life is difficult. There is not enough work for us and some of the old prejudice is still against us. The work that was more or less reserved for us, the railways, the police, has gone with the British. Our schools and way of life are threatened. We are pressed in on all sides. . . . Perhaps it would be better if we were gradually to die out and to vanish from the scene.[3]

---

[1] Sibly, *You'll Walk to Mandalay*, p. 120.

[2] Dennis Gray Stoll, *The Dove Found No Rest*, London, 1955, p. 80.

[3] Jon Godden, *The City and the Wave*, London, 1954, pp. 102–3.

Hinduism and Hindus play a larger role and are better treated than in either of the preceding periods. Two popular novelists, Somerset Maugham in *The Razor's Edge* and Nevil Shute in *The Chequer Board*, have continued the old image of India as the home of spiritualism from which the West has a great deal to learn. Many of the novels by Rumer and Jon Godden either deal favourably with Hinduism or attempt through their structure to reproduce a sense of timelessness which they feel is Hinduism. This can be seen particularly in the former's novel *The River* where the river itself never changes and the novel opens and closes with the same lines.[1] The favourable attitude towards Hindu spiritualism is not completely new, but for the first time there are sympathetic accounts of the more popular side of the religion, such as the carvings in the temples.

'It's always been thought disreputable to have a good word for Hindu temples, except architecturally. But it's precisely the disreputable things that tug, somewhere here,' and she touched the buckle of her belt. 'They make me feel like a child looking at, oh, a much too grown-up book.'[2]

A missionary woman is criticized for looking upon the Hindu temples as Towers of Babel when 'anybody with half an eye for proportion, and the other half for poetry, would have known what the Hindu architects were driving at'.[3]

Not only Hinduism, but Hindus too are far better treated in this period than ever before. Stephen Taverner in Payne's novel of the seventeenth century distinguishes between the Mogul and Hindu parts of Shah Jehan's character. The former is supposed to desire power and the latter to love people. The Englishman prefers the Hindu part and says that he loves the Hindus with all of his heart.[4] This same kind of an attitude is found in the description of a Hindu house. 'Here life was simple, almost austere; but here was so much depth, so much smoothness and ease of manner, that the house was pervaded with the finest traditions of ancient Hindu culture.'[5] This growing theme

---

[1] William York Tindall, 'Rumer Godden, Public Symbolist', *College English*, 13 March 1952, p. 298.
[2] Buchan, *Kumari*, pp. 125–6.   [3] Stoll, *The Dove Found No Rest*, p. 29.
[4] Pierre Stephen Robert Payne, *The Young Mogul*, London, 1950, p. 263.
[5] A. T. W. Simeons, *The Mask of a Lion*, London, 1952, p. 21.

may in part be a reflection of the British turning away from the Muslims who were seen as being responsible for destroying the fabric of unity which the British felt had been their most important gift to India.[1] Another explanation for this changing attitude may well be that, with independence as an accepted fact, it was no longer necessary to attack the Hindus who had been the greatest threat to British power.

Even so, a shadow of the former image remains here as it does in most places. Jon Godden's *The Seven Islands* is a beautiful short novel dealing with the attempt of a Hindu priest to establish a retreat on an island. The whole book is filled with respect for both Hinduism and Hindus. However, the villain of the piece is still that old character, the Bengali *babu*.

Just as the Era of Doubt saw a slight growth in the area of India which was described by the British authors, so in this period there is again an expansion. North India continues to be the centre of focus, but the actual setting in terms of geographical scope is not as important as it had been.

The most notable part of the setting is the continued importance of the jungle. Although the Indian jungle had long been central in the British image of India, in this period it, too, takes on a new, more important role. Only in the jungles can these last British writers find an India in which they still feel they have a place. Settings such as this will either have no Indian population or be populated by very primitive people. Masters' Rodney Savage explains his love for the jungle and its people:

> This was my India, not because of the capering or the drunkenness but because these people had no desire to become like me, nor I like them. There had been a place for me round such fires as this for three hundred years. The Ranjits and Surabhais, who were trying to change themselves, didn't light bonfires and dance round them. They read Paine and Burke and spoke in English because the ideas they were trying to express did not exist in their own language.[2]

The whole of Jon Godden's *The Peacock* is based upon this feeling.

Harry Black, in a novel by Walker, returns to India after

---

[1] For an excellent discussion of this development see K. K. Aziz, *Britain and Muslim India: A Study of British Public Opinion vis-à-vis the Development of Muslim Nationalism in India, 1857–1947*, London, 1963, especially p. 20 and p. 182.

[2] Masters, *Bhowani Junction*, p. 328.

independence. He welcomes independence because he believes that it has created a sense of equality between himself and his Indian friends. He loves the country and its people, but particularly he loves its jungles where he can stalk tigers accompanied only by his primitive guide: 'My best times have been spent in the forests of this country.'[1] Harry feels completely at home in the Indian jungle, but when he tries to talk about it with the Indian woman Somola she says that she does not like it at all. In fact, she is terrified of the jungle and far prefers the city. In this distinction is seen one attempt by the British to 'prove' that they actually do belong in India—that India is their country.

Only a few attempts are made to justify the position of the British in India. Older themes are still found. Most important among these older images is the idea that Britain was in India to protect the people from communal violence. Of more significance is the statement attributed to an English soldier after the Mutiny.

We've started them off again—ploughed them in if you like. They'll hate us for it, but they wouldn't have done anything for another hundred years or so if left to themselves. We've tried to go too quickly and force our way of life on them, but in a hundred years from now—or two hundred, or three—their history may show that Plassey wasn't an end or a defeat, but a beginning. Even this that is happening now was probably needed.[2]

The idea that the basic problem between the races was a personal one continued to be held by many British authors. Even if a man had come out to India determined to serve the country and its people and even if he were thought to be good with the Indians he did not have contact with the people.

The coolie children became shy and clung together when they saw him approach. . . . After a life's service in the city, the honest veteran would admit that his memories of coolie India were not those of the human affections. He knew the ways of these people in his charge as he knew the habits of tame animals, or not at all. Sometimes he would sublimate his own failure to know them by abusing them as innately vicious, filthy, heathen, immoral, inefficient, utterly irresponsible blacks; a race unworthy of the fine, clear, Christian, moral efficient, highly industrialized urban civilization of the West.[3]

[1] Harry David Walker, *Harry Black*, Boston, 1956, p. 172.
[2] Kaye, *Shadow of the Moon*, p. 331.   [3] Stoll, *The Dove Found No Rest*, p. 173.

British aid for the Indians is not received with gratitude. Although the Indians might appreciate what has been done for them, they dislike the way it was accomplished. An Indian describes his harsh life in the gutters of Calcutta and what the British have done for him.

I was picked out of the garbage and taken to school—and that was done by the detestable British . . . the Imperialistic British, who bothered to take up a gutter-boy and give him life.

Am I grateful? I need not be so very; the British have a passion for alteration. I was educated at the Slane Memorial Scottish School for Orphan Boys; they had my mind and my body for seven years, and for seven years I learnt to keep my heart shut away in darkness and starvation.[1]

This approach carries with it a continuation of the idea that the basic need was for personal friendship rather than political reform. Writing of the Mutiny, Masters says that it forged a chain of hatred which bound the British and Indians together. It could be broken only by love 'and there was no love'.[2] This is not very different from the attitude of Forster and Orwell that the Empire deserved to be and was lost because of a lack of affection by the British for the Indians.

We Hindus are hard political bargainers on the surface, but underneath we're eager to be friendly human beings. Mother India never fails to respond to strangers who touch her heart, holding a flame of love and understanding to her imagination. A few English men and women like C. F. Andrews and Sister Mary will always be welcome here. The rest of you we only endure because we must. You've patronized and bossed us for two centuries.[3]

A British resident in *The Wild Sweet Witch* explains to his wife why there is so much trouble between the two races. 'He's an emotional creature. They all are, of course, particularly when young. That's the mistake we make. Too cold. But it's our nature to be aloof with them, just as it's theirs to need that emotional appeal.'[4] In short, the relationship between the British and the Indians was believed to be similar to a love affair.

[1] Rumer Godden, *Breakfast With the Nikolides*, London, 1942, p. 36.
[2] John Masters, *Nightrunners of Bengal*, London and New York, 1951, p. vii of Preface to American edition.
[3] Stoll, *The Dove Found No Rest*, p. 205.
[4] Philip Mason, *The Wild Sweet Witch*, London, 1947, p. 106.

The whole thing is and always has been a love affair. First and last that's been what mattered. And it's taken the course, worse luck, of most love affairs, beginning with persuasion—none too gentle in this case—followed by delighted discovery, mutual esteem, ravishing plans for the future, the first really frightful row, and a long, miserable cooling off into polite bickering punctuated by sharp quarrels and joyless infidelities, each side withdrawing, steadily and continually, more and more of its real self.

The first great quarrel, the only one that mattered, was the Mutiny—that wound went deep and we've never ceased to suffer, in a way. By then we'd let our character change for the worse. We'd stopped wooing excitingly, violently, with real strength and a lot of poetry. We'd grown a great big, bland evangelical face and were going about doing and saying things to people—God forgive us—for *their own good*.[1]

One of the strongest supporters of the Empire, Masters, believed it was impossible for the two races to communicate with each other. The most recent of his long series of Rodney Savages finds this to be the case. 'After days and years and centuries, would there stand an opaque wall between true understanding, however clear the paintings each of us put on the surface of the wall, in an attempt to communicate.'[2]

Rumer Godden's *Kingfishers Catch Fire* is based on the misunderstandings between the races. Her heroine, Sophie, has come to Kashmir where she is determined to live like the Kashmiris. She refuses to have anything to do with the English community in Srinigar and believes that she is too poor to live in the city. Because of these ideas, along with an idealization of the Indian peasant, she takes a house in the hills. Sophie believes that she loves and respects the Indians. In order to show the people that she is not just a rich foreigner she takes her children for a walk through the village every afternoon. While they walked, however, the whole village stopped whatever it was doing to watch.

Sophie would have been astonished to know that her quiet afternoon walks were like a royal progress to the village. 'I have to do something. I may as well walk,' said Sophie, but for the villagers, to go walking was a luxury. . . .

'Then the clothes!' said the villagers. 'The beautiful clothes!'

---

[1] Buchan, *Kumari*, pp. 86–7.
[2] John Masters, *To the Coral Strand*, London, 1962, p. 133.

Sophie was worried about the children's growing shabbiness, but the villagers saw sumptuous woollen clothes, without a gap or rent in them.[1]

Sophie becomes a great source of money for the Kashmiris although she lives in what she thinks is a most frugal way. She cannot understand why they think she is rich. In fact she does not understand their way of life any better than they understand hers. When she tries to help them through setting up a small pharmacy, giving holidays to her servants, and trying to convince the people of the village to live in a more sanitary way, they only think that she is interfering in something that is none of her business.

Finally the Englishwoman who has attempted to become a part of India gets involved in a quarrel between two village families. Sophie does not even understand what this feud is about. One of her servants feeds her ground glass because he thinks that it is a love potion which will make her loyal to his side. Even greater tragedy almost results when her little daughter is attacked and seriously injured by the village children as she tries to protect her little brother from the violent courtship of the two feuding groups. The reason for all this trouble is explained to Sophie by her Indian friend, Profit David.

I told you you were like the emperors. The emperors suffered many things like this—poison and glass and influential drugs—and their children were always suffering too. . . . They had to expect it *because* they were emperors' children. . . . And the emperors had to expect it too, because they were emperors.[2]

When she has to leave the Kashmir and India which she loves, Profit David again expresses the idea. Sophie says that she is not an emperor. ' "No—but you might have been", said Profit David. Sophie felt he was disappointed in her.'[3]

As an emperor it would have been possible for the foreigner, Sophie, to live happily in Kashmir, but her unwillingness to accept the role which had been thrust upon her made it impossible for her to remain. She could either be an emperor or nothing. Although Sophie does not realize this, she does

[1] Rumer Godden, *Kingfishers Catch Fire*, London, 1953, pp. 100–1.
[2] Ibid., p. 245.   [3] Ibid., p. 277.

recognize that she could not comprehend what was going on. 'More than that. She was beginning to feel she was ringed round by something she did not understand.'[1] In her reaction to the attack on Teresa she uses the same phrase that earlier writers like Forster had used. Sophie sees no reason to prosecute the people who had injured her daughter because, as she says, 'It's a muddle.'[2]

In A. T. W. Simeons' *The Mask of a Lion* an Indian leper discovers a leprosarium after wandering the roads with no hope for the future. The hospital is run by an American and his sister. When he has been there for a time the Indian, Govind, begins to wonder why the Americans are sacrificing themselves for people who are not from their country. 'He wondered how much the mission paid Dr. Carter and his sister to do it. Surely some fabulous sum.'[3] The Indian simply does not understand the Americans' motivations. Despite the good care which he received in the American mission, Govind was very unhappy there and returned to the roads. Only after he finds an Indian-run hospital is he willing to remain for treatment. The assumption here is that Indians and not Westerners can cure the problems of India.

Again the reason for this lack of understanding is not merely personal, but racial. The Indians and the English are believed to think in completely different ways. The English resident in a princely Indian state writes back to England

that he has definitely learned the truth of the platitude . . . about people being like islands shouting at each other across oceans of misunderstanding. . . . And the people I'm thinking of are shut away from me by every kind of barrier—race, religion, upbringing, sex or age.[4]

In the seventeenth century, the Englishman Stephen Taverner has come to the court of Aurangzeb where he has fallen in love with the Indian Meriam. He has also learned that strange things happen in India. At the court of the Emperor he and Meriam have seen a fakir make an elephant disappear. Stephen recounts how the next day when he and Meriam were

---

[1] Rumer Godden, *Kingfishers Catch Fire*, p. 135.
[2] Ibid., p. 243.   [3] Simeons, *The Mask of a Lion*, p. 119.
[4] Philip Mason, *The Island of Chamba*, London, 1950, p. 108.

riding together he could not stop thinking about the disappear-
ance.

Seeing me disturbed, Meriam said, 'I have seen the Himalayas
when I was a child—'
'What has that to do with the elephant?'
'Everything. When you are a child and you see the Himalayas,
then you know that everything is possible. If he had made Aurangzeb disappear—God knows he was near enough to doing it—it
would have been remarkable, but no more remarkable than the
Himalayas.' She paused, turned her face, gazed at me as though
looking at me for the first time and went on: 'I never knew you were
such an Englishman! You haven't learned to think in our ways—'
'I do my best, but the truth is, I suppose that one becomes more
English the further one travels from England and tonight I travelled
further than I have ever been.'[1]

To Masters, the British in India were like people living in a
room upstairs who knew nothing of what was going on in the
house below. 'To feel India . . . you must become Indian,
gain one set of qualities and lose another. As a race we don't
do it—we can't.'[2]

As he sits in his hotel room above the streets of Calcutta,
another Englishman who loves the country finds himself cut
off from the people in a similar manner.

Armin cursed the symbolism of his situation five storeys up above
this ancient, unaltered life, surrounded with civilized comforts,
relatively rich and free, and yet utterly at the mercy of the humble,
unwilled enchantments rising from below. At times he longed to go
down and join the dark drummer and his friends. . . . Then he would
think how deeply shocked they would be, and how uncomprehend-
ing, and would cry, silently: 'There is no communication.'[3]

The problem of why it is impossible to join the two peoples
together is expressed by Masters in much the same terms as
those used by earlier writers.

William tried to understand, tried in the Western fashion to
separate the good from the evil, to balance the beauty of sacrifice
against the ugliness of waste, which is the essential of all sacrifice.

---

[1] Pierre Stephen Robert Payne, *Blood Royal*, New York, 1952, p. 93.
[2] Masters, *The Nightrunners of Bengal*, p. 30.   [3] Buchan, *Kumari*, p. 119.

But to these Hindus there was no conflict between God, who is all-powerful, and Satan, who yet flouts and perverts His intentions. Here, creation and destruction were opposite faces of the same medal, equal energies of the same universal spirit.[1]

William Savage comes to this conclusion when he is confronted by the problem of trying to uncover the Thugs. To do this he has decided that he must join the group. In order to accomplish this he attempts to become an Indian in thoughts and values as well as in dress. The interesting point is that he succeeds, going so far as to kill in honour of Kali. However, his success at becoming an Indian is done at the cost of something else—he is no longer an Englishman. Much of the novel is the story of the conflict between his newly found Indian ideas and his traditional Western values. In order to become a real Indian and understand the way in which they think he is forced to give up all that he had lived for. It finally takes a climactic event to bring him out of the world of the Indians and back into the world of the English—it was impossible for him to bring the two worlds together. The separation between the races is still believed to be something beyond the control of any person. At a party a European

noticed that a sort of segregation was slowly taking place. . . . The closer all these diverse elements were drawn together, the nearer they approached towards the ultimate unity, the more urgent became their unconscious resistance. It seemed as if some perverse and original memory asserted itself to remind them that moths are moths and bats are bats, that the devoted cranes which desert their crimson pools at sunset obey a wisdom which has determined to put more than space—to put form and substance—between life and life. The closer these people came to resembling one another the more strenuously they strove to separate. Only in the orgasm of love or of death could they ever forget their identity, and between themselves and this forgetfulness they had raised their fantastic barriers.[2]

Besides seeing that good relations between the races were impossible, the British authors of this period felt that the effect of India was basically destructive to the English character. Whereas the District Superintendent in *The Dove Found No Rest* might have a 'hidden Celtic flair for poetry . . . India had not brought it out'.[3] In another novel an Englishwoman feels that

---

[1] John Masters, *The Deceivers*, London, 1952, p. 25.
[2] Weston, *Indigo*, p. 219. [3] Stoll, *The Dove Found No Rest*, p. 169.

'no one could be herself here. No one could exist here and remain herself. I am dying.'[1]

The vastness of the country and its problems served to make everything the English believed in become meaningless. An English nurse notes:

> In the end nothing meaning everything: transit camps, transport, hospitals, malaria, jungle sickness, dysentery, prickly heat, amputations, pain, hysteria, home-sickness, death. Men came into your life, recovered, died, were time-expired; you crossed yourself and they were gone. Nothing meant anything except far off, ahead of you, a queer notion that you too would be time-expired, and you never were.[2]

It is not only the war, but the setting of the war which has caused the nurse to take this pessimistic view. India has the same effect on the nuns in Rumer Godden's *Black Narcissus*. They have come to a native state in the foothills of the Himalayas to teach the Indians. They soon find, however, that not only are they unsuccessful in their teaching, but that they are also falling under the spell of the Indian mountains. Sister Phillippa, who is supposed to be the most level-headed member the community, finds that she has become so fascinated with her work in the garden, where she can see the mountain Kanchenjungha, that she even hates to take time away from it to go to the chapel.

> She took to going in to chapel at the last minute, not even waiting to wash her hands. 'What am I thinking of?' she said, 'interrupting my *work* to go to chapel! What has come over me to make me think like that. It used to be, it ought to be, the other way round'. . . . Her cheeks burned from the sun and frost as she lay in bed at night, and the walls of her cubicle were bright with visions, not of saints but of flowers.
> Nowadays Sister Ruth was often ten minutes late ringing the bell. . . . Sister Clodaugh herself was sometimes curiously absent-minded as she read the prayers; occasionally she said a prayer through twice, and once, at the end of Compline, she kept them kneeling there for nearly ten minutes.[3]

Once Sister Phillippa became so involved with her gardening

[1] R. Godden, *Breakfast With the Nikolides*, p. 157.
[2] H. E. Bates, *The Scarlet Sword*, London, 1950, p. 224.
[3] Rumer Godden, *Black Narcissus*, London, 1939, pp. 115–16.

that she forgot to say her office altogether. Like Kipling's The Shrine of the Cow's Mouth and Forster's Caves, the mountains reduce everything to a meaningless void.[1] ' "I think you can see too far," said Sister Phillippa. "I look across there, and then I can't see the potato I'm planting and it doesn't seem to matter whether I plant it or not." '[2] Sister Clodaugh thinks to herself how the mountain dominates everything and seems to be stronger than God.

She tried to think how, to Him the mountain was as infinitesimal as the sparrows; instead she thought how the eagles, filled with His life, were beaten down before it.

It seemed to press through the window and fill her eyes with startling clearness like a railway poster, white and painted with blue on a blue sky. . . .

'We must fit curtains to the chapel window,' she said. 'The light is far too bright.'[3]

An Englishman who lives in the state warns Sister Clodaugh that it is an impossible place for a nunnery. Furthermore, he tells her that it will be impossible for the sisters to change the Indians in any way. If they continue to try to work there it will be like deliberately running into a stone wall. Sister Clodaugh sees things more clearly when she replies that it is rather more like running into a mist than into a stone wall.[4] Again, as for Kipling or Forster, the soul of India is thought of in negative rather than positive terms.

Sister Phillippa is the first to be defeated by the Indian environment. Explaining why she must leave the house, Mopu, where they have established themselves, she says:

Mopu had run away with me. I was obsessed with it and the mountains and my work in the garden. Yes, I think I was really obsessed. There's something in this place. I don't trust myself here. I mean it when I say I daren't stay. . . . I think there are only two ways to live in this place. . . . You must either live like Mr. Dean or like the Sunnyasi; either ignore it completely or give yourself up to it.[5]

Eventually the whole nunnery must follow her example. The nuns simply do not belong in India unless they are willing to give up everything they believe in. In this way Rumer

[1] Tindall, 'Rumer Godden', p. 301.   [2] Rumer Godden, *Black Narcissus*, p. 83.
[3] Ibid., pp. 86–7.   [4] Ibid., p. 230.   [5] Ibid., p. 202.

Godden's conception of India is not much different from that of Kipling or Forster. Her treatment of this perception is far more similar to Forster's than to Kipling's. Like the former she does not imagine that her English characters can remain constant to their Western civilization once they have come into contact with the soul of India. In this Godden shows the same lack of confidence in Western civilization as had filled the works of Forster. Unlike Kipling, she does not have her nuns flee because they are convinced of the correctness of their position, but because they are not.[1]

Through all of this there is the same feeling of racial consciousness that has been noted before. It is not so much that the 'racial values' of one race are believed to be superior to those of the other, but that the races cannot mix. No matter how much they might love India, all the English characters eventually are forced to leave as they realize they do not belong in an alien society. In *Bhowani Junction* the final decision by the Eurasian heroine to marry her Eurasian suitor rather than either the Indian or Englishman points this up. The Eurasian is far less capable than his Indian assistant and is dislikeable in almost every way. Yet the rule is that like must go with like. Similarly, in *Indigo* the friendship between Hardyal and Jacques is so deep that the two boys exchange clothes in a symbolic attempt to overcome the difficulties of friendship between the races, but in the end they fail. Jacques must return to his mother's indigo fields and Hardyal to a future as a nationalist.

There are a few highly favourable accounts of Indian nationalists, but the most common approach is an ambivalent one. Although most of the authors state that they favour independence, they clearly dislike the nationalists and continue to prefer those Indians who support the British. For Masters the 'good Indians' are not necessarily as servile as they had once been portrayed, but they are still pro-British. Govindaswami and Ranjit Singh in *Bhowani Junction*, Adam in *Far, Far the Mountain Peak*, Hussein in *The Deceivers*, and the villagers of Chalsigon in *Nightrunners of Bengal* all are shown to understand that only through working closely with the British, whom they respect, can India gain whatever she is seeking, be it peace or independence. These people are throughout depicted in highly

[1] See above, pp. 17–18 and 118–19.

flattering terms as sincere well-meaning people who really understand the situation. How unlike Orwell's ridicule of the pro-British Dr. Veraswami!

The nationalists and other anti-British characters such as Harnarayan in *Far, Far the Mountain Peak* or K. P. Roy in *Bhowani Junction* are shown as selfish men who are motivated by a desire for personal advancement rather than the good of India. Harnarayan refuses to help his fellow Indians following an earthquake so that the British will be blamed even at the cost of many Indian lives, and Roy uses brutal murder to attempt to widen the gulf between British and Indians. Masters feels that by their selfish actions they only prevent Indian advancement rather than further it. In the setting of the nationalist consciousness of the 1920s, an Indian prince, Adam, explains why he came to support the British and oppose the anti-British nationalists like Harnarayan.

This earthquake has altered my set of values a bit—as the war did in its way. Suppose—we the Congress—got everything we were asking for tomorrow, and you all went away on the next boat. Would that mean we didn't need an army or a police force or engineers or judges? Harnarayan says that Baber is a traitor to work for you—but it seems to me that he and people like him are strengthening our legs so that when we are free to walk alone we'll be able to.[1]

Harry Black thinks highly of Gandhi and the Congress Party, but when he talks to the woman nationalist, Somola, he sees a harsh side of this movement. She explains that an independent India cannot abide the continued existence of pockets of foreign control like Goa and Pondicherry which have remained. Despite the enormous size of India and the minuscule area of these foreign enclaves, she says that they are a threat to India. This far in her argument the reader might well take her speech as no more than the expression of the first flush of independent Indian nationalism. Her next statement puts the whole problem in a different light. Somola asks: 'What happened to Hitler's patience with the Poles?'[2]

The Indian nationalists in the mythical island state of Chamba are equally authoritarian. In his novel *The Island of*

---

[1] John Masters, *Far, Far the Mountain Peak*, London, 1957, p. 340.
[2] Walker, *Harry Black*, p. 168.

Chamba, Philip Mason has written one of the few political novels dealing with India in any period. It is the story of a princely state which has suddenly been given independence and forced to adjust itself to the modern world. It has changed little for centuries while under British protection. The island, populated largely by Hindus, has been ruled by Muslims since the days of the Moguls, but there has been no history of communal troubles up to the eve of independence. The Congress Party is attempting to stir up such trouble in order to take over the island and attach it to India. The Indian nationalists are a selfish group interested more in furthering their own power than in helping the people who are happy in their present state and want to be left alone. Although Mason does not present a detailed picture of an Indian nationalist, he does express what he believes to be their philosophy through a liberal English journalist, John, who supports the nationalists. The English Resident, Charles, expresses his opinion that it would be a tragedy for Chamba to become a part of India. The journalist is horrified at the thought of an independent Chamba which he believes would serve as a hostile base for all those who were opposed to India.

'India's going to be Hindu; make no mistake about it. . . . Well, how can Hindu India tolerate an island only seventy miles from her ruled as an independent state by Muslims? . . . The minorities in India would never settle down and become good citizens. They'd keep a separatist party head-quarters over here and there'd be no end to the trouble. The island would be a dagger pointed at the heart of Hindustan.'

'Haven't I heard that phrase before somewhere?' asked Charles politely. 'It seems to call to mind the memory of Czechoslovakia.'[1]

When John continues the discussion later with a plea that this is the ideal time for union, Charles replies: 'Poland. The creed of Napoleon, Bismarck, and Hitler.'[2] Earlier he has written to his fiancée in England that 'the Hindus have always talked of Chamba rather as Hitler talked about Czechoslovakia'.[3] A Chamban official continues this analogy when he says that the people of the island know that the British will not help them

---

[1] P. Mason, *The Island of Chamba*, p. 126.   [2] Ibid., p. 198.
[3] Ibid., p. 181.

against India 'just as you would not help the Czechs to resist Hitler'.[1]

In a less polemical novel Mason continues his attack on the nationalists. This novel, *The Wild Sweet Witch*, is the story of the Indian Jodh Singh who is disgusted with the failure of the British to put any real reforms into effect. The author is in full agreement with his complaints, but has serious reservations about the way the Indians go about trying to get these reforms.

You people want India to be free and manage her own affairs at once, but what sort of a showing do you make at managing a district, let alone a country? The deputy commissioners may not have been enthusiasts for education but they did keep roofs on the schools and see that the teachers were paid. How many schools are there that are falling down and how many teachers are there who are more than six months in arrears with their pay, now that the district board has taken over.[2]

Even such a likeable person as Jodh Singh seems to be accomplishing nothing practical despite the flowery words he used to stir up the people. When he finally does make an attempt to accomplish something useful—improving the position of a primitive minority, the Doms—he is frustrated more by the local Congress leader, Ram Parshad Singh, than by the British. The Congress leader 'was not an idealist and an enthusiast as Jodh Singh was; he was a careerist, a political adventurer. He wanted to represent this district at Lucknow and Jodh Singh was a dangerous rival whom it would be pleasant to discredit.'[3] In order to destroy Jodh Singh's popularity, Ram Parshad Singh encourages him to make an issue of the Doms' rights, well knowing that the result would be to alienate the rest of the community. Clearly, Ram Parshad Singh is more interested in his own personal power than in anything else.

The somewhat contradictory way in which the writers of this period looked at an independent India and Indian nationalism is an expression of the ambivalent image of India held by the British in 1960. The British feel themselves to be confused as to what they should be doing in India: 'Truly, in India, we know not what we do.'[4] Harry Black experiences the same confusion

---

[1] P. Mason, *The Island of Chamba*, p. 137.
[2] P. Mason, *The Wild Sweet Witch*, pp. 132–3.   [3] Ibid., pp. 117–18.
[4] Stoll, *The Dove Found No Rest*, p. 215.

when he tries to answer Somola's question: 'What thoughts will you take away of India?'

What thoughts would he take away? Of nepotism and corruption creeping higher. Of invariable courtesy and kindness? Of brilliant plans and hopeless execution? Of love my child and let my neighbours starve? Of caste abolished and going strong? Of Malthus waiting on a bad monsoon? 'I don't know,' he said. 'It's too difficult for me, Somola.'[1]

Following the Mutiny, Rodney Savage sums up this idea. 'There's been too much blood. I don't know now what's right for India—I thought I did once. I don't know who should decide—there are too many different voices.'[2] The change from optimism through doubt to melancholy is marked. The image of India which the authors of these different periods presented both reflected British opinion and also helped to shape it.

The Era of Confidence is distinguished by a feeling of security which did not make it necessary for the British to develop full-fledged theories of justification for their rule. It is true that in this period Kipling's idea of 'The White Man's Burden' was developed, but there is far less self-analysis than was to come later when the British felt that their position was being threatened. Because of their confidence they felt it unnecessary to deal with many problems which later became significant such as relations between the races and Indian nationalism. With anti-imperialism growing, particularly after the Boer War, and Western civilization going through the crisis of the First World War, this confidence began to ebb. Even in the late nineteenth century there was, beneath the main current of confidence, a feeling of doubt, but it was only under the additional stresses of the early twentieth century that doubt became an important element in shaping the British image of India. It affected both the imperialistic pro-Raj writers and the anti-imperialist anti-Raj writers. The former found it necessary to emphasize those themes which had been raised in the preceding period, while the latter attacked the very basis of British rule. Caught between these two groups was a third element which drew on both of them. These writers were unsure of the value of continued British control of India while,

[1] Walker, *Harry Black*, p. 169.   [2] Masters, *Nightrunners of Bengal*, p. 370.

at the same time, they were not happy with the thought that the connection between Britain and India might soon be ended. As far back as the early 1920s the feeling that Britain was already finished in India had been expressed. By the mid-1930s this idea had become so accepted by most of the British writers that the problem no longer had to be discussed. This may in part explain the lack of concern in England with which the independence of India was greeted. 'It must be the first time in history that an empire of this size passed away unwept and unsung. It was indeed an amazing phenomenon.'[1] Instead of concerning themselves with attacking or defending the right of Britain to remain in India, these writers looked backwards to what they thought had been better times.

Despite the differences in tone, as much as in theme, which marked these different periods, there are certain similarities which are common to all of them. All approached India from the point of view of Britain. If the image of India is derived from any one point, it is the British view of their own civilization. Even such a force as Indian nationalism was almost completely ignored so long as the British retained a large element of self-confidence. Once this confidence was weakened—a weakening which was not derived from Indian experiences—Indian nationalism seemed to be a great threat. It was not events in India but those in Britain which shaped the image. This is also seen in the concern with which all British writers looked on their national role. The writers of the Era of Confidence felt that the Empire in India was valuable chiefly because it gave Britons an outlet for the action they felt was most important to their own personal development—ruling over other people. In contrast, in the Era of Doubt, those British writers who took an anti-imperialist stance did not do so out of love for the Indians or because they felt that alien rule was bad for the Indians. Rather they believed that the exercise of the power that came from absolute control of India was destructive to the British as individuals and as a race. Even the most strongly anti-imperialist writers shared with their imperialist opponents at least some respect for what Britain had accomplished in India. They might not agree that what was being done was worthwhile or morally justifiable, but nevertheless, they did take some pride in the

[1] Aziz, *Britain and Muslim India*, p. 205.

responsibility with which the British had accepted what they thought they had to do.

One element lacking from the image of India at all times is humour. The British could never paint their picture of India in anything other than the darkest colours. Even in the earliest period, when the British could at least occasionally view their own position as being a pleasant one, India was not a happy land. The physical discomfort of the sub-continent is very real and when this is added to the separation first from England and later from both England and India, that the British felt that the situation lacked humour is understandable.

Finally, British novelists have tended to treat the Indians as Indians first and as individual men only second. In the earliest period and for many writers since, this has been an expression of a sense of racial superiority. Even for those not imbued with a sense of racial superiority, the continual emphasis on the difference between the races shows an element of racial consciousness. It is only in the most recent novels that this approach to the Indian people has been overcome to some degree. Although India has been independent now for almost twenty years, British fiction set in the sub-continent has continued to pour forth. Considering that there is still a large British community in India and also that there are many British who are no longer in India but who lived a great part of their lives there, it is unlikely that the British image of India has reached the end of its development.

BIOGRAPHICAL NOTES

Francis W. Bain (1863–1940) entered the Indian Educational Service in 1892 and served as Professor of History and Political Economy at Deccan College, Poona, for twenty-seven years. Eventually Bain became Senior Principal of the School and received the C.I.E. For many years it was thought that the thirteen stories of his cycle of Indian stories were translations from ancient Sanskrit legends and not written by him. The whole series was very popular and the first of its stories, *A Digit of the Moon*, became immediately famous.

H. E. Bates (1905–   ), one of the most popular of contemporary British writers, was the first short-story writer commissioned by the British Government to write about the R.A.F. and was sent to Burma to write about the war there. *The Purple Plain* and two other novels set in Burma and India were the result of his wartime experiences.

L. Adams Beck (?–1931) is known as much as a mystic as a novelist. She became acquainted with the Orient as a child when her father, Admiral John Moresby, was stationed there. She spent much of her life travelling in India, Ceylon, Burma, Japan, and Tibet until her death in Kyoto. Miss Beck was thoroughly versed in Oriental ideology and through her writing of such books as *The Ninth Vibration* expressed her conception of Asian mysticism.

William Buchan, son of the famous author John Buchan, served in Burma during the Second World War in the R.A.F. Out of his wartime experiences he wrote his first novel, *Kumari*, which is set in India.

Edmund Candler (1874–1926) was educated at Cambridge where his favourite reading was romantic literature of travel in Asia, the writings of Kipling, and a biography of John Nicholson. He entered educational work in India as Classical Master at St. Paul's School in Darjeeling. Later he became the private tutor to a rajah and then served on a newspaper in Bengal. Unhappy in Bengal, Candler was pleased to get a post in the

Punjab where he ultimately became the principal of Mohimara College in Patiala. In 1920 he was awarded the C.B.E. and was appointed Director of Publicity to the Punjab Government. He held this position for less than two years, partly because he antagonized Gandhi by a reference to his daughter. His works, particularly *Siri Ram*, which was originally thought to be a memoir by an Indian, caused great debate in England.

Gordon Casserly (?–1947) was a professional army officer who transfered to the Indian Army after going to the subcontinent with his regiment. Because of ill-health he retired after the First World War and became a leading member of the Kipling Society, contributing frequent articles to its journal.

Bithia Mae Croker (?–1920) spent fourteen years in the East as the wife of an officer in the army. She wrote over twenty romantic novels dealing with India.

Wilfrid David is the author of *Monsoon*, which was published in 1933.

Ethel M. Dell (?–1939) was a best-selling novelist during the First World War. Her first book, *The Way of an Eagle*, was her best known and sold hundreds of thousands of copies.

Maud Diver (1867?–1945) was born at a hill station in the Himalayas where her father served as a soldier-civilian. Her great-aunt was Honoria Lawrence, the wife of Sir Henry Lawrence. After being educated in England, Mrs. Diver returned to India at the age of sixteen. Her companion on this trip was her life-long friend, Mrs. Fleming, Rudyard Kipling's sister, who served as critic for Diver's early works. Mrs. Diver married a subaltern and, after his regiment returned to England, began to write about India. In addition to her novels on romantic subjects, she is known for her sympathetic study of the princes of India, *Royal India*.

Arthur Conan Doyle (1859–1930) was a doctor, writer, and mystic best known as the creator of Sherlock Holmes. He was knighted in 1902 for his defence of Britain in a study of the Boer War.

John Eyton (1890–   ) was a very popular writer about the Indian scene in the 1920s. His allegiance to Kipling is conspicuous in several novels, such as *Bulbulla*, which follow the general pattern of *Kim*.

E. M. Forster (1879–   ) spent a short time in India in 1912 and returned there in 1921 for a somewhat longer stay. During this latter visit he served as private secretary to the Maharajah of Dewas for about six months. Forster has recounted his experiences in *The Hill of Devi* and many of its episodes form the basis for parts of *A Passage to India*.

Jon Godden (1906–), the older sister of Rumer Godden, was born in Bengal and made her first voyage to England when she was six months old. After a short formal education in England she returned with her sister to India during the First World War. Since then she has lived in both India and England.

Rumer Godden (1907–) was born in Sussex, but raised on the banks of the Ganges. When she was sent to England for her education she found life there dull and colourless. She was happy to return to India and has since divided her time between these countries, being always a little homesick for one or the other. Two of her Indian novels, *The River* and *Black Narcissus*, have been made into films.

Hilda Caroline Gregg (1856–1933), who wrote under the pseudonym 'Sydney C. Grier', was a novelist with a large following. In addition to many novels on India and other parts of the world, she edited the letters of Warren Hastings.

Thomas Anstey Guthrie (1856–1934), writing under the pseudonym 'F. Anstey', created in his *babus* a type of character that has become a classic. He was associated with *Punch* from 1887 to 1930 and is the outstanding humorist to have concerned himself with Indian themes.

G. A. Henty (1832–1902) was the greatest writer of boys' books of his day, and through his glorification of the British Empire did much to popularize it. During the Crimean War he first served in the commissariat department and then became a war correspondent. In 1875 he accompanied Edward, Prince of Wales, on his tour of India and with him travelled the length and breadth of the country. His books on India cover virtually every event of historical importance in the history of British expansion in South Asia.

Sir William W. Hunter (1840–1900) entered the Indian Civil Service in 1861. Among the many positions which he held was that of Assistant-Magistrate Collector in the Bengali district which he described in his short novel, *The Old Missionary*, which was an immediate success when first published in *The*

Contemporary Review in 1889. From 1869 to 1881 he supervised and helped to compile the important statistical survey of the Indian Empire which was published in nine volumes. In 1887 he returned to England where he was able to complete two volumes of his *History of British India* before his death.

F. Tennyson Jesse (?–1958) is best known for her works, fictional and otherwise, on criminology. Because of an interest in the area she decided to write a novel dealing with the annexation of Upper Burma. To do this she made several trips to Burma where she claims to have seen secret files and spoken with some of the Burmese participants in the action. She says that her novel, *The Lacquer Lady* published in 1929, tells the truth about the annexation. Miss Jesse has also written a short popular history of Burma.

Mary Margaret Kaye lived most of her life in India where she was born, the daughter of Sir Cecil Kaye, the last non-police head of the Criminal Intelligence Department in India. She is a descendant of Major Edward Kaye, who commanded a battery at the Siege of Delhi, and of Sir William Kaye, author of a history of the Indian Mutiny.

Dennis Kincaid (1905–1937) came from a family long associated with India. His father, Charles Augustus Kincaid, was a member of the I.C.S. and well known as the author of many works, particularly on the Mahrattas; and his grandfather was Major-General William Kincaid, Resident of Bhopal. In 1928 Dennis Kincaid came to Bombay as a judicial member of the I.C.S. There he studied Indian civilization and wrote a number of novels and a *Social History of the British in India*. He was one of the few British authors who wrote about the Bombay region.

Rudyard Kipling (1865–1936), the most influential British author to write about India, was born in Bombay where his father was a professor of architectural sculpture in an Indian school. Except for one short visit to England, Kipling lived in India until he was seven. After a typical Anglo-Indian education in England, away from his family, he returned to India in 1882 where he worked for the next seven years as a journalist. His earliest works, all dealing with India, come from this period. In 1889 he left India and, except for a brief return two years later, lived the rest of his life first in the United States and then in England. He burst upon the literary scene with the publication of his collections of short stories, *Plain Tales from the Hills* and *Soldiers Three*, which made India for the first time a major theme in English literature, and won the Nobel Prize for literature in 1907.

Alfred Edward Woodley Mason (1865–1948), one of the most successful popular novelists and short-story writers of his generation, went to India in the early years of this century in order to become known as an authority on India in Parliament. Subsequently he served as a Member of the House of Commons from 1906 to 1910, and his novel, *The Broken Road*, was praised by Lord Curzon for its accuracy.

Philip Mason (1906–) wrote most of his fictional works on India under the pseudonym 'Philip Woodruff'. He was a member of the I.C.S. from 1928 to 1947, holding such important posts as Under-Secretary in the War Department, Deputy Commissioner in Garhwal, and Deputy Secretary in the Defence and War Department. Since 1958 he has been the Director of the Institute of Race Relations in London. Besides his novels on India, 'Philip Woodruff' is best known for his apologia for the I.C.S. in *The Men Who Ruled India*.

John Masters (1914–) was born in Calcutta in 1914 of a family which had served in India for five generations. After an education at Sandhurst, he returned to India in 1934 and served in the Indian Army until the transfer of power. Following Independence, he felt that he had no place in India and went to the United States rather than England. Only after leaving India did he begin to write. Originally, Masters planned to write a saga of the Savage family in India in many volumes. His novel of the independence movement, *Bhowani Junction*, was made into a successful film.

W. Somerset Maugham (1874–1965) was one of the leading British writers of this century. He spent a large part of his life travelling in the United States, the South Seas, and China, and settled in the South of France for long periods. His many short stories dealing with the British in South-East Asia and the Pacific shed light on important aspects of the British imperial mind.

Talbot Mundy (1874–1940), after entering the government service in Baroda, India, wandered over the entire sub-continent and Tibet. He was fascinated by Indian occultism and later served in Kenya, where he found African magic to be as exciting as Indian. He became a citizen of the United States in 1917.

Leopold H. Myers (1881–1944) developed the idea of writing novels based on the Mogul court from the publication in English of the Japanese classic, *Tales of Genji*. His series of novels on India, *The Root and the Flower* and *The Pool of Visnu*, are not actually attempts to re-create the Indian scene, but rather India provides the setting for his philosophical ideals. Nevertheless, his depiction of India reflects the then contemporary image of the sub-continent.

Nevil Shute Norway (1899–1960), who wrote under the pseudonym of 'Nevil Shute', is best known for his books set in Australia where he settled following the war. Not only a writer, but also a successful aircraft manufacturer, Norway saw action in the Second World War, which resulted in his one novel dealing in part with Burma, *The Chequer Board*.

Alfred Ollivant (1874–1927) is remembered for his first novel, *Bob, Son of Battle*. After being commissioned an officer in the Royal Artillery, Ollivant was injured in a fall from his horse and forced to resign from the army. His military background is obvious in his novel on India, *Old For-Ever*.

George Orwell (1903–1950) was born in Motihari, Bengal, but went to England with his parents when he was only a few years old and his father retired from the Indian Customs. He came to Burma in 1922 and remained there until 1927 as a police officer with the Indian Imperial Police. On his return to England, after resigning from this post, he felt that he had to get his experience in Burma out of his system. To do this he wrote the novel *Burmese Days* and several essays including 'Shooting an Elephant'.

Pierre Stephen Robert Payne (1911–   ) has written nearly a hundred books on a wide variety of subjects, but he is predominantly associated with Asia. Raised in a cosmopolitan atmosphere, he spent half his childhood in France and most of his adult life has been spent in travelling. After spending the Second World War in China, he moved to the United States where he now lives.

Alice Perrin (1867–1934) was of old John Company stock, being the daughter of General John Innes Robinson of the Bengal Cavalry. Her husband was a member of the Medical Service of the I.C.S., who later became associated with the

Ministry of Health. She wrote a large number of novels set in India, most of which deal with British social life in the subcontinent. After her return from India she lived in Switzerland until her death.

Ethil Savi (1865–1954) wrote over one hundred novels dealing with India. She was born in Calcutta of British and American parents and remained in India until 1909. Returning to England she began to write and turned out at least a novel a year until her death.

Hugh S. Scott (1862–1903) wrote under the pseudonym of 'Henry Seton Merriman' and in the late nineteenth century was considered to be one of the most popular of the then current romanticists. He did much careful research for his novels, which were set in many foreign places.

John Sibly (1920–   ) left Cambridge before his graduation and joined the Gloucestershire Regiment in Burma, where he was wounded. He recovered in an Indian hospital and from these experiences wrote his novel *You'll Walk to Mandalay*.

Albert Theodore William Simeons is a doctor specializing in the treatment of leprosy. His knowledge of this disease and its treatment in India form the background of his only novel, *The Mask of a Lion*.

Flora Annie Steel (1847–1927) was, in her day, compared favourably with Kipling, and some critics consider her the greatest novelist, in the literal sense of that word, that Anglo-Indian literature has produced. In 1867 she married a member of the I.C.S. and in the following year came out to India. Most of her time was spent in the Punjab where she advocated education for Indian women. She was the first inspector of girls' schools and in 1884 became a member of the Provincial Educational Board with John Lockwood Kipling, Rudyard's father. In 1889, upon her husband's retirement, she returned to England. In order to do research for her novel of the Indian Mutiny, *On the Face of the Waters*, she returned to India to talk with the surviving members of the Mogul nobility.

Dennis Gray Stoll (1912–   ) is a composer, writer on music, and conductor, who has written a number of articles on Oriental music. He has also been a lecturer on Oriental music for the Royal India and Pakistan Society. In the 1940s he wrote several novels, including *The Dove Found No Rest*, in which he attempted to popularize the Indian independence movement.

Edward John Thompson (1886–1946) served as an educational missionary at Bankura College, Bengal, from 1910 to 1922, except for the wartime period when he was with the army in the Near East. In 1932 he was appointed a special correspondent in India for the *Manchester Guardian*, regularly exchanging letters with Nehru and becoming one of the leading propagandists in England for the Congress position. In addition to his novels, he wrote several historical works including *The Other Side of the Medal* in which he began the re-evaluation of the Indian Mutiny by showing British acts of brutality.

Harry David Walker (1911–   ) served in the British Army in India from 1932 to 1936 and was later captured in France during the Second World War. These experiences are reflected in his novel *Harry Black*. He was Comptroller to the Viceroy of India from 1946 to 1947.

Patricia Wentworth (?–1961) was a successful writer of detective novels from the early years of this century. Only in her early work, *The Devil's Wind*, did she write about the India where she was born while her father was stationed there in the army.

Christine Weston (1904–   ) was born, as her parents had been, in India. Her father was an officer in the Indian Imperial Police and later a barrister in India. Except for brief periods in England, she lived in India until 1923 when she married an American and moved to the United States.

Leonard Woolf (1880–   ) went out to Ceylon in 1904 as a cadet in the Ceylon Civil Service. He served in Jaffna until 1906 and then transferred first to the Northern Provinces and then to Kandy. From 1908 to 1911 he served as the Acting Assistant Government Agent in the Hambantota District. Returning to England on furlough, he began to write *The Village in the Jungle*, and tried to overcome his increasing obsession with Ceylon in the same way as Orwell did later, by writing about what he had seen. While writing he became convinced of his growing anti-imperialist sentiment and resigned his position. Besides his novel and short stories about Ceylon, his autobiography and diary of his years in Hambantota are important documents for understanding British imperialist sentiment in the early twentieth century.

Percival Christopher Wren (1885–1941), best known for his

story of the French Foreign Legion, *Beau Geste*, spent ten years in India as an assistant director of education and physical culture to the Bombay Government. His earliest novels and also some which were published posthumously all have an Indian background.

BIBLIOGRAPHY

Primary Sources

Included in this section are novels, short stories, essays, and articles by the authors covered in this study. Autobiographical accounts are listed in a following section. This is in no way a complete bibliography of fictional works dealing with India. For a fuller bibliography see Bhupal Singh's *A Survey of Anglo-Indian Fiction*, which carries the list down to the mid-1930s. For the period since then, *The Book Review Digest*, which lists books according to their locale, is helpful.

BAIN, F. W., *Bubbles of the Foam*, London, Methuen and Company, 1912.
—— *The Descent of the Sun: A Cycle of Birth*, London, J. Parker and Company, 1903.
——*A Digit of the Moon: A Hindoo Love Story*, London, J. Parker and Company, 1899.
—— *A Heifer of the Dawn*, London, J. Parker and Company, Oxford, Parker and Son, 1904.
—— *The Livery of Eve*, London, Methuen and Company, 1917.
—— *A Syrup of the Bees*, London, Methuen and Company, 1914.
BATES, H. E., *The Jacaranda Tree*, London, Michael Joseph, 1949.
—— *The Purple Plain*, London, Michael Joseph, 1947.
—— *The Scarlet Sword*, London, Michael Joseph, 1950.
BECK, L. ADAMS, *The House of Fulfilment: The Romance of a Soul*, London, T. Fisher Unwin, 1927.
—— *The Ninth Vibration and Other Stories*, London, T. Fisher Unwin, 1928.
—— *The Perfume of the Rainbow and Other Stories*, London, Ernest Benn, 1931.
BUCHAN, WILLIAM, *Kumari*, London, Gerald Duckworth and Company, 1955.
CANDLER, EDMUND, *Abdication*, London, Constable and Company, 1922.

CANDLER, EDMUND, *Siri Ram Revolutionist: A Transcript From Life 1907–1910*, London, Constable and Company, 1912.

CASSERLY, GORDON, *The Elephant God*, London, P. Allan and Company, 1920.

CROKER, BITHIA MAE, *Diana Barrington: A Romance of Central India*, London, Ward and Downey, 3 vols., 1888.

—— *Mr. Jervis*, London, Chatto and Windus, 3 vols., 1894.

DAVID, WILFRID, *Monsoon*, London, Hamish Hamilton, 1933.

DELL, ETHEL M., *The Safety Curtain and Other Stories*, London, T. Fisher Unwin, 1917.

—— *The Way of an Eagle*, London, T. Fisher Unwin, 1912.

DIVER, MAUD, *The Dream Prevails: A Story of India*, London, John Murray, 1938.

—— *Far to Seek: A Romance of England and India*, Edinburgh and London, W. Blackwood and Sons, 1921.

—— *The Great Amulet*, revised edition, New York and London, G. P. Putnam's Sons, 1914.

—— *Lilamani: A Study in Possibilities*, London, Hutchinson and Company, 1911.

—— *Siege Perilous and Other Stories*, London, John Murray, 1924.

—— *The Singer Passes: An Indian Tapestry*, Edinburgh and London, W. Blackwood and Sons, 1934.

DOYLE, ARTHUR CONAN, *The Adventures of Sherlock Holmes*, London, George Newnes, 1892.

—— *The Return of Sherlock Holmes*, London, George Newnes, 1905.

—— *The Sign of Four*, London, Spencer Blackett, 1890.

—— *A Study in Scarlet*, London, Ward, Lock, and Company, 1888.

EYTON, JOHN, *Bulbulla*, London, Arrowsmith, 1928.

—— *The Dancing Fakir and Other Stories*, London, Longmans, Green and Company, 1922.

FORSTER, E. M., *Abinger Harvest*, London, E. Arnold and Company, 1936. (Contains several essays on India published from 1914 to 1922 originally.)

—— Foreword to *Flowers and Elephants* by Constance Sitwell, London, Jonathan Cape, 1927.

—— *A Passage to India*, London, E. Arnold and Company, 1924.

—— 'Reflections in India: I—Too Late?' *The Nation and the Athenaeum*, XXX (21 January 1922), pp. 612–16.

GODDEN, JON, *The City and the Wave*, London, Michael Joseph, 1954.

—— *The Peacock*, London, Michael Joseph, 1950.

—— *The Seven Islands*, London, Chatto and Windus, 1950.

GODDEN, RUMER, *Black Narcissus*, London, Peter Davies, 1939.

—— *Breakfast With the Nikolides*, London, Peter Davies, 1942.

—— *Kingfishers Catch Fire*, London, Macmillan and Company, 1953.

GODDEN, RUMER, *The Lady and the Unicorn*, London, Peter Davies, 1937.
—— *Mooltiki: Stories and Poems from India*, New York, Viking Press, 1957.
—— *The River*, London, Michael Joseph, 1946.
GREGG, HILDA C. (under the pseudonym 'Sydney C. Grier'), *In Furthest Ind: The Narrative of Mr. Edward Carlyon of the Honourable East India Company's Service*, Edinburgh, William Blackwood and Sons, 1894.
GUTHRIE THOMAS ANSTEY (under the pseudonym 'F. Anstey'), *A Bayard From Bengal*, London, Methuen and Company, 1902. (Originally published serially in *Punch* in 1900.)
—— *Baboo Hurry Bungsho Jabberjee, B.A.*, London, J. M. Dent and Company, 1897.
HENTY, G. A., *At the Point of the Bayonet: A Tale of the Mahratta War*, London, Blackie and Son, 1902.
—— *Colonel Thorndyke's Secret*, London, Chatto and Windus, 1898.
—— *On the Irrawaddy: A Story of the First Burmese War*, London, Blackie and Son, 1897.
—— *Through the Sikh War: A Tale of the Conquest of the Punjab*, London, Blackie and Son, 1894.
—— *With Clive in India: or The Beginnings of an Empire*, London, Blackie and Son, 1884.
HUNTER, SIR WILLIAM W., *The Old Missionary*, London, Henry Frowde, 1895. (Originally published in the *Contemporary Review* in 1889.)
JESSE F. TENNYSON, *The Lacquer Lady*, London, William Heinemann, 1929.
KAYE, MARY MARGARET, *Shadow of the Moon*, London and New York, Staples Press, 1953.
KINCAID, DENNIS, *Cactus Land*, London, Chatto and Windus, 1933.
—— *Durbar*, London, Chatto and Windus, 1933.
—— *Their Ways Divide*, London, Chatto and Windus, 1936.
—— *Tropic Rome*, London, Chatto and Windus, 1935.
KIPLING, RUDYARD, *The Bombay Edition of the Works of Rudyard Kipling in Prose and Verse*, London, Macmillan and Company, vols. 1–23, 1913–14; vols. 24–31, 1937–8.
MASON, A. E. W., *The Broken Road*, London, Smith, Elder, and Company, 1907.
—— *The Sapphire*, London, Hodder and Stoughton, 1933.
MASON, PHILIP (under the pseudonym 'Philip Woodruff'), *Call the Next Witness*, London, Jonathan Cape, 1945.
—— *The Island of Chamba*, London, Jonathan Cape, 1950.
—— *The Wild Sweet Witch*, London, Jonathan Cape, 1947.
MASTERS, JOHN, *Bhowani Junction*, London, Michael Joseph, 1954.

*P

MASTERS, JOHN, *Coromandel!*, London, Michael Joseph, 1955.

—— *The Deceivers*, London, Michael Joseph, 1952.

—— *Far, Far the Mountain Peak*, London, Michael Joseph, 1957.

—— *The Lotus and the Wind*, London, Michael Joseph, 1953.

—— *The Nightrunners of Bengal*, London, Michael Joseph, 1951.

—— *To the Coral Strand*, London, Michael Joseph, 1962.

—— *The Venus of Konpara*, London, Michael Joseph, 1960.

MAUGHAM, W. SOMERSET, *The Razor's Edge*, London, William Heinemann, 1944.

MUNDY, TALBOT, *Hira Singh's Tale*, London, Cassell and Company, 1918.

—— *King—of the Khyber Rifles: A Romance of Adventure*, London, Constable and Company, 1917.

—— *Om, the Secret of Abhor Valley*, London, Hutchinson and Company, 1924.

—— *Rung Ho!*, London, Cassell and Company, 1914.

—— *Told in the East*, New York, McKinlay, Stone and MacKenzie, 1920.

MYERS, L. H., *The Pool of Visnu*, London, Jonathan Cape, 1940.

—— *The Root and the Flower*, London, Jonathan Cape, 1935 (Contains *The Near and the Far* originally published by Jonathan Cape, London, in 1929; *Prince Jali* originally published by Jonathan Cape, London, in 1931; and *Rajah Amar* published for the first time in this volume.)

NORWAY, NEVIL SHUTE (under the pseudonym 'Nevil Shute'), *The Chequer Board*, London and Toronto, William Heinemann, 1947.

OLLIVANT, ALFRED, *Old For-Ever: An Epic of Beyond the Indus*, London, G. Allen and Unwin, 1923.

ORWELL, GEORGE, *Burmese Days*, London, Victor Gollancz, 1935.

—— *Shooting an Elephant and Other Essays*, London, Secker and Warburg, 1950. (Contains essays on Burma originally written from 1932 to 1935.)

PAYNE, PIERRE STEPHEN ROBERT, *Blood Royal*, New York, Prentice-Hall, 1952.

—— *The Great Mogul*, London, William Heinemann, 1950.

PERRIN, ALICE, *Idolatry*, London, Chatto and Windus, 1909.

SAVI, ETHIL W., *By Torchlight*, London, Hurst and Blackett, 1931.

SCOTT, HUGH S. (under the pseudonym 'Henry Seton Merriman'), *Flotsam: The Study of a Life*, London, Longmans and Company, 1896.

SIBLY, JOHN, *You'll Walk to Mandalay*, London, Hamilton and Company, 1963.

SIMEONS, A. T. W., *The Mask of a Lion*, London, Victor Gollancz, 1952.

STEEL, FLORA ANNIE, *The Flower of Forgiveness and Other Stories*, London, Macmillan and Company, 2 vols., 1894.

—— *From the Five Rivers*, London, William Heinemann, 1893.

—— *The Hosts of the Lord*, London, William Heinemann, 1900.

—— *In the Guardianship of God*, London, William Heinemann, 1903.

—— *Indian Scene: Collected Short Stories*, London, E. Arnold, 1933.

—— *King-Errant*, London, William Heinemann, 1912.

—— *On the Face of the Waters*, London, William Heinemann, 1897.

—— *The Potter's Thumb*, London, William Heinemann, 3 vols., 1894.

—— *A Prince of Dreamers*, London, William Heinemann, 1908.

STOLL, DENNIS GRAY, *The Dove Found No Rest*, London, Victor Gollancz, 1946.

THOMPSON, EDWARD, *An End of the Hours*, London, Macmillan and Company, 1938.

—— *A Farewell to India*, London, Ernest Benn, 1930.

—— *An Indian Day*, London, A. A. Knopf, 1927.

—— *Krishna Kumari: An Historical Drama in Four Acts*, London, Ernest Benn, 1924.

—— *Night Falls on Siva's Hill*, London, William Heinemann, 1929.

WALKER, HARRY DAVID, *Harry Black*, Boston, Houghton Mifflin, 1956.

WENTWORTH, PATRICIA, *The Devil's Wind*, London, Andrew Melrose, 1912.

WESTON, CHRISTINE, *Indigo*, London, Collins, 1944.

—— *There and Then*, London, Collins, 1948.

—— *The World is a Bridge*, London, Collins, 1950.

WOOLF, LEONARD, *Stories From the East*, Richmond, L. and V. Woolf, 1921.

—— *The Village in the Jungle*, London, Edward Arnold, 1913.

WREN, PERCIVAL CHRISTOPHER, *The Dark Woman*, Philadelphia, Macrae Smith Company, 1943.

—— *Odd—But Even So: Stories Stranger Than Fiction*, London, John Murray, 1941.

Secondary Sources

There are few secondary accounts dealing with Anglo-Indian literature. Bhupal Singh's discussion is the only one to attempt a survey of the whole range of such literature. It, however, is marred by having been written from the point of view of an Indian nationalist, who is intent on proving that no one understands the Indians. Nevertheless, for its bibliography and plot outlines it remains a valuable work.

Howe's introduction to the problem of literature and imperialism covers not only English, but also French, German, and Italian novels. Finally, Cooperman's article is a most exciting one in which he has much of interest to say about the changing British image of India.

General Surveys of Anglo-Indian Literature

GARRATT, GEOFFREY THEODORE, ed., *The Legacy of India*, London, Oxford University Press, 1937.

GUPTA, BRIJEN K., *Modern India in English Fiction: An Annotated Bibliography*, privately mimeographed, 1964.

HOWE, SUSANNE, *Novels of Empire*, New York, Columbia University Press, 1949.

'The Indian Mutiny in Fiction', *Blackwood's Edinburgh Magazine*, CLXI (February 1897), pp. 218–31.

OATEN, EDWARD FARLEY, *A Sketch of Anglo-Indian Literature*, London, Kegan Paul and Company, 1908.

RAU, SANTHA RAMA, 'New Voices from Asia', *American Association of University Women Journal*, October 1964, pp. 3–8.

SINGH, BHUPAL, *A Survey of Anglo-Indian Fiction*, London, Oxford University Press, 1934.

Criticism, Biography, and Autobiography (arranged by Author)

GENERAL

ETHRIDGE, JAMES M. and BARBARA KOPALA, eds., *Contemporary Authors*, Detroit, Gale Research Company, 1962–6.

KUNITZ, STANLEY J., ed., *British Authors of the Nineteenth Century*, New York, H. W. Wilson, 1936.

KUNITZ, STANLEY J. and VINETA COLBY, eds., *Twentieth Century Authors, Supplement*, New York, H. W. Wilson, 1955.

KUNITZ, STANLEY J. and HOWARD HAYCRAFT, *Twentieth Century Authors*, New York, H. W. Wilson, 1942.

EDMUND CANDLER

'An Indian Jigsaw', *Nation and Athenaeum*, 31 (22 April 1922), p. 126. (Review of Candler's *Abdication*.)

CANDLER, EDMUND, *Youth and the East: An Unconventional Autobiography*, Edinburgh and London, W. Blackwood and Sons, 1924.

A. CONAN DOYLE

STARRETT, VINCENT, *The Private Life of Sherlock Holmes*, London, J. Nicholson and Watson, 1934.

E. M. FORSTER

BRANDER, LAURENCE, 'E. M. Forster and India', *A Review of English Literature*, III (October 1962), pp. 76–83.

BURRA, PETER, 'The Novels of E. M. Forster', *The Nineteenth Century and After*, CXVI (November 1934), pp. 581–94.

CHAUDHURI, NIRAD G., 'Passage To and From India', *Encounter*, II (June 1954), pp. 19–24.

COOPERMAN, STANLEY, 'The Imperial Posture and The Shrine of Darkness: Kipling's *The Naulahka* and E. M. Forster's *A Passage to India*', *English Literature in Transition*, 6 (1963), pp. 9–13.

COWLEY, MALCOLM, 'E. M. Forster's Answer', *New Republic*, 109 (29 November 1943), pp. 749–50.

DAUMIER, LOUISE, 'What Happened in The Caves? Reflections on *A Passage to India*', *Modern Fiction Studies*, 7 (Autumn 1961), pp. 258–70.

FORSTER, E. M., *The Hill of Devi*, London, Edward Arnold and Company, 1953. (Autobiographical account of his visit to India.)
—— 'Indian Entries', *Encounter*, 18 (May–June 1962), pp. 20–7. (Excerpts from his diary kept on his trip to India.)

MACAULAY, ROSE, *The Writings of E. M. Forster*, London, Hogarth Press, 1938.

MCLUHAN, HERBERT MARSHALL, 'Kipling and Forster', *Sewanee Review*, LII (Summer 1944), pp. 332–43.

TRILLING, LIONEL, *E. M. Forster*, London, Hogarth Press, 1944.

WHITE, GERTRUDE, '*A Passage to India*: Analysis and Revaluation', *Publications of the Modern Language Association of America*, LXX (December 1955), pp. 934–54.

WOOLF, VIRGINIA, *The Death of the Moth and Other Essays*, London, Hogarth Press, 1947 (1942).

RUMER GODDEN

GODDEN, RUMER, *Rungli-Rungli: Thus Far and No Further*, London, Peter Davies, 1943. (Autobiographical account of her life in Kashmir.)
—— and Jon, *Two Under the Indian Sun*, London, Macmillan and Company, 1966. (Autobiographical account of their youth in India.)

TINDALL, WILLIAM YORK, 'Rumer Godden, Public Symbolist', *College English*, 13 (March 1952), pp. 297–303.

THOMAS ANSTEY GUTHRIE ('F. ANSTEY')

GUTHRIE, THOMAS ANSTEY (under the pseudonym 'F. Anstey'), *A Long Retrospect*, London, Oxford University Press, 1936.

G. A. HENTY

DAVIS, GODFREY, 'G. A. Henty and History', *Huntington Library Quarterly*, XVIII (February 1955), pp. 159–67.

FENN, G. MANVILLE, *George Alfred Henty: The Story of an Active Life*, London, Blackie and Son Limited, 1907.

NADIS, MARK, 'G. A. Henty's Idea of India', *Victorian Studies*, VII (September 1964), pp. 49–58.

SIR WILLIAM W. HUNTER

SKRINE, FRANCIS HENRY, *Life of Sir William Wilson Hunter*, London, Longmans, Green and Company, 1901.

RUDYARD KIPLING

ANNAN, NOEL, 'Rudyard Kipling as a Sociologist', *Kipling Journal*, 111 (October 1954), pp. 5–6.

CARRINGTON, C. E., *Rudyard Kipling: His Life and Work*, London, Macmillan and Company, 1955.

COOK, RICHARD, 'Rudyard Kipling and George Orwell', *Modern Fiction Studies*, 7 (Summer 1961), pp. 125–35.

COOPERMAN, STANLEY, 'The Imperial Posture and The Shrine of Darkness: Kipling's *The Naulahka* and E. M. Forster's *A Passage to India*', *English Literature in Transition*, 6 (1963), pp. 9–13.

CORNELL, LOUIS L., *Kipling in India*, London, Macmillan and Company, 1966.

DEUTSCH, KARL W. and NORBERT WIENER, 'The Lonely Nationalism of Rudyard Kipling', *Yale Review*, LII (June 1963), pp. 499–517.

DOBRÉE, BONAMY, *Rudyard Kipling*, London, Longmans, Green and Company, 1951.

EDWARDES, MICHAEL, 'Rudyard Kipling and the Imperial Imagination', *The Twentieth Century*, CLIII (June 1953), pp. 443–54.

HAWARD, EDWIN, 'Kipling Myths and Traditions in India', *The Nineteenth Century and After*, CXXV (February 1939), pp. 194–202.

HOLLIS, CHRISTOPHER, 'Kim and the apolitical Man', *Kipling Journal*, 119 (October 1956), pp. 5–7.

LE GALLIENNE, RICHARD, *Rudyard Kipling: A Criticism*, London, John Lane, 1900.

MACMUNN, SIR GEORGE, 'Some Kipling Origins: The Irish Soldier', *Kipling Journal*, 1 (March 1927), pp. 13–14.

McLUHAN, HERBERT MARSHALL, 'Kipling and Forster', *Sewanee Review*, LII (Summer 1944), pp. 332–43.

ORWELL, GEORGE, *Critical Essays*, London, Secker and Warburg, 1946. (Contains essay entitled 'Rudyard Kipling' which was written in 1942.)

RAO, K. BHASKARA, *Rudyard Kipling's India*, Norman, University of Oklahoma Press, 1967.

RUTHERFORD, ANDREW, ed., *Kipling's Mind and Art*, Edinburgh and London, Oliver and Boyd, 1964.

SHANKS, EDWARD, *Rudyard Kipling: A Study in Literature and Political Ideals*, London, Macmillan and Company, 1940.

SOLOMON, ERIC, 'The Regulars: A Note on "Soldiers Three" and "Military Tales" ', *Kipling Journal*, 139 (June 1959), pp. 8–12.

A. E. W. MASON

BROOKES, BENJAMIN GILBERT, 'Three English Novelists and the Pakistani Scene', in *Crescent and Green: A Miscellany of Writings on Pakistan*, London, Cassell and Company, 1955.

GREEN, ROGER LANCELYN, *A. E. W. Mason*, London, Max Parrish, 1952.

JOHN MASTERS

'The Colonel's Campaign', *Time*, 65 (28 March 1955), pp. 102–4. (Review of *Coromandel!*)

DEMPSEY, DAVID, 'File on Masters', in 'In and Out of Books', *New York Times Book Review*, 11 January 1953, p. 8.

MASTERS, JOHN, *Bugles and a Tiger*, London, New English Library, 1962.

—— *The Road Past Mandalay: A Personal Narrative*, London, Michael Joseph, 1961. (These two volumes are the author's autobiographical account of his life in Burma and India during the Second World War.)

NICHOLS, LEWIS, 'Talk with John Masters', *New York Times Book Review*, 28 March 1954, p. 15.

'The Soldier's Trade', *Time*, 67 (9 January 1956), pp. 90–2. (Review of *Bugles and a Tiger*.)

L. H. MYERS

BANTOCK, G. H., *L. H. Myers: A Critical Study*, London, Jonathan Cape, 1956.

BOTTRALL, RICHARD, 'L. H. Myers', *A Review of English Literature*, II (April 1961), pp. 47–58.

HARDING, D. W., 'The Work of L. H. Myers', *Scrutiny*, III (June 1934), pp. 44–63.

GEORGE ORWELL

BRANDER, LAURENCE, *George Orwell*, London, Longmans, Green and Company, 1954.

Cook, Richard, 'Rudyard Kipling and George Orwell', *Modern Fiction Studies*, 7 (Summer 1961), pp. 125–35.

Hollis, Christopher, *A Study of George Orwell: The Man and His Works*, London, Hollis and Carter, 1956.

Hopkinson, Tom, *George Orwell*, London, Longmans, Green and Company, 1953.

Orwell, George, *The Road to Wigan Pier*, London, Victor Gollancz, 1937. (Sociology of England and Autobiography.)

Stevens, A. Wilber, 'George Orwell and Southeast Asia', *Yearbook of Comparative and General Literature*, XI (1962), pp. 133–41.

Trilling, Lionel, *The Opposing Self: Nine Essays in Criticism*, London, Secker and Warburg, 1955.

Voorhees, Richard J., *The Paradox of George Orwell*, Lafayette, Indiana, Purdue Research Foundation, 1961.

FLORA ANNIE STEEL

Steel, Flora Annie, *The Garden of Fidelity*, London, Macmillan and Company, 1930. (Autobiography.)

Webster, Mabel, 'Biographical Introduction' to Flora Annie Steel, *Indian Scene: Collected Short Stories*, London, E. Arnold and Company, 1933.

EDWARD THOMPSON

Nehru, Jawaharlal, *A Bunch of Old Letters Written Mostly to Jawaharlal Nehru and Some Written By Him*, Bombay, Asia Publishing House, 1958. (Contains a series of letters from Nehru to Thompson on the question of Indian independence.)

LEONARD WOOLF

de Silva, Mervyn, 'Introduction to *Diaries in Ceylon* by Leonard Woolf', *Ceylon Historical Journal*, IX (July 1959–April 1960), pp. xlviii–lx.

Elkin, P. K., 'Leonard Woolf's Masterpiece', *Journal of the Australasian Universities Language and Literature Association (AUMLA)*, 13 (May 1960), pp. 46–55.

Woolf, Leonard, *Beginning Again: An Autobiography of the Years 1911–1918*, London, Hogarth Press, 1964.

—— *Diaries in Ceylon*, *Ceylon Historical Journal*, IX (July 1959–April 1960), pp. 1–253.

—— *Growing: An Autobiography of the Years 1904–1911*, London, Hogarth Press, 1961.

—— *Sowing: An Autobiography of the Years 1880–1904*, London, Hogarth Press, 1960.

General Works

ARBERRY, A. J., *British Orientalists*, London, William Collins, 1943.

AZIZ, K. K., *Britain and Muslim India: A Study of British Public Opinion vis-à-vis the Development of Muslim Nationalism in India, 1857–1947*, Heinemann, 1963.

BOULDING, KENNETH, *The Image: Knowledge in Life and Society*, Ann Arbor, University of Michigan Press, 1961.

CHATURVEDI, BENARSIDAS and MARJORIE SYKES, *Charles Freer Andrews: A Narrative*, London, George Allen and Unwin, 1949.

CHAUDHURI, NIRAD C., 'On Understanding the Hindus', *Encounter*, XXIV (July 1965), pp. 20–3.

CURTIN, PHILIP D., *The Image of Africa: British Ideas and Action, 1780–1850*, London, Macmillan and Company, 1965.

DANGERFIELD, GEORGE, *The Strange Death of Liberal England*, London, Constable and Company, 1936.

FREYRE, GILBERTO, *Brazil: An Interpretation*, New York, Alfred A. Knopf, 1945.

ISAACS, HAROLD R., *Images of Asia: American Views of China and India*, New York, Capricorn Books, 1962. (Originally published as *Scratches on Our Minds* in 1958.)

JONES, DOROTHY B., *The Portrayal of China and India on the American Screen, 1896–1955: The Evolution of Chinese and Indian Themes, Locales, and Characters as Portrayed on the American Screen*, Cambridge Center for International Studies, Massachusetts Institute of Technology, 1955.

KINCAID, DENNIS, *British Social Life in India, 1608–1937*, London, George Routledge and Sons, 1939.

Letters of an Indian Judge to an English Gentlewoman, London, L. Dickinson Limited, 1934

MACK, EDWARD, *Public Schools and British Opinion Since 1860: The Relationship Between Contemporary Ideas and The Evolution of an English Institution*, New York, Columbia University Press, 1941.

MANNONI, O., *Prospero and Caliban: The Psychology of Colonization*, translated from the French by Pamela Powesland, New York, Frederick A. Praeger, 1964 (1950).

MAUNIER, RENÉ, *The Sociology of Colonies: An Introduction to the Study of Race Contact*, edited and translated from the French by E. O. Lorimer, London, Routledge and Kegan Paul Limited, 1949. (Two volumes in the original published in 1932 and 1942.)

NEWSOME, DAVID, *Godliness and Good Learning: Four Studies on a Victorian Ideal*, London, John Murray, 1961.

PEARSON, R., *Eastern Interlude: A Social History of the European Community in Calcutta*, Calcutta, Thacker, Spink, and Company, 1954.

RUDOLPH, SUSANNE HOEBER, 'The New Courage: An Essay on Gandhi's Psychology', *World Politics*, XVI (October 1963), pp. 98–117.

STANFORD, J. K., *Ladies in the Sun: The Memsahibs' India, 1760–1860*, London, The Galley Press, 1962.

STEIN, MAURICE R., ARTHUR J. VIDICH and DAVID MANNING WHITE, eds., *Identity and Anxiety: Survival of the Person in Mass Society*, Glencoe, Illinois, The Free Press, 1960.

TAGORE, RABINDRANATH, *Letters to a Friend*, edited by C. F. Andrews, London, George Allen and Unwin, 1928.

THOMPSON, EDWARD, *The Other Side of the Medal*, London, L. and V. Woolf, 1925.

WILKINSON, RUPERT, *The Prefects, British Leadership and the Public School Tradition: A Comparative Study in the Making of Rulers*, London, Oxford University Press, 1964.

WINT, GUY, *The British in Asia*, London, Faber and Faber, 1954.

WORSLEY, T. C., *Barbarians and Philistines: Democracy and the Public Schools*, London, Robert Hale, 1940.

INDEX

873- 5355

A.H.-7294-2238